Masters of the
Shoot-'Em-Up

Masters of the Shoot-'Em-Up

Conversations with Directors, Actors and Writers of Vintage Action Movies and Television Shows

TADHG TAYLOR

McFarland & Company, Inc., Publishers
Jefferson, North Carolina

All photographs are from the author's collection unless otherwise noted.

LIBRARY OF CONGRESS CATALOGUING-IN-PUBLICATION DATA

Taylor, Tadhg.
    Masters of the shoot-'em-up : conversations with directors, actors and writers of vintage action movies and television shows / Tadhg Taylor.
    p. cm.
    Includes bibliographical references and index.

    ISBN 978-0-7864-9406-4 (softcover : acid free paper) ∞
    ISBN 978-1-4766-2098-5 (ebook)

    1. Action and adventure films—History and criticism. 2. Action and adventure television programs—History and criticism. 3. Screenwriters—Interviews. 4. Television writers—Interviews. 5. Motion picture producers and directors—Interviews. 6. Television producers and directors—Interviews. 7. Actors—Interviews. I. Title.

PN1995.9.A3T39 2015
791.43'655—dc23   2015035295

BRITISH LIBRARY CATALOGUING DATA ARE AVAILABLE

© 2015 Tadhg Taylor. All rights reserved

No part of this book may be reproduced or transmitted in any form or by any means, electronic or mechanical, including photocopying or recording, or by any information storage and retrieval system, without permission in writing from the publisher.

Cover image: Hector Elizondo and Tom Mason in *Freebie and the Bean* (1980-81), a Warner Bros. TV series based on the 1974 movie starring James Caan and Alan Arkin

Printed in the United States of America

McFarland & Company, Inc., Publishers
  Box 611, Jefferson, North Carolina 28640
    www.mcfarlandpub.com

For Terry Taylor
who loved shoot-'em-ups, and
Bill Norton who wrote them.
Erin go bragh.

Acknowledgments

I'd like to thank the following for their part in making this book happen.

All the interviewees, of course.

B.L. Norton.

Stephen Bowie from the Classic TV History Blog—enthusiastic, concise and impeccably researched writing about vintage television.

Director Harry Falk and his wife Candace. Harry's *Death Squad* (1973), starring Robert Forster, is one of the best crime telefeatures you'll ever see—tough, fast and expertly delivered. If it was a black-and-white programmer from the 1950s, noir buffs would be lining up to sing its praises.

Brian McFarlane, whose classic book *An Autobiography of British Cinema* inspired my modus operandi, and Tise Vahimagi who always stood up for action television.

John Bonis, Phillipa Berry and Anthony Story for loaning me so many movies.

My mum, for letting me use her phone in the period between all the phone booths disappearing and my discovery of Skype.

And most of all, Rallou: "I like it already … he's familiar … bit slow.… I think I'll read my book."

Table of Contents

Acknowledgments — vii
Preface — 1

Richard Harris—Writer — 3
Bill Norton—Writer — 10
Leigh Chapman—Writer — 16
Peter Yeldham—Writer — 26
Stewart Raffill—Director — 36
Dick Clement—Director — 44
Chris Leitch—Director — 51
Steve Carver—Director — 59
Michael Preece—Director — 70
Gary Conway—Director — 80
Alvin Rakoff—Director — 91
Robert M. Lewis—Director — 98
Jeff Kanew—Director — 108
Paul Annett—Director — 118
Bruce Kessler—Director — 129
Joseph Scanlan—Director — 135
Les Sheldon—Director — 143
Ron Satlof—Director — 151
Jerome M. Siegel—Assistant Director — 161
Mike McStay—Actor — 168
Jeffrey Byron—Actor — 178
Tony Russel—Actor — 187

Table of Contents

Peter DeAnda—Actor	195
Linda Marlowe—Actor	201
Peter Mark Richman—Actor	207
Bibliography	215
Index	217

Preface

This is a book about action movies, episodic television, busted pilots and telefeatures; a collection of interviews with writers, directors and actors that have done notable work in the genre; a book for movie and television marginaliacs and would-be Don Siegels who want to learn how it's done.

It covers work from the late 1950s to the mid–1980s, but the main focus is the '60s and '70s—the age of Bullitt and Bond, Mannix and the Professionals; characters rooted in the mythology and morality of westerns, John Buchan "shockers" (*sans* the snobbery and racism) and the hardboiled detective novel; quick-witted tough guys defending right against wrong and weak against strong.

The cut-off point is the mid–'80s because after that, you're into a different era—big muscles, big explosions and big budgets. At times I do stray into the late '80s, and even the '90s, but only for works like *Hunter* (1984–91) and *Walker, Texas Ranger* (1993–2000) that utilized vintage tropes and veteran talent. Bottom line: I like those tropes and that talent.

I've tried to come at the subject from lots of angles, everything from spy comedies to "good ol' boy" movies, and to avoid going over old ground. There isn't much more to say about *The French Connection* (1971) so why not turn our attention to *The London Connection* (1979), a Bond-inspired Disney movie helmed by *Enter the Dragon* (1973) director Robert Clouse?

I've spoken to Americans, Brits and a couple of Aussies. Yes, action movies are international and yes, the French and Italians made some of the best of the period—Sergio Sollima's *Revolver* (1973), Philippe Labro's *The Predator* (1976) and Enzo G. Castellari's *The Day of the Cobra* (1980), for example. But I'll cover that lot next time, when I've got an army of interpreters on the payroll.

Television is given as much space as movies, and rightly so. Top-class television didn't begin with HBO and top-class television is made by top-class talent. Television has been called "the producer's medium" and in this book you'll read about creative producers like Jack Webb, Roy Huggins, Stephen J. Cannell, Glen A. Larson, Quinn Martin and Dean Hargrove—great talents with signature styles who exerted a huge influence on the shows they worked on and in some cases created. But without good scripts, well-paced, punchy direction and dynamic performances, those shows would have gotten nowhere. *Kojak* (1973–78) episodes written by crime novelist Joe Gores stand out for their big-city grit; *Kojak* episodes directed by Richard Donner bristle with energy in their staging, camera style and editing; *Kojak* without Telly Savalas is unthinkable.

Before I sign off, I'd like to suggest a drinking game: mix a jug of vodka martini and pour yourself a glass. Read the book from cover to cover and take a swig each time James Bond is mentioned. Better make it two jugs.

Richard Harris
Writer

In the 1960s and '70s, British scripter Richard Harris supplied superior thrills and kills to every kind of crime and action series on television: from Carnaby Street comic strips like *The Avengers* (1961–69) to shoot-and-shout cop shows like *The Sweeney* (1975–78) and *Target* (1977–78).

He penned episodes of *No Hiding Place* (1959–66), *The Saint* (1962–69), *Redcap* (1965–66), *Public Eye* (1965–75), *Fraud Squad* (1969–70) and *Hunter's Walk* (1973–76). The latter was a police series created by Ted Willis, estimable playwright, television and movie scripter, spy-fi novelist and Labour Party peer.

Harris created the espionage series *Spyder's Web* (1972) and co-created *Man in a Suitcase* (1967–68), a private eye effort that stood out from the ITC pack thanks to lead Richard Bradford's intense and naturalistic portrayal of the tersely monkered, ex–secret service agent McGill.

Harris knew his way around a "dirty London" story and was an excellent choice for script editor on *Hazell* (1978–79), a series based on the fast, funny "egg and chips" crime novels of P.B. Yuill aka Gordon Williams and Terry Venables.

Man in a Suitcase *was a good show.*

Dennis Spooner and I came up with the idea, which occupied no more than one side of a piece of A4 typing paper. My agent took it to Lew Grade who, with just a shake of the hand, bought it there and then. That certainly wouldn't happen nowadays, it'd have to go through forty-three committees! You were much less hog-tied then than you are today.

Hog-tied?

I haven't been in television for a long time, out of choice. There was a time when you wrote a script and you worked to a producer and that was it. Now, the producer has to refer to all sorts of people, and all of them are saying, "We want this, we want that." I remember on the last thing I wrote they said to me, "Can you write a part for Dawn French in this script?" I said, "Why?" and they said, "Because it will bring the Dawn French audience." Well, that's no way to create stuff, is it? So I thought, "I've had a good time but I don't want to do it anymore, and I'm old enough and rich enough to not have to do it anymore." I was part of the golden years, the 1960s, when television was really very vibrant and exciting to be in. A lot of people had moved over from the theater and there was a terrific sense of putting a show together. To do an hour show, it would take maybe three or four hours to record and at the end of it you'd all have a drink and talk about it. Now it's totally different, there's so much filming to be done, you're racing against the clock, and the last person they want to see is the writer. I'd go along to the filming of a show like *A Touch of Frost* (1992–2010), for which I wrote the pilot script and first two series, and I'd think, "What am I doing here?" It's thunderously boring watching other people filming, isn't it? Unless you've got a job to do, and what can you do as a writer? You can't say, "Ooh, can we change that bit there?" You'd soon get a flea in your ear.

Did they not try and enlist you to rewrite on the set?
Certainly not, not on a series. You might do a tiny bit, but it's a tight schedule. If it was a play or something maybe, but even then, by the time it's got on the floor they've got to get on with the thing; all that stuff [re-writing] should be done in the rehearsal. In the theater, which is what I've mainly been concerned with in my later years, you can rework stuff on its feet [but] in television you can't, people see your mistakes. Sometimes you do something and it doesn't work and you think, "I wish I'd done that differently," but you've just got to hope you're given the chance of having another go at it. It gets harder and harder. Today it's all money-based, you need instant success, instant ratings. People talk about the standard of television, what rubbish it is, but I don't agree. There are a lot of dreadful shows that you can see are put together by numbers, so cynical, and there's lot of style over content. I just shake my head at the urgency of the camerawork; you don't need it. Look at Woody Allen, the camera is an eye, it doesn't have to be jerking about all over the place. It's supposed to be exciting but all it does is give me a headache.

But there's rubbish in every field. If you went to the library, you'd find a fair amount there too, and when you think about how something like *Eastenders* [1985–] is done, it's extraordinary; they just get up and do it, they don't rehearse, they don't have time. I don't think my first play, the play that set off my career, was any better than a good *Eastenders*. The amount of talent I had to offer, I certainly wouldn't be noticed now, I'd just get lost in the rush.

You say that, but they could film one of the scripts you wrote for The Sweeney *or* Public Eye *today, and not only would they not be dated, they'd stand head and shoulders above the pack.*

I was terribly lucky because I came around at the time when commercial television was opening up and at the same time the working class was being given a voice—the kitchen sink dramas if you like. As with so many things in life, I happened to be there at the right time … timing is so important. I sold the first thing I ever wrote and before I knew it I was being asked to write other scripts, without the faintest idea what I was doing. I called myself an apprentice with a master's ticket, one minute I was working in an office, the next minute I was a television writer and I never stopped writing for, God knows, fifty years I think. I was so privileged to learn as I went along. Classes for writers never existed in my day, now you get degrees in television writing and sometimes *my* stuff is done on drama courses, it just makes me laugh. I'm not knocking modern writers, I've had my time and the world changes, but I was incredibly lucky to have found that world at a time when the likes of me were few and far between. I don't mean because of my extraordinary talent, I mean the people who wanted to do it. Now people want to be writers, back then you didn't know who the writer was, the writer was the backstage boy. But now, in this world of celebrity, writers have become personalities, you get pictures of writers in the *Radio Times*.

How did you sell the first script?

I just sent it in. I had nothing to do with the arts, no creative background, but I knew that the director was somebody important, so I sent my play to the director of a play I saw on television. The director's name was Peter Potter and he read my play and gave it to a man named Cecil Clarke who ran H.M. Tennant, the drama wing of ATV. Cecil Clarke bought it, and suddenly I had something on television. The play was seen by Ted Willis, of *Dixon of Dock Green* [1955–76] fame, and he asked me to write another play for a series he was working on. I said yes without realizing what I was doing, it was just the innocence, the naivety of youth. That play starred an unknown young actor called Ian Hendry. Ian liked my script and when he was offered a series on ABC television called *Police Surgeon* [1960] he asked them if I could contribute, which I did. *Police Surgeon* sort of grew, evolved into *The Avengers*.

You wrote for The Avengers *from the Ian Hendry days to the Linda Thorson episodes.*
  I wrote some scripts at the beginning and then drifted away from it. Brian Clemens was the leading light, although the man who produced it was John Bryce. He was mad as a brush and I think he had a lot of input. *The Avengers* took a bit of time to develop. When I wrote for it at the beginning, it was quite ordinary in terms of its style, it was just goodies chasing baddies. Then under the auspices of John Bryce and Brian Clemens it became *The Avengers* as we know it. I contributed to the subsequent series but not as a mainstream writer. That sort of show wasn't really my bag, I was more doing what you might call straight drama.

You wrote a lot of cop shows. What are the key ingredients of a good one?
  Well, with a cop show there are only so many plots. It can only be a robbery or a murder or a missing kid, you know what I mean? There are only so many ways you can say, "What did you do on the night of the twenty-fourth?" So I think the success of a cop show has a lot to do with the charisma of your leading actor.

Do you think in the case of The Sweeney *it was John Thaw and Dennis Waterman that gave it the edge over other cop shows you worked on in that period, like* Target *or* New Scotland Yard *[1972–74]?*
  Yeah, I think so, but it was also very well produced by Ted Childs, it just hit all the right buttons. But two very important buttons were the leading men. If you get guys who deliver the goods like they did, it makes writers want to write for them. I know as a writer, if there's an actor on a series I think is really good and is gonna deliver the lines well, then I'm gonna want to write for him, aren't I?

You were very involved with the series Hazell.

I wrote the first episodes and then took over as script editor, so I wrote loads of scripts and was also in charge of the scripts. I commissioned the other writers which is quite a hateful job because sometimes writers, especially inexperienced writers, don't realize that it might be a good script but is it a good *Hazell*? It's like if you said to Mozart, "Listen, my daughter's getting married. Can you knock me up a two-minute tune?" He's not gonna deliver a symphony, is he? A lot of writers say, "Oh, I couldn't write for series" and I always say, "Well, Mozart didn't mind being asked to write a bit of music for a couple of quid." As long as you try and write a good whatever-it-is you're trying to write, then you can hold your head up.

Can you explain how you, as the script editor, worked with the writers?
The script editor would say, "This is the style" and there'd be scripts to show them as examples. With *Hazell*, everything was from his point of view: We had a voiceover, he carried the story, but he also carried every single scene. You never cut away to the villain or whatever, it was always Hazell. We decided that would be our house style and it was quite a challenge. I tried to get a solid team of writers whose work I was familiar with, the pros if you like, and at the same time I tried to get in some fresh talent. Because of the demands of television, once the wheels are turning, you can't stop, so you have to have a backbone of people you know are going to deliver. That way, if the guys you're giving a leg up to don't work out, then you've got others to fall back on.

I always found that the more experienced the writer, the less precious they were about their work. I did try and introduce new talent but often they were the ones who effed and blinded about their work being destroyed. I'd say to them, "If you want to write a play, terrific, go and write a play."

Who were the guys you wanted when you were commissioning scripts? The pros?
Oh, I can't remember now, you're talking about forty years ago! I mean, there were guys I thought were terrific writers but I wouldn't ask them to write a *Hazell* because I didn't think they were right for the show, or they wouldn't enjoy doing it.

Roger Marshall?

Now there's a writer I have a great deal of time for. I think he's an excellent writer; in fact, I think he didn't do what he should've done. There's a writer called P.J. Hammond, Peter Hammond, who I think is another very good writer, very quirky writer, very interesting. Also Bill Craig, who never wrote that sort of stuff. There were a handful, and in those days it was only a handful.

What can you tell us about how you write? The process.

You start in all sorts of different ways. I always say that if you're a dentist and you go to a party and you're talking to people, you're subconsciously or unconsciously looking at their teeth saying, "Ooh, I wonder who did that filling" or "They need those straightened out"—I think you tune into what you do for a living. And if you're a writer, your antennae are up so you hear a little snippet of news or whatever and suddenly you think, "That really interests me as a script." Now why it interests you I don't know, because different writers are interested in different sorts of stories. My ideas could come from half an overheard conversation or, of course, many times, something that's actually happened in life. They say a writer's a man who takes a notebook on his honeymoon. A writer's always sitting on his own shoulder. I think, even in the most dreadful circumstances, you're thinking, "That's a good story." That's what you do, isn't it? You're telling a story. It doesn't have to be a cheap story, but you have to engage and hold your audience, and if you want to get something across, the way to do it is by sucking them along with you. And then it's down to the sheer business of writing. I know people who take three years to write something and I know people who write really good stuff in a weekend. What I do, when I've got an idea, I never stop thinking about it, consciously or otherwise, and I kind of build up a little file in my head until the point arrives when I think I'm ready to put some of it down on paper. When I'm writing, I'm like somebody standing on the edge of a swimming pool in cold weather, I walk around the edge hesitating, then suddenly there's a moment where I think, "Right!" and I dive in. There's a moment, and I don't know when it'll arrive, when I know I'm ready to actually start writing. I could sit at my desk for hours before that moment and I don't think I'd write much.

Have you ever sat on ideas for years and not known how to make them work?

Oh yeah, absolutely, I've got a book full of them, and they're the ones you think are the best ideas you've ever had. I wrote a stage play that I just couldn't get right. I rewrote it three times over the years but I never got it right. It was performed but I knew I hadn't really cracked it. Sometimes it's good to talk out loud, to try an idea out on other people. It can be quite embarrassing because it often sounds terrible when you're telling it, but sometimes the sheer process of speaking sets you free. I always say to young writers that I find that the actual physical business of writing sets the creative juices flowing. Just writing something down can suddenly set you on your way.

Bill Norton
Writer

The 1970s was *the* decade for action movies of grit and substance and nobody wrote more classic specimens than Bill Norton. His scripts were straightforward, full of rowdy humor and always on the side of the underdog.

He kicked off the decade's "good ol' boy" road rebel craze with the Burt Reynolds classic *White Lightning* (1973), written like many of Norton's scripts for the production team of Jules Levy, Arthur Gardner and Arnold Laven. He revisited the genre with the *White Lightning* sequel *Gator* (1976), *A Small Town in Texas* (1976) and *Moving Violation* (1976). His multi-talented son B.L. Norton got in on the act as well, scripting Sam Peckinpah's *Convoy* (1978) and the enjoyable *Outlaw Blues* (1977).

Bill wrote the westerns *The Scalphunters* (1968) and *Sam Whiskey* (1969), the World War II P.O.W. movie *The McKenzie Break* (1970) and the Corman classic *Big Bad Mama* (1974)—a *Bonnie and Clyde* (1967) riff that far surpasses its model in energy and punch.

He also added his two cents to the likes of *The Hunting Party* (1971), *Trader Horn* (1973), *Night of the Juggler* (1980) and Douglas Hickox's one-of-a-kind *Brannigan* (1975) with John Wayne as an Irish American cop in London. It's not quite as good as it sounds, but what could be?

Where did you grow up? Are you a country guy?
  I was born in Ogden, Utah. There was sagebrush and a few dozen families. In school there were nine grades in three rooms. Herbert Hoover was president and everyone was poor as hell. My father ran a general store because the Depression had lost him his job in San Francisco. My father was not a man who used swear words but he said, "They can shit on you but they can't make you like it."

How did you get your start as a writer?

I taught myself the structure of film writing from the example of James Agee's script for *The African Queen* [1951] which I admired very much. When I was in high school I got the notion of wanting to be a writer because of Jack London, George Bernard Shaw and Eugene O'Neill. So it was with me during all those times, but the first time I had a short story published was when the blacklisted writers of Hollywood started a magazine called *The California Quarterly*. I had a story in the same issue as Dalton Trumbo when he was doing a year in jail because of the Red Scare nonsense.

Were you questioned by HUAC?

I was called as an unfriendly witness while I was working as a park ranger with a wife and three children. Earlier the FBI had visited me and said I should tell them the names of other people in the Peace Club meetings and picket lines in front of the Federal Building, or else this was the last chance and my family could go to a concentration camp. I didn't believe that bullshit for a minute. When I was an infantry soldier I'd been shot at by machine guns on night patrol attacks, carried wounded men, had holes shot in my clothes and shot an SS officer in the Hartz Mountains. They could kiss my ass in their neat suits. I thought the whole idea of hating Russia and wanting to have a nuke war was fucking stupid and I told them so. At the hearing I said I'd write ten thousand words explaining the history of the American radical movement but I wasn't going to give them any names. They dismissed me after I made the audience laugh. I was a nobody of no consequence so I got away with it. The whole Red Scare war drive was utter bullshit, and General Eisenhower knew it. He calmed down the quack brains a little. Anyhow, I worked as a construction laborer, roofer, warehouseman, truck driver, newspaper reporter, truck tire changer, shipyard worker, and then park ranger for eleven years, all the time raising the children and writing stories, plays, little theater, low-budget films.

What can you tell us about The Scalphunters [1968]*?*

It took five years of the script being taken around Hollywood until Levy-Gardner-Laven bought it and I worked on their television series *The Big Valley* [1965–69]. Then Burt Lancaster said he'd do it and I worked on rewrites with him. UA produced it and Sydney Pollack shot it in Mexico. I felt lucky to be finally making a living as a writer. Lancaster was an intelligent honest guy to work for, I respected him. I didn't know Pollack much, but I've seen him a few times since then, once in Havana when I lived there after jail and was still wanted by the FBI so I couldn't come back to the States.

You went to jail?

After I retired at sixty, I went off on a modest Writers Guild pension to do political activist things like transport arms for Guatemala rebels and El Salvador rebels and Irish rebels. I ended up doing a couple of years for it in the jail in Le Havre, France, where I'd earlier landed as a PFC rifleman in the 71st division. I tried to be a medic when I was drafted into the army, because of philosophical reasons, but I later volunteered for infantry. After I got back to the U.S. and the FBI didn't want me any more, my old agent Mike Wise got me a job on a western idea a producer had. It was the first job I'd had in ten years, but I walked out because the producer said the two old-timer western guys in the story were rich and lived in a rich house. That's not what a western story is about. He had a lot of rich antique furniture in his office. I told him he needed to find a different writer.

I wrote a script that Richard Dreyfuss said he was going to do about my wife and I running guns, going to jail, living in Nicaragua and Cuba. Dreyfuss backed out but I never believed the project was real, it was just bullshit.

Any other unproduced Bill Norton scripts lying around?

I have so many unproduced scripts that a mule couldn't carry them. After *The Scalphunters* I wrote *Sam Whiskey* and a script called *Nitro* that Raquel Welch and Burt Reynolds almost did but didn't. I did rewrites for Raquel Welch on *Kansas City Bomber* [1972]. She was intelligent and a nice person in story meetings, I thought. The director Jerrold Freedman fired me because he saw it as a soap opera and I saw it as an action film with a super-girl star. Don't argue with directors.

What was Nitro *about?*

Nitro was about a woman who disguised herself as a nun to carry nitro explosives in Bibles, a crate of them on a train into Mexico for the Mexican revolution of Zapata and Pancho Villa. She meets an American oil wildcat driller and persuades him to help her when the train is stopped and searched by the Mexican army of the dictator Diaz. I guess it wasn't made either because UA thought it was too radical or Reynolds and Raquel took a dislike to each other. I wasn't ever on the inside of things with the producers.

White Lightning *set the tone for all of the Burt Reynolds "good ol' boy" movies.*

I was doing a rewrite called *The Hunting Party* [1971] that was shot in Spain with Oliver Reed, Gene Hackman and Candice Bergen, directed by a good guy, Don Medford. While we were there, Jules Levy asked me to do a story about moonshine runners because UA said *Thunder Road* (1958) with Robert Mitchum had been successful. So I wrote *White Lightning* and later went with Arnold Laven to visit moonshine people and federal cops and locations in Georgia. Arnold was going to direct it but I guess UA wouldn't let him, and Joe Sargent did.

He did a great job.

I thought he did a hell of a great job. Then later Art Gardner wanted to do another picture with Burt Reynolds, so I wrote *Gator*. The producers didn't want me to go on location when the films were shot for some reason, maybe because I was rude to Jules's son and told him to sit down and shut up when we were having a story meeting. He was there from school in Switzerland. Maybe that's not polite to say to the son of your boss.

It's the 1970s, Burt Reynolds is sitting in a car, but he's not behind the wheel! Jack Weston takes his turn in the United Artists production *Gator* (1976), written by Bill Norton.

Tell us about working for Roger Corman on Big Bad Mama *[1974].*

I did that after Levy-Gardner-Laven didn't renew my UA contract. Frances Doel, a lady who worked for Roger, had done the story and I screenplayed it out. Later, Roger's wife produced one called *Moving Violation* and she was very nice to work for, and so was Roger, a good guy. I got along okay with people because I like people, and I don't get picky about artistic things. I never saw some films I worked on because you have absolutely no control over what happens, good or bad. The filming process itself is out of my hands and I never had any interest in being a director. I was always trying to put some kind of a humanitarian message in a story but I didn't fight with people over it because I always knew it was a no-win situation. During the writing process, you have to make yourself agreeable to the producer, the producer's son, the star. If you don't, they fire you.

Anyone ever fire you?

The director Dick Sarafian fired me because I didn't agree with his idea that Burt Reynolds should act mean towards Sarah Miles and not give her a blanket when she was cold in a rewrite called *The Man Who Loved Cat Dancing* [1973]. I told him Gary Cooper wouldn't act that way in a western. He [Sarafian] was a long-haired hippie in those days and I guess he had inner feelings. I worked on a rewrite in Canada with Genevieve Bujold and her director husband, he was an okay guy, but they fired me because I warped the story so it wasn't an anti–Russia diatribe. As a Patton's Army infantryman, I wouldn't stomach that shit from some civilian asshole who never heard a shot fired in anger. Maybe they wouldn't let me put in my humanistic propaganda but I sure as hell wasn't going to put in any warmonger propaganda. Arnold Laven suggested one time that we do a story about pilots in Vietnam who got shot down behind the lines. Arnold's a nice guy but I told him I didn't care if the Viet Cong hanged them. That whole war was stupid. I got to know John Milius a little bit while he was switching the "Heart of Darkness" story. Later when he did *Red Dawn* [1984] I wrote him a letter saying I would shoot it out with him with M1s in the street but I never got a reply. I don't like warmonger propaganda shit. I got fired from a Brian Keith film called *Suppose They Gave a War and Nobody Came* [1970].

Is anything in the finished product yours? It's a good film.

I never saw it. My version of the script was rejected by the army—

they had script approval because they were providing the hardware, the tanks, for Paramount. The director was Hy Averback and he said that was the order.

What can you tell us about Brannigan *[1975]? Did you have much to do with John Wayne?*

I liked Doug Hickox who directed it but I didn't get to go to England with them. I saw John Wayne in the office when I was working on it but I didn't have story meetings with him. I did shake hands with Elvis when I did a rewrite on one of his pictures.

Which Elvis film?

Maybe the title was *Clambake* [1967]. I never saw it. I think it had motorboats in it.

Leigh Chapman
Writer

Other femme screenwriters specialized in action: Rita Fink, Marguerite Roberts, Harriet Frank, Leigh Brackett ... but as far as I know, only the late Leigh Chapman racked up multiple action credits as a writer *and* an actress.

She acted in the series *Ripcord* (1961–62), *Burke's Law* (1963–66), *Combat!* (1962–66), *The Man from U.N.C.L.E.* (1964–68) and *The Iron Horse* (1966–67), and in movies like *Law of the Lawless* (1964) and *The Professionals* (1966).

As a television writer she cooked up episodes of *Burke's Law*, *The Wild Wild West* (1965–70), *Mission: Impossible* (1966–72) and *It Takes a Thief* (1965–69). Her big screen credits include the Afro-action classic *Truck Turner* (1974), *Dirty Mary Crazy Larry* (1974), directed by John Hough, *The Octagon* (1980), starring Chuck Norris and Lee Van Cleef, and *Steel* (1980), directed by Steve Carver.

Early in her career she wrote a screenplay for Howard Hawks that was unfortunately never filmed. That's Howard Hawks whose pet themes and scenes are recycled in action movies to this day. Scripting skills aside, it's obvious why Hawks recruited her: She could have stepped out of one of his movies. The classic Hawksian heroine was a slim beauty with backbone and bite, holding her own in a male-dominated sphere. Actress Leigh Chapman was born for the part, screenwriter Leigh Chapman lived it.

You started off as an actor.
 I come from a town of a thousand people, in South Carolina. On a blind date I met the person who became my ex-husband. His father wanted him to be a doctor but he wanted go to Los Angeles to be an actor and I was like, "Let's go!" All the wedding gifts got left behind and we split for Los Angeles. When we got there, we didn't have any money

so I went to an employment agency and, relying on high school typing, I got a job at the William Morris Agency—the attorneys, not the agents. I remember going back to the employment agency and saying, "I don't know if I want to work there. It's kinda stuffy," and they said, "Are you crazy? You say your husband wants to be an actor and you don't wanna take a job at William Morris?" So I took the job and worked there for about a year but I had to be one of the world's worst secretaries. Messages would come in and, I mean, they weren't for me so I'd forget to give 'em to the attorneys! The only reason I didn't get fired was that both of the attorneys that I worked for would rather sit and discuss philosophy with me than actually do their work.

I was working through the daytime and both my husband and I were going to acting classes at night, and after that we were working delivering newspapers in Beverly Hills—and there are condos in Beverly Hills, you can't just toss the paper out of the car. So I was living on about two hours sleep. After about a year he wanted to go back home and I wanted to stay in Los Angeles, and we got a divorce. When we got divorced, I was still working at William Morris and with their permission I started seeking out acting work. They were very protective of me because they knew how naïve I was, but I got hired, and that was cool for a while. I had a part for a year, year and a half, on *The Man from U.N.C.L.E.* I had no concept of cameras and camera position and key lighting, all of that was very bewildering, and I hated getting up in the morning to go to hair and makeup. If I have to get up at five in the morning, the only way I'm going to give a good performance is to

A publicity shot of Leigh Chapman on MGM's *The Man from U.N.C.L.E.* (1964–68) (courtesy Stephen Bowie).

do a death scene or something! I did commercials and I was under contract to Screen Gems and guest starred on some shows. Apparently they thought they had a Katharine Hepburn type; however, they weren't doing any shows where you could possibly cast a Katharine Hepburn type! Not that I'm arrogant enough to think I was anything like she was. I realized I really hated being in front of the camera, and I got hired to do some stage plays, professional theater, and I hated that too—I used to think, "Oh no, I have to go to the theater again tonight and do the same thing all over again!" I don't like doing the same thing twice, it's my personality, that's why I was always a freelance writer. I'd have a heck of a lot more money if I'd taken some of the jobs that were offered to me on shows.

How did you go about making the move to writing?
I was dating a guy who was a successful writer, he did a bunch of episodes of *Combat!* [1962–67]. I needed money, and he was paying me to type some scripts. I typed about six scripts and I thought, "I think I know how this works." I've heard he claimed he taught me how to write. *Excuse me?* You can't teach someone how to write. You can teach someone a formula, but whether or not they can write is a whole other ball of wax. I thought, "I'll write between one and fifty scripts and if I haven't sold a script after fifty I guess I'm not a writer." Well, I studied the format of the show *Burke's Law*, wrote a script and bingo! One of my roommates was still working at William Morris and she gave my first script to the associate producer of *Burke's Law*. We had a meeting and he said, "I really like your script, but it needs some work. Are you willing to make the changes that I suggest, without any guarantee that I'll buy your script?" I made the changes and he bought the script and I think I did a second *Burke's Law* and then I was off and running and William Morris became my agent. They shot the first script I sold and when I watched it on television I was so naïve that I thought, "Oh no! That line was meant to be tongue in cheek. Oh no, what are you doing? This is terrible!" I got so angry that I wanted to kick in the television and I thought, "Leigh, do not watch your own stuff." As a writer you provide a blueprint but for the most part the director runs the show and if you're going to get upset by that, you're not going to have a career. So I just didn't watch the product.

You wrote quite a few scripts for The Wild Wild West.

I had a great time on that. I mostly dealt with a story editor called Henry Sharp. Henry was a marvelous gentleman and the story conferences were an absolute scream. I remember I was in the outer office one day, waiting to go in for a story conference, and somebody came up behind me. I turned around and it was the star of the show, Robert Conrad, and I literally gasped. I thought, "This man is more beautiful than any female I have ever seen!"

Any other memories of Robert Conrad?

He was very pleasant but I never got to know him. I always kept a distance between myself and the people I was working with, it was safer that way. Not that anybody ever hit on me, except for one horrible man. He was producing a pilot for a series and I had a part in it. I was already a writer, I'd just gotten bored and said, "Find me an acting job." We were on location in Mexico and I'm wondering, "Why have I got this big room to myself when everyone else is doubling up?" I soon found out! I didn't know that women weren't writing action-adventure, I didn't know what the rest of the world was doing, I was too busy working and I had no clue that I was kind of an anomaly. If you throw around a few big words and some quotes that you remember from college, Aristotle, Socrates, whatever, then you become a brain, and your ideas are as important as their ideas. That was my method of leveling the playing field, and ultimately, regardless of how I chose to present myself, my pages went in before I did.

You wrote the first version of the script for Truck Turner, *right?*

I think I wrote that as a spec script about a Steve McQueen–type bounty hunter and Freddie Weintraub either bought it outright or had it under option—I think he bought it outright—for a pittance. The next thing I knew, I heard they were going to turn it into a black flick and I remember saying to Weintraub, "I'm not re-writing this" and Weintraub said, "Well, Larry blah blah doesn't want you to anyway." So much for my big declaration! I got a co-credit on the story for that, but the film was so wildly different from my original script that I remember looking at Weintraub's partner at the screening and saying, "There's enough left, you could still make my movie." God, I was a snot sometimes!

Masters of the Shoot-'Em-Up

Take a number, ladies. Isaac Hayes under pressure in American International's *Truck Turner* (1974).

A few writers worked on Dirty Mary Crazy Larry *as well, didn't they?*

I was working for Howard Hawks, writing a script. I don't know where these things go chronologically—I don't even wear a watch! For some reason I went on an acting interview, the movie was *Red Line* 7000 [1965]. He wanted me to lower my voice, to sound like Lauren Bacall, so he told me I should go home and say my lines while pushing my diaphragm into an ironing board, and that would lower my voice. Well, it temporarily lowered it, but only when I had the ironing board in front of me! Somehow it came up that I was a writer and he said to me, "You know, you're a lousy actress but I'd like to read a script from you." I don't remember the script I gave him but the next thing I knew, he hired me to write a script about Vietnam, about two guys and a female. It was called *Night Crawler* but it didn't get made because it didn't get military support. I think the reason for that was that John Wayne had *The Green Berets* [1968] going at the same time and—I remember the quote because it was quite funny—the Hawks script wasn't Hawkish enough! He was living in Palm Springs and I had to go down there on weekends and deliver what I'd done that week. I mention that because he taught me how to ride a dirt bike! He was a lovely man and we got along great, principally I'm told because I was a typical Hawks female in that I'm opinionated and I argued with him. I was young, I was in my twenties, and I thought I knew everything. I didn't know who he was. Technically I knew he was a legendary director, but coming from a town of a thousand people, with a Southern Baptist father, I did not get to go to the movies. I might have seen a John Wayne Western but I didn't have that background. So I had no clue who I was working for, I was just uppity enough that we got along. He wouldn't let me cook, he'd say, "Women are lousy cooks," which suited me just fine, and he'd tell these stories at the dinner table about Bogart and Bacall and Hepburn and all these people, and I thought, "What do I care about all these people? I've never seen their movies. Thanks for telling me the stories but basically I'm not that interested." I'd never seen *Red River* [1948] and he kept talking about something called *Bringing Up Baby* [1938] which sounded *so stupid*. Years later I see it on television and I go, "Oh no!"—wow, was I wrong, it's a classic comedy flick. What was his last movie?

Rio Lobo *[1970]*.
He wanted me to write that but I dropped out and went to Hawaii and did drugs instead. I now know in retrospect that I was burnt out from three and a half years of constantly writing, because I'm not a prolific writer. I'll labor over a line of dialogue for an hour or two hours. So he wanted me to do *Rio Lobo* and in the interim he mentioned this thing he had an option on called *Dirty Mary Crazy Larry*. That wasn't the original title, originally it came from a book called *The Chase*, which I later read, after I'd written the script! He'd already commissioned a script by a very good writer named Leigh Brackett, but he gave me the impression that he'd created the character of Mary. I lived in Hawaii for a year, and yes, I had some fun. I came back when the money ran out and I thought, "Oh-oh, I gotta get some work!" The irony is that my original script for *Truck Turner* was given to a man I very much admire, an excellent line producer named Norman Herman. Norman wanted me to do a black version of *The Godfather* [1972], so I wrote a script

called *Blackfather*! It didn't get made but then *Dirty Mary Crazy Larry* fell into his hands and I rewrote the Leigh Brackett script that went back to the Hawks days. There was a co-credit on there, Antonio Santean, who was apparently one in a long line of people who had optioned this book and had scripts done. Supposedly it was him, not Hawks, who created the character of Mary. I don't know which story is true, but the first time I heard about it was with Howard Hawks.

Give us an idea of how you go about writing a script.
Dialogue is my strong suit and my weakness is plot, unless it's someone else's material that I'm analyzing and restructuring. I usually got hired to rewrite somebody else or adapt a novel, but if I was doing a spec script I would start backwards: I would think, "Oh wow, that would make an interesting chase scene" or murder scene or whatever, and then I'd work backwards—with character and plot—off of that scene. I'd build my story to have that scene occur two-thirds of the way through or have it as the final scene. If I was writing a scene and my characters wouldn't talk to each other, then I knew I'd made a mistake, that the scene either shouldn't be there at all or it should be somewhere else, because in my head they talked to each other and sometimes I'd take a wrong turn and they just wouldn't talk. My characters had a life of their own and if I was trying to make them do something that wasn't who they were, they'd just shut up. I don't know what other writers do, I imagine they're far more disciplined than I am, but sometimes I'd have to go back and revise whole acts to get them to talk to each other. And no, I did not go to Sid Fields' writing course, I never did any of that, I just fumbled around!

Steel was a troubled production.
I got a call from the producers saying, "Help!" They were in Kentucky with a week of film in the can and the script was too long, it was like a hundred twenty pages; so I got on the plane to Kentucky that afternoon and spent the next two weeks being the most popular person at a Holiday Inn, because basically it was *The Magnificent Seven* [1960], right?, so every actor is wondering, "Is my part gone? Am I dead? What's she going to do?" There was a rift between the producers and the director, I reported only to the producers. I was rewriting every night based on what I could do with what was already in the can. The director liked to

storyboard and the pages would get put under his door every morning, which of course pissed him off enormously. I was constantly rewriting because I'd hand in a revised scene and the completion bond guarantor would say, "Sorry, gotta cut it back some more." He was making the action smaller and smaller and smaller because "Budget won't handle it" so it was an interesting two weeks! Then I got a call saying a film called *Boardwalk* [1979] was in trouble, so I went straight to New York and started doing what I could to rewrite a portion of that. I've forgotten how much film they had in the can on that but it was certainly a lot more than *Steel*. I was a pretty tired camper!

Was there anything energizing about that sort of pressure, or was it just stress?

Oh no, I'm a pressure junkie. Was I exhausted? You bet! I was taking Dexedrine, supplemented by … let's say another substance. I remember the first night working on *Steel* I thought, "Oh shit, there's I don't know *how* many thousands of dollars a day being spent on this movie. What if my brain doesn't work?" But it worked. Was the finished product anything that anyone had hoped for? Well, no, but films happen in strange ways. There are movies where they start off with a dreadful script and a brilliant director and they end up with a brilliant movie. This wasn't supposed to be a brilliant script, it was just supposed to entertain, and I think it did on some level. So much of it is serendipity, the circumstances, all the weird things that go into how great movies happen or don't happen. That's what the movie business is like, and that's what my involvement is like.

How did you get involved with The Octagon?

I don't remember. All I remember was that I was hired and within twenty-four hours I was in a car heading to a meeting in Del Mar with just two words, "Chuck Norris" and "Ninjas," and ten people waiting for me to throw out a plot line. I don't know how I got through that one. I don't do pitch meetings. Story conferences I have no problem with whatsoever—because you're dealing with some degree of a finished product and I can have an opinion—but I don't know how to pitch anything. Nobody told me at that point that Chuck's brother had written a story, I never read it, I don't know what it was about. I did the script start to finish in two weeks. I didn't have a chance to rewrite, they shot the first draft. The dialogue is mine because the director told Chuck to say what I'd written, but the ending is not the ending I'd hoped for. I saw it once afterwards on television and I thought, "Oh, no, this is moving too slowly. Oh God." I wish I'd had a chance to rewrite it and pull out some of the stuff that was slowing the thing down, but those are the rules. If they truly are shooting, as opposed to "Oh, this movie's going to get made"—if they truly are shooting, you gotta hand in stuff.

Was it through Chuck Norris that you got the job on Walker, Texas Ranger *[1993–2000]?*

No, that was because of Al Ruddy. I've worked with Al Ruddy three times now, he always gets me cheap! I loved working with Ruddy, I worked for him early on, in my very first year of writing, on a script that Clint Eastwood was supposed to do. I don't remember the bloody plot, but it was action. Ruddy was also a writer and he kinda rewrote what I did. I was in the office every day paying no attention to Clint Eastwood, which was funny because he was a very good-looking man then. That never got made but then we did *Impulse* [1990] and the *Walker, Texas Ranger* pilot. With that one, he called me up and said, "There's a one-hour pilot, read it 'cause it needs to be rewritten" so I read it and I called him and said, "Ruddy, this is a really good script! There's nothing wrong with this script, I don't see what to rewrite." He said, "Well, CBS suddenly decided they want a two-hour pilot." So I re-wrote it and used the name Louise McCarn, that's my mother's name.

Why didn't you want the credit?

I didn't like the result, I thought it was too saccharine, and I felt I didn't need that credit at that time. I'd have a lot more money if I had gotten into writing pilots. I got offered show-runner on that, by Ruddy and Leslie Greif; I liked working with them, and Chuck's a nice man, but I didn't want to be a show-runner and I didn't want to move to Texas. I mean, it's a lot of money, and God knows I do love money, but I never wanted an executive position. Do you know who David Gerber was?

Police Story *[1973–77],* Eischied *[1979–83],* David Cassidy—Man Undercover *[1978–79]!*

I took a meeting with David Gerber, I don't know why, I think he was doing that female cop show. Anyway, I was sitting in his office wondering why I had agreed to let my agent set up this meeting and he said, "Okay now, I want you to be the story editor on blah blah blah and you'll have a great big office and wonderful furniture" and I said, "I don't do offices" and without skipping a beat he said, "Okay, you'll have a small office!"

Peter Yeldham
Writer

Peter Yeldham is an Australian who, like so many of his generation, took his talents to London. Once there he joined the ranks of the Spike Milligan-Eric Sykes–founded writers agency Associated London Scripts and penned episodes of British television thick-ears like *Shadow Squad* (1957), *Dial 999* (1958–59), *The Third Man* (1959–60, starring Michael Rennie as Harry Lime … crime-buster!), *International Detective* (1959–60), *No Hiding Place* (1959–66), *Echo Four-Two* (1961), *Top Secret* (1961–62), *Ghost Squad* (1961–63) and *Espionage* (1963–64).

On the action movie front he wrote *Code Seven, Victim Five* (1964), *Mozambique* (1964), *24 Hours to Kill* (1965) and *Our Man in Marrakesh* (1966), all for indefatigable B-movie producer Harry Alan Towers, and *The Liquidator* (1965), an enjoyable super-spy send-up based on a book by future 007 scribe John Gardner.

Returning to television in the early 1970s, he wrote "Read and Destroy" (hidden microfilm, glamourpuss lady agents, a comic butler), one of the best ever episodes of *The Persuaders!* (1971–72), and contributed scripts to *Van Der Valk* (1972–77) and *Zodiac* (1974), a mystery series that scored points by teaming Bond bird Anoushka Hempel with Anton Rodgers, one of the great comic smoothies of his day.

What can you tell us about Associated London Scripts?
When I first went to England, I had a young wife and two very young kids and things were a bit tough. Through a friend we met Spike Milligan. His parents had just emigrated to Australia and he liked the country a lot. He introduced me to his agent, Beryl Vertue, and she took me on. She was a great, great agent. She had a whole team of comedy writers: Johnny Speight, Ray Galton and Alan Simpson. I was a drama writer so I kind of got special attention. I was trying to write plays and getting a lot of them turned down and not a lot was happening. My wife was typ-

ing Spike's scripts for him so that helped us survive. The office was over a fruit shop in Shepherd's Bush, a pretty down-market sort of area at that time. Then they moved to a building in Bayswater that Spike and Eric Sykes owned. I took an office there but Johnny Speight would write his shows so quickly that he'd want to spend the rest of the day chatting, which was great fun for a while but eventually I said, "Listen, I think I better work from home because I'm not doing any work here." One day Beryl rang in the morning and told me that Granada wanted to buy a play that almost everyone had rejected. Then she called again in the afternoon, almost hysterical, and said, "You won't believe this but the BBC want to buy one too"—two in the one day. We were living in a small flat in Earls Court at the time and we'd been thinking of going home as soon we could afford it, but we said, "Right, that's it, cancel everything, we're staying," and I stayed twenty years. All our Australian mates came over and had drinks that night and I had a hangover I think I can still remember.

You wrote a lot of series television in the late 1950s and early '60s.

The big problem to begin with was that there was no tape. When I first started it was all live-to-air. The first show I had on was for Granada Television, a thriller called *Shadow Squad* directed by Herbert Wise, who went on to do some very big productions. In the middle of it, the cast jumped about a page. We nearly went berserk in the control room but they somehow picked it up and nobody noticed. Later on, when shows were pre-recorded, the actors used to say that directors would only stop the tape and record again if somebody took their clothes off or said *fuck*. I sold some plays to the BBC and Granada and that got me heaps of work, mainly on thriller series.

Any of the series stand out?

There was a show called *Probation Officer* [1959–62] which was slightly different because it dealt with social issues and was way ahead of its time. I got a British Guild award for an episode of that. Sadly, there are no copies of it in existence; they had tape by then but they didn't keep them. The other shows like *Top Secret* and *Dial* 999 and so on, they were good fun but they weren't really what I wanted to do with the rest of my life. Eventually a friend of mine, Ted Willis, said to me, "You're getting into a rut again with these series." I'd told him that I was getting into a rut in Australia when I was writing radio and that's why I'd left.

Masters of the Shoot-'Em-Up

He told me I should start writing plays again. I did and I sold quite a few because in those days there was about four or five single plays on British television each week. You could write a play on spec and have a good chance of selling it because you had four or five doors to go to.

Were you under the gun writing for these shows?

No, after working in Australian radio I found it very leisurely. You could really work on something, take a month to do it and get well paid, instead of having to write it in a day like I did in Sydney, which is a big difference, believe me.

Dial 999 *was produced by Harry Alan Towers.*

Harry was an incredible character. He used to come to Australia and do radio shows, he was called "Towers of London" in those days. I never did anything for him here but when I was going to England, my accountant, who was also his accountant, said I should give him a call. I mentioned that I'd just read in the paper that he was bankrupt, and he said, "Well, how long will it take you to get there? A few months? He'll be all right by then"—that was Harry. When I did get there, he asked me to do a few radio shows and that probably helped me to survive for the first year. Then he started to do films and hired me to work on those. I did them between writing films I liked! He'd always give you a four-line outline which was the idea for the film, that way he could claim a part writing credit. Some of them were okay but they were always a bit dodgy because he'd be financing the end of one picture with the money he got for the next one. It was a well-known thing that you held the finished script in one hand and he paid you in the other. Some actors wouldn't go and work for him unless they were paid before they left home.

Are the stories about him true?

Yes. They're all true. I don't know about when he was supposed to be caught with a girl that...

The "call girl racket"?

Yeah, I don't think that was Harry, to be honest. I mean, he was a shifty bugger, but he always had a great sense of humor, and I think that's what kept me going back to him. The films I wrote for Harry sort of paid the rent, films like *24 Hours to Kill*. I actually went to Beirut to research that, and Beirut in those days was an absolutely beautiful city, nice people and no trouble. Lex Barker was in it, along with what I used to call Harry's rep company: Wilfrid Hyde-White, John Le Mesurier, Herbert Lom…

Did adapting Agatha Christie's Ten Little Indians *present any challenges?*
It did for me because I'm not a great admirer. We did muck around with it a bit but we had to follow the story because you couldn't do anything else with it. But we had some nice actors in it—Harry's rep company was in that in full flow because he had those ten roles to cast! Boris Karloff was in it and I got to meet him, which was amazing. He was a very old man in a wheelchair by then. He was living in Knightsbridge, I was living in Kensington, and he asked if I could come and talk to him about the script. Well, when I got there, we had a drink and he didn't want to talk about the script at all, he wanted to talk about the cricket. He was a mad cricket fan and the Ashes was on that year and he wanted to know if I knew about the Australian cricketers and so on. So that's what we talked about all afternoon. In the end I said, "Well, what about the script?" and he said, "Oh it's fine, I haven't got a lot to do but that's fine." [Ultimately Karloff did not appear in the movie.]

You worked with the Australian director Don Sharp on Our Man in Marrakesh.
Don had been a friend of mine for years. We were going to do another film for Harry, but it fell through.

What was that?
I can't remember. I've got half a dozen scripts that were never made tucked away here, or they may be down at the film archive. Some of them are better than the things that *were* made. There was a nice one called *Fever Grass*. David Frost rang me and asked if I would write this script, he had a West Indian girlfriend at the time, an actress, and she was going to star in it. It was a good story and Frost was good to work with, very much on the ball. We worked three or four months and I got paid for it, but then his girlfriend gave him the heave-ho and the film was never made.

He didn't want to do it with his new girlfriend?
No, it was all to do with that girlfriend. There's been a few of those along the way, but there've been so many produced I can't complain.

Masters of the Shoot-'Em-Up

Spy-jinks. Terry-Thomas and Senta Berger in *Our Man in Marrakesh* (1966) a.k.a. *Bang, Bang, You're Dead*, written by Peter Yeldham.

Did you go to Marrakesh?

Yeah, Don and I went out to Marrakesh on a recce and spent a couple of weeks there. Harry always made films outside of England, something to do with the tax department and all the rest of it. But he always had contra deals so we stayed at the best hotels and flew on the best airlines, first class, very, very posh. It was only when it came time to pay you that there was sometimes a problem. Once, I forget which film it was, he hadn't paid me for the last draft and my agent sent in the bailiffs. Harry was on the phone to us saying, "Please, this is ruining me, they're going to take my furniture." Of course then he paid, he found it from somewhere. Years later he came to Australia again. He called me up and I said, "Good God, who let you in?" He was doing something here and wanted me to work on it, but I was too busy and recommended a friend of mine instead. I told my friend to make sure he got the money first, but of course he didn't and spent the next five years chasing Harry for it!

Was there a social community of Australian movie people in London in the 1960s?

Yeah, there was. Buddy Tingwell was there, we saw a lot of each other. John Mellion was there, we used to often meet. Ray Barrett was a close friend of mine. Ray's first job in England was in a show written by me, just by chance, as was Guy Doleman's.

What about Reg Lye?

Oh, wonderful Reg Lye, he was in a couple of television plays I wrote. He was a lovely actor, one of the best.

You worked with Rod Taylor, the most famous Australian actor of the day, on The Liquidator.

Jon Pennington, an English producer, got hold of the book, read it on a plane, got off the plane and made an offer which was accepted. Meanwhile, a quite high-powered character at MGM read the same book on a plane, got off and tried to make an offer but found that Jon Pennington had beaten him to it; so MGM got onto Pennington and said they wanted to back it. From the time I started to write it to the time it went into production, it was only about four or five months—that was a record for me. Everything went well except that unknown to us, Jon Pennington had a partner who had 51 percent. He had nothing to do with the film business but halfway through it he took over and kicked out Pennington. In those days contracts weren't always signed before the thing began because they were dealing with producers they could trust. Then along came this new boy who proceeded to sort of hijack MGM and hold them to ransom. It made the picture eighteen months late, by which time a couple of spoofs on Bond had beaten us to it, which was a great shame.

They'd originally planned to make a series of films, right?

Yes. I met the producer Sydney Box somewhere and we became friendly. He was keen for me to write something and made me an amazing offer. He took my agent and me to the most expensive restaurant in London and asked me to write the next two scripts of *The Liquidator*. I'd co-produce the first one and produce the second one. After that we were going to do a film called *The Pulse of Danger*, which was based on a book by John Cleary. My agent Beryl Vertue was used to big offers by this time but we came out of there and she said, "Golly, this is the stars, isn't it?" But terrible things happened because Sydney got ill and virtually retired from the business, so all that fell apart, though it did lead, in a roundabout way, to *The Long Duel* because he'd already asked me to write that.

Your epic.

Yes, it was something different for me, cowboys and Indians stuff in a way. Ken Annakin was hired to direct it which to me was a very good thing because he'd directed some great films. In the film business they're as rough as guts and they called him "Panickin' Annakin," but I don't think he was a panic merchant at all, I think he was a really nice guy and a good director. The money was all set—Arthur Rank was going to be the distributor and put up a lot of the money. The Maharaja of Beroda was going to put up a healthy chunk as well. So a small group of us went out to India on a recce. We went to Delhi and into the Himalayas, about a day's drive by Jeep, where there was this massive hotel, a quite mad thing built by the last of the mad English I think, the last of the Raj. It was about two hundred rooms, all of it empty except for us. There was a dining room about the size of the Melbourne Cricket Ground, with twenty waiters, and the six of us would sit there feeling very strange and lonely. On the first night the fog came down and soaked our beds, and it went downhill from there. We found some great places but bad rumors started going round. The Maharaja of Beroda was missing and so was his money. We'd done all our recce by this time, all we could, and we just wondered when the hell we were going to get out of there. There was a bit of a fight with Rank about who was responsible and it took about ten extra days to sort it out. Ten days with nothing to do but lie around the swimming pool and worry about it. In the end we made the film in Spain, we tricked up the Alhambra, but it didn't have the same appeal.

Is there a film where you think the script, actors and director really gelled?

The first film I ever did, which was *The Comedy Man* (1964) with Kenneth More, directed by Alvin Rakoff, who was a Canadian living in England. He and I really had a rapport on that film. Kenny was terrific. I liked writing it because although it was based on a book, it was about an actor who was out of work a lot and having been a writer who was out of work a lot in the first couple of years I was in England, I felt it was my sort of story too.

I love the script you wrote for The Persuaders! *[1971–72]. Was that commissioned by Terry Nation? He was also with Associated London Scripts, wasn't he?*

Yes, he was. Nice guy, Terry, we were good friends, we had adjoining offices. I was asked to write *Doctor Who* [1963–] and one of my agents at the time, not Beryl, said, "Oh no, he's writing films and television plays now and he doesn't want to get into that." I agreed actually and Terry took it on instead of me, invented the Daleks and lived on that for the rest of his life! But I only did that one episode of *The Persuaders!* because again, I was mainly interested in doing films at that time.

How do you start work on a script? Do you start with ideas for scenes, or characters, or do you sketch in the plot?

Sometimes you're adapting a book so you have to have discussions to talk about what you're going to do with it. But if I can write an original, then I try to start with the characters and often I start writing before I have the entire plot figured out. That's what I do with novels. I'm nearly always unsure how the book is going to end because that gives me a kick when I'm writing, to sit down and write something and suddenly think, "God, I never thought of that before" and feel excited about it. That for me is fun, that's why I enjoy writing.

Screenwriters put up with a lot of interference and producers' notes these days.

Too many.

It must kill the fun.

Absolutely kills it for me. When I did *Jessica* [2004], the adaptation, I had so many notes from so many producers and executive producers—some of whom aren't really in the film business, you know, they've raised the money or whatever—that it just drove me mad frankly. So these days, books are great because it's just the editor, the publisher and me.

And no actors?

Oh, I didn't mind actors, good actors. I never minded read-throughs where an actor would ask to change something. Trevor Howard was one of my favorite actors and was in two films of mine. He used to ring me up—usually at about dawn because he'd be on the set early—and say, "Can I just change this line a little bit?" All he ever wanted to do was paraphrase it, just shift a few words around. I'd generally tell him that I'd come up and we'd talk about it, and when I did we'd have lunch together and we wouldn't talk about it at all!

Were there any instances where you felt an actor really brought your script to life?
There was a Canadian actress called Katharine Blake who gave the most wonderful performance as an outback Australian woman in a television play I wrote called *Stella* [1963], and Ray Barrett in a play called *Reunion Day* [1962]. They were kind of the highlights of the television plays I wrote in Britain.

What can you tell us about The Age of Consent?
I went to meet Mickey Powell and we got on. I'd written all these films set in other places and I loved the idea that, at last, Australia again. The first meeting with James Mason was going to be at his agent's office in Park Lane. We turned up and she'd left her keys behind so we had the meeting in the corridor outside. I was sitting there on the floor thinking, "I wonder if this is an omen?" In a way it was, because I was never that satisfied with *The Age of Consent*, mainly because of Mason's accent. I spent a lot of time with James talking about this and absolutely convinced him that he could use his own accent. His voice was his great asset, one of the best-known voices in the English-speaking world, and it seemed a pity not to keep it. But on the way out to Australia, Michael—I'm sure it was Michael—persuaded James to play it Australian. I wasn't there for the shoot, they told me there wasn't quite enough money for the writer to come and I said, "Oh yes, well, I have struck this before." I saw it when they'd finished at Columbia's main office in Soho, just Michael and the suits from Columbia in this little theaterette. That was the first time I heard this appalling Australian accent and I thought, "Oh my God." At the end of it, the lights came up and the head of Columbia asked me what I thought and I said, "Well, I think it's very beautiful but I think it's a terrible shame that James used that Australian accent" and Michael said, "That's writer's paranoia, take no notice of Peter" and I

said, "The other thing is, you've misspelled my name on the titles so you'll have to do that again." That caused an uproar because they knew they had to redo the titles because the Writers Guild would've been on them like a flash. They didn't take any notice of my comments about the accent but the spelling was all-important.

Directors are usually viewed as the sole author of a film. Do you think writers get a raw deal?
I do, absolutely. It started in a way in France, with the auteur thing, and we didn't realize it was gonna spread quite like it did. I found it more and more difficult to work in films because of it. You had much more freedom in television; films really became the domain of the director, and the writer was hardly ever mentioned in reviews, it's "A Ken Annakin Film."

It's particularly galling when a review is praising the film's story, dialogue, themes, gee, who thought of them?!
And you think, well, I did, but nobody's going to say so. It's very unfair. I know a writer who very bitterly wrote to the paper and said, "Everyone loved the script but nobody mentioned who wrote it."

Stewart Raffill
Director

Two movies, released in 1980, anticipated the exuberant tone and breathless pace that defined 1980s action: *Raiders of the Lost Ark* and *High Risk*. The latter was written and directed by Stewart Raffill, a British-born filmmaker who'd already had great success with a number of independently produced outdoor adventure movies. Both *Raiders of the Lost Ark* and *High Risk* are about Americans facing danger in remote corners of foreign lands, and both are built around outrageous action set pieces; but whereas *Raiders of the Lost Ark* is a pumped-up adventure serial-comic book-rollercoaster ride, full stop, *High Risk* maintains a residue of 1970s grit. Yes, it's larger than life, and the final shoot-out is rock 'n' roll in the extreme, but it's got an undercurrent of social commentary absent in Spielberg's movie, and its depiction of violence is, for the most part, less flippant. It's messy and everybody pays for it, physically or emotionally. *Raiders of the Lost Ark* is kiddie hokum, *High Risk* is grownup hokum, a category that got harder to fill as the 1980s progressed.

James Brolin leads a great cast that includes James Coburn, Anthony Quinn, Ernest Borgnine and Lindsay Wagner. Brolin handles his *High Risk* derring do like a master; did it land him his *Octopussy* (1983) test? Burt Reynolds, Adam West, Robert Wagner, John Gavin … life would have been so much easier for "Cubby" Broccoli if James Bond was American: The late, great Robert Urich, star of Raffill's sci-fi adventure comedy *The Ice Pirates* (1984), would have been a shoo-in.

There's more social-political context in High Risk *than there is in most of the action movies that came out in the 1980s.*
It was about a bunch of working class guys taking off on an incredible adventure and I wrote it at a time, like today, when there was high unemployment in America. In those days, people took a little more time with

the characters and their backgrounds. Action adventure films today are really just about pure action without any sort of characterization; the action, pace and CGI work take precedence over everything and people fear the very idea of slowing down to develop a character. But the films would be better if they did. *High Risk* isn't absolutely real, it's a slightly grander-than-life piece with a sense of humor, but it's still rooted in real human sentiments.

And it's still incredibly fast and uncluttered.

I did try to keep it well-paced. Having four characters allowed me to split the action between them, which made the picture faster than it would've been if I'd had a single hero.

Several of your movies are about men and women facing the wild. High Risk *is like* The Adventures of the Wilderness Family *[1975] with automatic weapons!*

I've always liked the outdoors so I set a lot of my films there. When you're sitting down to write something, the first and most important thing you need to come up with is your characters, but the next thing that you need to decide is where your story takes place. The action will then flow from envisioning your characters in that place so you need to pick one where they can have a rollicking good adventure. I always wanted to have great adventures and always tried to write films with settings that would provide me with them. Working on films has allowed me to have adventures on the sea, in the jungle, in the deserts of Africa and South America. A lot of people making movies today, without knowing it, see the world through other movies and glean their ideas from other movies whereas I had all these crazy things happen to me in real life. I was working as a cameraman on a documentary film and was hired to go to Spain to interview people who were in prison for smuggling hashish out of Morocco. At the end of this odyssey, I found out that the people who'd hired me were actually drug dealers themselves trying to learn all about smuggling hashish out of North Africa! That experience was my initial inspiration for writing *High Risk*. The pilot characters were inspired by some people I'd met that smuggled pot out of Columbia by plane. *High Risk* was set in Columbia but was shot in Mexico. The entire crew was Mexican, including the cameraman, so I had to learn a bit of Spanish to do it. I'd spent a lot of time in Mexico and the Latino

Masters of the Shoot-'Em-Up

attitude to life had always fascinated me. Anthony Quinn is, of course, originally from Mexico and the humor that flows from his character in the film is really soaked in the feeling of Mexico, the attitudes of Mexican culture. In my experience, people from the third world usually have a better sense of humor about their position in the world than people from other countries.

Quinn gives a great, full-blooded performance.

Anthony Quinn was one of the most colorful and powerful actors I ever worked with. He got so wrapped up in the character he was playing that, for the two or three weeks we shot him, he literally became that character. It was nerve-wracking in a way because there was a measure of danger in that character, you never knew what he was going to do. He'd get mad and actually fire people off the set! I'd tell them not to worry about it because I knew that when they came back the next morning he'd have forgotten about it. The first scene I did with him was over three pages long and he wasn't very happy about that, but I told him just to play with it, and have fun. It was the scene where he asks his assistant, "How many gringos are there?" and he answers, "Seven" but only holds up four fingers. I told the actor playing his assistant to do that just before we shot the scene and Anthony was taken by surprise, which was good because he quickly recovered and went off on an improvised rant that was great for the scene. When he finished, he asked me what I thought. I thought his performance was a bit too big in that instance so I just pointed down slightly and he said, "Got it." He did it again, pulled it down a bit and it was perfect. You have to be very delicate in how you direct actors, particularly in front of other people.

You've got screen legends Ernest Borgnine and James Coburn in there too.

Ernest Borgnine was an incredibly basic, forthright guy and that's how he played his character. James Coburn on the other hand was more of an intellectual actor, the opposite of Anthony who was visceral and emotional.

What do you mean when you say James Coburn was "more of an intellectual actor"?

He was a wonderful character as well but he was a more contained actor, he wasn't somebody who'd throw himself into a part and lose con-

James Brolin (left) should've done more films like Stewart Raffill's rollicking *High Risk* (1980). James Coburn did plenty.

trol like Anthony Quinn. Few actors will. James was also not particularly well when we did the film, he had terrible arthritis and it slowed him down.

I really appreciate that the dog lives!

Disney did kill Bambi and Old Yeller, and killing people in the millions seems to be the thing in movies today, but I still think people would much prefer an animal make it through to the end. Somehow killing off animals seems crueler than killing off people.

You began your career in movies as an animal trainer.

Yes. I'm from England originally, I grew up in the Midlands near Coventry. There was no adventure in England, people have lived on every inch of it from the dawn of time, there's no real wilderness, it's a very limited world and I detested the weather! When I was growing up I always said I'd leave as soon as I could and when I was 18 I headed for the docks. I ended up in California and the first job I got was training animals for the movie business. In some ways the movie business was a lot easier to get into back then, partly because there weren't as many people who wanted to get into it. Eventually I started my own company and had elephants, tigers, reptiles.... I'd put my lion in the back of a station wagon and take him for a walk down Hollywood Boulevard on a chain! I worked for Walt Disney a lot in the early days and I also did a picture called *The Lion* [1962] with Bill Holden, Trevor Howard and Capucine. I took three lions from California to Africa to do that and one night, after being out real late with Trevor Howard, I ran into a wild lion who'd come to visit my lions! I used to do all the Tarzan movies, wrestling tigers, swinging from vines and all that shit.

How do you go from Coventry to wrestling tigers?
My uncle had a farm outside of Coventry and I spent a lot of my time there. We used to train horses and I always loved animals. I paid for my ticket to America with money I made by fixing up a broken-down racehorse who ended up winning a couple of races. I always wanted to be a jockey but I ended up being six foot six so it didn't work out. The horse looked like a centipede with me on it!

High Risk *has some textbook edge-of-the-seat scenes. How do you go about creating tension and suspense?*
You have to strive to outdo yourself, to say, "They won't be expecting this!" I don't like the audience to be ahead of me, I like to make it so they're not sure what's going to happen, so there are surprises and twists and it's visceral. And you have to make them care about the characters, that's the most important thing. If they don't care about the characters, they won't give a damn about what happens to them.

How did you raise the money for High Risk?
Independent films usually get made either as a tax investment or because you have enough name actors connected to it that somebody is willing to give you the money. *High Risk* was made very inexpensively. I just happened to meet somebody in Mexico who had the money and was looking for something to do with it. They liked the script, I went down there for two or three weeks to cast and find locations, and we started shooting probably five or six weeks after we made the deal. When you're in the business of independent filmmaking, you have to adjust

the film to fit the circumstances of the financing. If you don't find the budget you need for the film, you fit the film to the budget that's available. I did a very cheap movie in Africa once that came about because I met the Duke of Northumberland, the queen's godson, and he wanted to do a movie about African elephants. He wanted to do it immediately so I wrote him a script and we shot it. People have particular needs and you try and meet them. You have to complete and deliver the film in a finite amount of time and you don't have the lavish amounts of money that the studios do. They spend so much money that the films have to be perfect and they just keep spending till they are.

High Risk *had some release problems, didn't it?*

You have no control over your films once you've made them. If you're working for a studio, they will usually baby them and maintain them, but independents are so fleeting in their presence, especially nowadays, that it's very easy for films to get lost because the business side of things

Fun with guns. Lindsay Wagner and Chick Vennera in *High Risk* (1980).

isn't working. *High Risk* came out theatrically and was doing well, but within a week the company that distributed it went under and the film just ended up in no man's land. Audiences liked it though, and it was talked about and because of that I got the job directing *The Ice Pirates* for MGM. One of the studio heads had seen *High Risk*, he showed me the [*Ice Pirates*] script and asked if I could do it for eight million—they were having financial problems and that's all they could spend. I said I could, but I'd have to do a rewrite—it was a big space adventure story and I changed it into a more comedic thing, which made the special effects less important and less expensive.

How would you compare directing your own script to directing somebody else's?

When I work with someone else's piece, I try to render the author's vision as best I can. But even with my own screenplays, there are times a scene doesn't work as expected and a rewrite becomes essential. I'm always open to new ideas, particularly on things I've written myself, and if somebody in the crew has a better idea, I'm going to use it. If an actor can't get his tongue around a line, I'm going to change it. But I still try to keep the same essence. I enjoy that process and I think it works well for actors because they have enough pressure on them to perform without being held to specific dialogue. What *is* a problem is when you write something and an actor interprets it completely differently than you intended, delivering the words with a different consciousness behind them. You then have to either adjust your story to what they're doing or ask them to change their whole sense of the character, which puts pressure on them and potentially interferes with getting their best performance. Either way, it's a dilemma because it's hard to tell an actor to make these changes, especially if he's a big star.

Would you like to have a period of rehearsal to fine-tune the script and performances?

It would be lovely to do that but on most independent films you just simply don't have the time or the money. In television they do a read-through on the set to see how it runs and nail the dialogue, and that's great because you can see things that don't work, gaps in a character's thinking, things that didn't really pan out, subtle things that you might not notice otherwise.

Robert Urich and James Brolin were both dashing leading men who might've been even more famous had they come along a few decades earlier.

The studio wanted me to use Bob Urich. I didn't know him but he surprised me, he had a deliciously expressive sense of humor. I was very pleased with his work and we became good friends. Jim Brolin is also a good friend. I met him when I first came to America and we're still partners in business today. He grew up around horses and he's the classic all–American cowboy sort of character: tough, understated and honorable to the core.

What are some of the differences between making movies independently and making them for a studio?

As a director working for a studio, you're very locked in, there's a lot of pressure on you to deliver a film that fits their pre-conceptions of what they want. There's nothing wrong with that but a lot of the time they're judging it before it's finished, they look at the rushes without any idea of what it's going to look like all cut together. On the other hand, the problem with making independent films today is that within a week of finishing your project, someone will steal it and put it on the Internet. You call these people up and tell them that it's not their movie to give away or sell and as soon as they've taken it off one site they put it on another. Intellectual property has gone out the window and it's very hard to make any money. I can't see this changing, unfortunately, because the big companies that control the Internet, and allow all of this to happen, have more finance and political clout than film studios.

But it's still an adventure!

It's a grand adventure and it's like fighting a guerrilla war. Once you're in the field, you sort of live off the land and respond to what happens, you have to be ready to adapt, to change procedures, you have to be fleet-footed and fleet-minded. That's the rush, that's the joy.

Dick Clement
Director

Dick Clement and his writing partner Ian La Frenais are responsible for some of the best sitcoms British television has produced, banter-packed portraits of strained but sturdy male friendships like *Whatever Happened to the Likely Lads* (1973–74), *Porridge* (1974–77) and *Thick as Thieves* (1974).

They're not the first names that spring to mind when you think about action movies, but a close look at their back catalogue reveals they've been there (or thereabouts), done that, and delivered the goods every time: *The Jokers* (1966), *Hannibal Brooks* (1968), *Villain* (1971, one of the best British gangster movies ever made), *Never Say Never Again* (1983) and *The Bank Job* (2008) starring modern action great Jason Statham, inheritor of Charles Bronson's "all bite, no bark" crown. Even the broadly comic *Bullshot* (1983) comes close, spoofing as it does Sapper's "clubland hero" Bulldog Drummond.

If I'd asked Dick about all his action achievements, we'd still be talking. Instead I focused on *Otley* (1968) starring Tom Courtenay, and *Catch Me a Spy* (1971) starring Kirk Douglas and Marlène Jobert, the two "joke-and-dagger" movies that he wrote (with La Frenais) and directed. Both are spy stories with very high spirits and an abundance of flamboyant character turns.

Tom Courtenay was so right for Otley.

Tom's a smashing bloke and a joy to work with. He's a wonderful actor and completely collaborative. He didn't act like a star at all, but then he didn't really want to be a film star. He's a very serious actor and shortly after *Otley* he went and did a lot of theater in Manchester, to learn his craft.

Every actor in the movie is impressive.

The biggest favor a director can do themselves is to cast every part with the best actor available, even down to small parts, one-line parts. Irene Lamb cast it and she did a great job. Romy Schneider was not my idea, I would've rather have had an English girl. She was under contract to Columbia and owed them a film or something so she was kind of wished upon us. She was absolutely beautiful but inevitably, by being European, you had to write lines to explain what she was doing here, though it probably didn't matter in the end. I wanted Johnston the assassin to be played by somebody associated with comedy, I wanted him to be funny but then quite sinister at the same time. I approached Ronnie Barker first but he wasn't free and I ended up with Len Rossiter, who was a marvelous actor and quite subtle. I'd admired him in various things on television, as I had Freddie Jones.

Freddie Jones gives a great camp performance. Did you encourage him to pull out the stops?

Yes, he offered that up and it was fairly outrageous but I thought it was great. You give actors room to offer something up and then some of them need bringing up and some of them need taking down a bit. It's up to you to know which is which.

How did Otley *come about?*

Bruce Cohn Curtis, the producer, approached Ian La Frenais and myself to write the screenplay. We really had to be inventive because it's not a good book, it's really pretty crappy, but we did like the character of Otley and the idea of an innocent being dragged into various things that surprise you, spies and all that stuff. It's interesting, we've adapted good books and we've adapted bad books and sometimes a good book can make a bad movie and a bad book can make a good movie, if it has a very good premise, a very cinematic premise. Bruce was a first-time producer so they gave us Carl Foreman as executive producer—he was their insurance policy. His job was to steer the film in the right direction, to act as a sort of godfather to us. He'd written *High Noon* [1952] and *The Bridge on the River Kwai* [1957] and we were very honored to work with him. We went to see him—he'd been blacklisted so he lived in London—and he said he liked the script, he thought it was very good, but what it needed was a chariot race. Now, what did he mean by a chariot race? He meant a sequence that makes people say, "What about that bit when…" as they walk out of the theater. We thought that was a great note and went away and wrote the car chase in the middle. We already had a line in the script where Otley mentions that he has to take his driving test and we thought, "What if the heavies chase him while he's taking it?" That was our chariot race and it's probably the best sequence in the movie. After we'd written the screenplay, I put myself forward to direct it. I'd done a lot of stuff on television but I hadn't directed a movie before, and to my great delight I got the gig.

Was there anything about the move from television to film that threw you?
On the first day we were shooting outside a pub at Notting Hill Gate and I couldn't believe the amount of lights they were putting up. I'd done a certain amount of location work in television, but that had been snatched very quickly. Suddenly I was working with a full-sized movie crew and things took a lot longer to do than I was used to. It was a new experience, but I learned as I went along and I had enormous fun. The crew were great and helped me a lot because I didn't know one lens from another when I started. If you approach crews the right way, they're very supportive.

The opening at the second-hand market really sets the mood for the film. It's so exuberant.
We put a camera in the back of a van and drove it very slowly through the crowd. I told Tom that if anyone shouted out to him as he walked along, that he should just acknowledge them as if he'd seen a mate. I think there was a moment where somebody said, "Hi Tom, how you doing?" and he just sort of signaled to them that he couldn't stop. We managed to keep the film going for something like three minutes and it was kind of a nice shot, I'm rather proud of it. We stole a shot outside Buckingham Palace, on a day when people were turning up for investiture, and that was fun too.

Did your collaboration with Ian La Frenais extend to his chipping in with directing advice?
Yes, quite a bit. If ever I had a problem with the script, it was nice to be able to get another opinion. The great thing about directing your own script is that if you find something doesn't work, you have no compunction whatsoever about getting rid of it. That said, the script was very tight. Ian and I have always written very tight scripts and I like

that. I shot something like ninety-eight minutes and cut it down to ninety-three and as a ratio that's pretty tight, especially when you compare it to films where they shoot twice what they're going to use.

Carmen Dillon was the art director on both Otley *and* Catch Me a Spy.

She was a lovely lady. Again they wanted to give me somebody with a lot of experience and the first thing she said to me was, "Why do you want me? I've been doing this since Noah was a sailor." She'd done *Henry V* [1944] for Olivier and was a marvelous art director. She worked for the director, not for the budget, not for the line producer; she was there to make sure the director got whatever he said he wanted. She found the farm we used and that was a great piece of art direction because it wasn't really that far from London, I had to be careful where I put the camera so that there wouldn't be buildings in the background.

Otley *is one of the few 1960s spy comedies that's actually funny.*

As a kid listening to the radio, I was always a great fan of comedy thrillers. I always thought that exciting and funny was a great combination and I still do. When we were writing it, we were trying to make sure that every character was as interesting as possible, even down to giving the assassin character that Ronnie Lacey was playing a cold. He wasn't a particularly obvious assassin—neither of them were. Rather than casting two heavies, we tried to give them a little bit of personality and character which I think is our approach to writing.

You mentioned how tight the script was, but it's also very rich.

Yeah, it's trying not to waste a moment. I shot a movie called *Bullshot* for Handmade Films, it was a parody of Bulldog Drummond, an outrageous comedy, so there wasn't one day shooting where you could say to yourself, "Oh, we're doing the romantic scene, that's fairly easy, I can relax." Every scene was either funny or it wasn't working and it was relentless.

Was the novel that Catch Me a Spy *is based on humorous?*

Not to me! Again we were asked to read the book and we didn't like it, it really wasn't a good book and at first we turned it down. But there was a film I did want to do and my agent told me that the producer would do it if we did *Catch Me a Spy*. So we did it but of course the other film never happened! What we set out to write was something like

Charade [1963]—there's a good comedy thriller for you. But we had more trouble writing it than *Otley* because the basic premise was flimsier.

It was a French-British co-production, wasn't it?
Yes, it was. The producer was a Belgian and he was tricky, money didn't always come through on time and so on.

Was it more difficult to get a film made by 1971 than it had been in the 1960s?
A little more difficult. The 1960s was a very good time for making movies, but by '71 it was harder. Marlène Jobert was a big star in France and it was on the basis of her involvement that the film got green-lit. It's always the same with movies: You don't really care where the money comes from as long as you get it. There are films where you don't get it till the last minute, sometimes it collapses, it's always a battle.

Did the fact that it was a co-production with an international cast present any special difficulties?
Marlène's English was a problem, in regards to both communication—my French is at best sort of adequate—and learning lines. It's always tough if somebody has to learn lines in a language that isn't their own. You've got to be very careful when you're writing for them, unless they speak it really, really well.

What about post-syncing?
I'm sure we did a bit but there's a limit to what you can achieve. The actor has to be very comfortable with the dialogue because it's not just the words you're after but all the nuances behind them.

Bernadette LaFont is a marvel.
She was a lovely actress, yes, terrific. To qualify for the French money I had to have at least three French actors. Bernard Blier was another one. In France it was called *Les Doigts Croisés*, "Fingers Crossed," which is almost a better title actually!

How did Kirk Douglas get involved?
I wanted somebody like George Segal for the lead but whatever happened we didn't get him and the producer told me he'd cast Kirk Douglas. Kirk is a terrific screen actor but he doesn't exactly have a light touch, he's not Cary Grant. I had to shoot him in quite a tight period of time

Kirk Douglas and Marlène Jobert in Dick Clement's *Catch Me a Spy* (1971), one of the best comic thrillers of the 1970s.

and the first thing he said to me when I met him was, "I can't play comedy." What could I say to that? "Oh, I'm sure you can, Kirk, I'm sure I'll get you there"? I think he was feeling insecure and because of that, he could sometimes be difficult. He knew he was a Hollywood star and from time to time he'd pull rank, he'd say, "I've done forty-six goddamn movies, I think I know what I'm talking about," that sort of thing. Some afternoons he'd be sweet as pie and I'd think, "I've broken through, I've got a good relationship with Kirk now," but it was only because he'd had a joint at lunchtime and the next morning we'd be back to square one again. He gave it his all, though, bless his heart, but I just would've liked a different sort of actor. I wanted to make it more of a romantic comedy and I don't think that really came off because there wasn't enough chemistry between him and Marlène Jobert. I was aiming for Cary Grant and Audrey Hepburn in *Charade* and I don't think I got anywhere near that.

Where was it shot?

We shot the spy exchange on water up in Scotland, in a loch that was so deep we couldn't drop anchor. That was a nightmare because we had to keep stopping and moving the boats back to roughly where they'd been in the previous shot. The spy exchange on ice was done in Sweden and that was also very hard because I didn't have one of the actors. I had to shoot close-ups of him in England and I think it looks a little ropey. The hotel we used was the Great Northern which is just outside Kings Cross, and that was the genius of Carmen, my art director, because she had to find locations, on our budget, that looked like Eastern Europe—which it did, if you didn't move the camera too much in the wrong direction!

What had you learned as a director between Otley *and* Catch Me a Spy?

Well, much more about lenses, much more about the sheer craft of directing. On *Otley* I had a camera operator called Freddie Cooper who was marvelous and taught me a lot. He'd read the script very carefully, which was extremely rare. So every time we came to do a scene, he'd know what scene went before it and if we'd already shot it he'd say, "We ended that on a close-up, so we should start this widely." He was actually thinking about how to cut the film on the floor. Some directors don't want to know about that kind of collaboration, but I found it stimulating and I tried to work with the crew in that way on each film I did. You need to know the story you want to tell, hang onto that, but let the technicians become part of your team. Listen to them, get them on your side, work alongside them as collaborators, because it will help.

Chris Leitch
Director

Actor Ron O'Neal was smooth and intense with glower-power to rival Oliver Reed. Not enough movies revolve around him so the ones that do are all worth a peek. Everyone knows *Superfly* (1972), one of the early high points of the *Shaft*-inspired Afro-action cycle; everyone *should* know *The Hitter* (1979), one of the last and best of the breed.

The Hitter was written (with Ben Harris) and directed by Chris Leitch. Its subject is bare-knuckle boxing and there's humor, pathos and back-alley atmosphere to spare—think *Hard Times* (1975) without the relentlessly tight-lipped, austere style. The performances are all grade A but Adolph Caesar takes first prize as O'Neal's hustling manager; the guy's got nuggetty pizzazz like no tomorrow. The score by Garfield Ruff is excellent and deftly utilized.

The Hitter was Leitch's first feature but you'd never know it. From the just-so opening (that pins down O'Neal and Caesar's characters in a handful of dialogue-free shots) onwards, it's able, confident work.

Leitch directed other movies that fit the bill for discussion in this book, *Border Cop* (1980) with Telly Savalas for example, but his experiences making *The Hitter* are worth dwelling on, especially for aspiring filmmakers. They constitute what might be called a cautionary tale: Once you've got film in the can, your star has leverage … you better hope he's nice.

The Hitter *is a very impressive first feature.*
It started life as a story about a white street fighter, trying to hustle and make a way for himself in the world. I'd had a lot of experience teaching. Half the time I was in coal mining towns in West Virginia and the other half of the time I was in Ohio, parts of America which were very tough, unsophisticated environments. There were a couple of people that I met then that I sort of modeled the character on, but it was

just easier to get the money with a black cast. As long as it had some of the elements of a black exploitation film, there was an audience out there; and if you could do it for under a half a million dollars, there was a reasonable chance you could make these pictures.

How did you end up with Ron O'Neal in the lead?
We needed a star. As you know, it's a chicken and egg game. They say that you can have the money if you get a star, and when you talk to agents they ask if you've got the money and you say, "No, not until we get the star." But it's always easier, and still is today unfortunately, to cast black actors because they just don't get as many opportunities. Ron O'Neal was already a star, quote unquote, because of *Superfly*. Ron had a tremendous theater background in New York, Off Broadway and Broadway credits, and then when *Superfly* came out he was suddenly turned into this black exploitation star. This was about two, maybe three years after *Superfly*. He was the first piece of the puzzle and obviously the most important piece as far as finance. His agent at the time checked me out and checked out my financing sources and I think I was able to convince them to actually come up with money to make an offer to Ron for his services. I think he said he wouldn't read the script unless he had an offer and they said okay and put an offer on the table. I think we put a sixty-day limit on it or a thirty-day reading offer. Anyway, he read it, we met, he said okay, and we made a deal with him. Then it came time to cast the movie and Ron really responded to the script and the character from the point of view of playing an existential kind of guy. Ron was at the point in his career where he was doing some work in television, he was doing work in other features, but still there was quite a bit of a racial barrier between mainstream movies and black actors. Unless you were Sidney Poitier it was not easy, even though at this point in time, 1977, you would have thought the color barrier would have been more broken down, but obviously not. There just weren't a lot of parts.

He's very good. There's a particularly nice scene where he's sitting up in bed telling Sheila Frazer about his past.
He did a great job. I remember that scene. She's the only person that he ever really opens up to and obviously that marks a change in his character and I believe from that point on, the movie gets into its darker mode!

Adolph Caesar is even better.

My producing partner Gary Herman was in New York and he told me that there was an actor he'd just seen in an Off Broadway play that I should take a look at. I was coming back to New York anyway and we knew we had Ron O'Neal so we were sort of 99 percent sure we were going to make this movie. I saw Adolph in the play, we talked about it and I gave him a copy of the script. When we made the movie, I think Adolph Caesar was probably about forty years old but playing a sixty-year-old guy! Again, tremendous theater credits, Off Broadway and Broadway stuff, a really solid actor. We cast him and then we were able to get Sheila Frazer, who'd been in *Superfly* with Ron. Again, a lot of this comes together because unfortunately they just weren't getting the kind of work they deserved.

The casting inevitably leads to comparisons with Superfly.

I take my hat off to those early movies, obviously *Superfly* and the movies that were done by Gordon Parks and Melvin Van Peebles. They were trying to tell real stories and they weren't thinking genre and they weren't thinking exploitation, but in order to be able to make the movies that they wanted to make, the elements had to be there. We were coming in under the radar: It looked like a black exploitation film, it sounded like a black exploitation film on paper, but I'm a filmmaker and I just wanted to make the best film I could under the circumstances. I thought, "Well, this might be my first, last and only chance to do this," so I sort of threw caution to the wind.

Tell us about the shoot.

The shoot! Well, there's a story there and quite an interesting story and a lot of first-time filmmakers can identify with this sort of thing. By the time you hit the floor on your first feature, you really don't know what you're doing to a certain extent except that you have to trust in the script, the characters, the story and the actors. All the other elements are pretty new. We were going along really well for about the first, oh, ten days of shooting, but Ron O'Neal, as it turned out, was not the easiest guy in the world to work with. He wasn't the best collaborator and he was throwing his star weight around. However, Adolph Caesar, it was clear after the first few days of shooting, was kinda stealing the picture. When I say stealing, it was almost like Ron was giving it to him. As a result, I could see that the character Adolph was playing had a lot to offer and was just more interesting to look at half the time and that Ron's character worked best when he was just reacting to Adolph. Adolph was playing the jokester, the clown, and Ron was playing the straight man to a certain extent, except in his physicality, he had a lot of presence. Adolph was very good at being a real buddy to Ron, he'd be a really calming influence. He was very good at keeping everybody's spirits up, a really good cheerleader. He was also very good at saying, "Hey man, let's keep our eyes on the prize, this is you and me up there on the screen, and if you're just going to walk through the scene, I'm going to take it," and he was very open about it and Ron got it.

So anyway, the first ten days went pretty well and then we were shooting a fight scene, one of many. Ron would do three-quarters of the fight and then the stunt double would come in and do some stuff. I think it was the second or third fight scene we were shooting and Ron said he'd worked it out with the stunt coordinator and he could do the fall, which was basically just a fall into the crowd. Normally when you'd do something like that, part of the crowd would be stunt actors who'd catch your principal actor. Well, we were so low-budget that we only had one stunt actor and the long and the short of it is that when Ron fell back into the crowd he missed the stunt actor and fell into just regular extras, fell onto some guy's knee and cracked a vertebrae. Of course we didn't know that at the time, but Ron was in pain and we barely finished that day. I think it was a Saturday and we all had Sunday off because we were on location. The stunt coordinator said, "Yeah, little bruise back there. Put some ice on it"—it didn't seem that big. Sunday morning, I got a call from a production manager who was with Ron in the hospital. The doctor said he couldn't work for four weeks and as you can imagine, it was devastating. The insurance company told us to shut down for four weeks, Ron went back to California and the rest of the cast went their way. Everybody promised to come back and schedules were redone and again the only lucky thing for us was that so many of these talented people just weren't booked and weren't working as much as they should've been. So for four weeks we were down and in retrospect it was kind of a good opportunity for me to sit down with my editor, see what worked and what didn't work, at the expense of Ron's injury. We returned after four weeks, and we had another two weeks to shoot—it must have been like a twenty-five day shoot. Now, when Ron returned he was a bit of a changed man, and that's being polite. He was very angry, very demanding, and took the star thing to another level.

How do you deal with that?
Well, you do it one day at a time. As a director, your job is to be a supportive, sometime father figure to your cast, which means you can be a loving father figure or a stern father figure or taskmaster. You find yourself learning this by the seat of your pants. It's a trial by fire, you gotta do it, because this is your life, your career on the line, so you've gotta reach down deep and suck it up. You take a lot of abuse. When an actor has these sorts of problems and he's your star, you try and take it off the set. You see the warning signs and you say, "Let's all go take a break, Ron, let's go talk it out." Sometimes those things worked and sometimes they didn't and sometimes you just continue on. Another crisis occurred on the last day of shooting. It was the climactic fight scene in the movie where he's been set up by the villain of the piece, Louisiana Slim I think was the name of the character, another wonderful actor. We started that day about seven a.m. About halfway through the day, Ron O'Neal just lost it, he hated the choreography of the fight and started screaming at everybody and being very abusive. We tried to work around him but it was becoming clear to me that he was in a spiraling downward dark place. People were coming up to me, my AD, my producer, and saying, "I don't know if we're going to make it through this." We took a lot of breaks and the filming was really being stalled. It was a non-union crew but when you're working with such low budget margins, you're still concerned. Then, around hour thirteen, Ron started to pick on my wife for some reason or other. I was married at the time and she was the wardrobe and costume supervisor. I was pretty frazzled, burned out, and I just said, "You've just crossed the line, bud. Don't say that," and he looked at me and he said, "Who's gonna stop me?" And I said, "I will," and he attacked me. I'm a fairly big guy, I'm about 6'2" and at that time I was in a ton better shape but I certainly wasn't a boxer or a fighter. But when he attacked me, I decided I was going to defend myself. He ran across the set, knocking down Adolph Caesar who was trying to be the peacemaker, and took a swing at me. I got out of the way and then, in one of these split second decisions, I hit him. I must've

hit him enough to knock him back because the next thing I remember, the crew were pulling us apart, like a bar brawl.

Then suddenly my wife screamed out because when Ron had charged across the set and knocked Adolph Caesar to the ground, he'd knocked him unconscious. Adolph was not a big guy and the floor was concrete. At that point all the attention went to Adolph. We called an ambulance, Ron stormed off the set to his trailer, and everybody was looking at me. It was beyond disaster, it was tragic. The paramedics came and took Adolph away, I was following them and as they were about to put him in the ambulance, I felt his hand reach out and grab mine. He then opened one eye and said, "Come in the ambulance and close the doors, I wanna talk to you." I mean, I couldn't have scripted this.

He got me in the ambulance and said, "I just did this to get everyone's attention away from you and Ron. What are we gonna do? We gotta finish this movie, finish this scene." I said, "Well, are you okay?" and he said, "Hell yes, I'm okay, I'm just acting! You've gotta go into that trailer and you've got to apologize to him and you've gotta get his ass back." We came up with a plan where the line producer would go to the trailer, knock on the door, and tell Ron that Adolph was in the ambulance and wanted to talk to him. Ron felt bad about knocking Adolph over, he didn't feel bad about attacking me at all. So Ron went to the ambulance to talk to Adolph and Adolph probably gave the performance of his life in convincing Ron that we had to finish the film. Ron said, "Fuck it, I'm walking off, I'm not working with that director" and blah blah. Then it was my turn to go into Ron's trailer and basically get down on my knees and beg him to return and apologize and listen to Ron rant and rave for about fifteen minutes. Then he said, "Okay, we'll go back. You call the entire crew together and you apologize in front of them" and he listed all these things I had to apologize for. I had no choice, really, it was beyond embarrassment. I just wanted to finish this movie and I knew that it was the only way this actor would work. Of course the crew knew what it was all about; they were loyal to me, they basically hated Ron at this point too. So we shot for about another twelve hours, an entire twenty-four hours straight—longest day I'd ever experienced on a film set. Never want to do it again.

So the film's in the can.

Chris Leitch • Director

The film's in the can and edited and, surprise surprise, we ran out of money. To get a distribution deal, we had to really turn it into a black exploitation film. We had to re-shoot the ending, add more violence. I didn't really want to go in that direction but I was broke. We did the new ending, the shoot-out. It was like a day shoot, it was easy, we shot it in Hollywood, and it was all fine. It was almost like, for Ron, it kinda never happened. I mean, he was in total denial that there'd been a problem.

What sort of release did it get?

The number of theater screens that were available to a film of this type was limited to major cities with huge black populations. So the release of the movie was really limited to New York, Chicago, Baltimore, Washington, Detroit, initially. Then from that point on they rolled it out to other black cities in the South.

What was the response?

The movie was entered, I believe, in the Miami Film Festival and this was purely a fluke; the movie was not intended to hit the festival circuit but the distributor who came on board actually liked the movie enough in the end to enter it. Adolph Caesar won Best Actor, Ron O'Neal was nominated and I got Best First Feature over a film by Bobby Roth, who's a colleague of mine now. He had a film, a more "legitimate" movie about his experiences growing up in New York and working in the garment industry, and lo and behold what everybody assumed was this black exploitation film walked away with the equivalent of the Sundance Audience award. It was kinda nice. That didn't translate to anything beyond that festival though! We did go to the Chicago Film Festival and we got a Best First Feature mention, but from that point on, there wasn't the same publicity media machine that there is nowadays, and the film just played out to the audience it was primarily intended for.

Did you go see it in a theater, with a paying audience?

Yes, I saw it in the theaters and there was no crossover. I saw it in Baltimore and in New York, and I was the only white guy in the audience.

Did the audience get into it?

Totally. The experience in those days of going to see a black exploitation film with an audience was that the audience talked to the screen, talked to the characters, the whole time.

It's a great way to see a movie, an action movie.

Unfortunately now in the theaters, if they're talking, it's on their cell phones, but in those days they really got into it, particularly in the fight scenes. They're yelling, they're screaming, they're on their feet, it's a very 3D experience. They related, which was very gratifying. It's probably from my directing experience the only time I've watched a movie I made with that sort of outrageous, over-the-top reaction. To see a movie that you made connect with the audience in such a visceral way is amazing.

Steve Carver
Director

Roger Corman productions of the 1970s have a rowdy, ragged energy that can't be beat. It's the energy of young directors, excited to be making movies, undaunted by restrictions of time and money—great talents like Jonathan Kaplan, Jonathan Demme, George Armitage, Paul Bartel (he was younger than he looked!) and Steve Carver, director of *The Arena* (1973), *Big Bad Mama* (1974), *Capone* (1975) and *Fast Charlie, The Moonbeam Rider* (1978). Most of these guys made action movies (and the odd "frisky nurse" opus) for Corman, then moved into straight dramas and comedies. Steve Carver on the other hand worked in and around action for most of his career, more often than not with Sam Peckinpah veterans L.Q. Jones and R.G. Armstrong in tow. *Drum* (1976) and *Steel* (1980) are getting there, *Oceans of Fire* (1986), *Bullet Proof* (1988), *River of Death* (1989) and *Dead Center* (1993) are right on target.

Then there are the Chuck Norris starrers *An Eye for an Eye* (1981) and *Lone Wolf McQuade* (1983). The latter, with its spaghetti western visual style and sad-rousing Francesco De Masi score, was the turning point for Norris. Before *Lone Wolf McQuade* he was a star, after *Lone Wolf McQuade* he was an icon.

How did you end up shooting your first feature The Arena *in Italy?*

I started out trying to make it in Tel Aviv, Israel, with Menahem Golan, but it was too expensive to put together some of the sets and costumes we needed, being a gladiator picture, so Roger sent me on to Italy. In Italy, Mark Damon was the producer. He was a nice guy; he was basically an actor trying to make some money on the side by helping Roger produce films, horror films, *Lady Frankenstein* (1971), movies like that. Mark tried to talk Roger into making the picture bigger and Roger, being money-minded, said, "Forget it" and sent me on to Spain. In Spain,

Masters of the Shoot-'Em-Up

Gregorio Sacristan was the producer on the show and he couldn't put it together either. When it got too expensive, Roger would flag me on. Then Mark Damon called Roger and said he could make it for half the price of whatever he'd said before, so I went back to Italy and we made it. Five months had gone by, Israel to Italy to Spain and then back to Italy.

You shot it at Cinecittà?
And I was just in awe, and nervous like hell, it being my first commercial picture. Fellini was on the next set shooting *Amarcord* [1973] and because he liked big-breasted women fighting he used to come onto the set and stand next to me by the camera. He would always show up whenever I had the girls fighting, he somehow knew about the schedule.

The score was by Francesco De Masi, who later did such a wonderful job on Lone Wolf McQuade.
Francesco De Masi was [Ennio] Morricone's orchestrator and conductor. When I went to Rome to record with De Masi, Morricone was there and was very influential with regard to all the people he had worked with, the harmonica player, the guitarist, the whistler and so on.

Did shooting in Italy make it harder?
No, actually it was a lot easier. If I'd shot it in America, it would've been Roger Corman on me twenty-seven hours a day to get everything shot in three days or whatever. I had more money to work with because the dollar went a long way, they already had all the sets and costumes, and the people were great. The cameraman was Aristide Massacesi, who'd done a lot of westerns at Elios Studios. In the United States, I would have been working with people who were just coming into the business—that's the way Roger gets them cheap. Or I would have been working with people who are making a deal and don't give a damn about filmmaking. That's what I found out from making pictures in the States with Roger afterwards. When I came back and did *Big Bad Mama*, I didn't have as many days to shoot and I didn't have the real sound, seasoned crew to work with; I had great actors, that was it. In Italy it was a breeze because they were devoted, passionate people. Italians have

class when they make pictures. Everything is done with passion, nothing is done haphazardly or is a job, clock strikes five they go home—no way. The way the Italians make pictures is fun. I had a lot of superstitious Southern Italian people on the crew and when I say superstitious, I mean really superstitious. You can't wear purple on the set, whenever they make the first shot the operator is the only one that can look in the direction where the camera's pointing, everyone else has to look in the opposite direction, you can't bring an umbrella on the set…

What about a purple umbrella?

Oh man, I woulda gotten shot! I mean, I was wearing a purple shirt once and they pulled it off of me and everybody on the crew had to come over and stomp on it. And I became superstitious too, I wouldn't allow purple on the set!

Pam Grier was one of the stars of The Arena *and you worked with her again on* Drum.

Pam was great to work with, a sweetheart. [Quentin] Tarantino told me that when he worked with Pam she'd recount the things I'd done with her in Italy and he was amazed that I got her to do them, nude pillow fights and stuff like that. She did all her own stunts because there weren't very many black stunt doubles. She'd done a lot of pictures in the Philippines, women-in-cages movies, so she was used to doing that physical stuff.

Did you learn anything from working with Roger Corman?

Absolutely. Roger's the greatest teacher of making films. He teaches you not to waste time and he teaches you a lot of tricks. When he shot his period films *Bloody Mama* [1970] and *The St. Valentine's Day Massacre* [1967], he had cars painted one color on one side and another color on the other side and he had them go around in a circle so he got twice as many cars in the shot. The other thing he did was put bullet hits on one side of the car, but not on the other, so he could use it twice. He'd use extras in a similar fashion, have them walk through the scene, put on different clothes and go back into the scene. So basically Roger taught you how to double production values with these tricks. And when I did *Big Bad Mama* and *Capone*, with two pennies and not a lot of time, it was a lot of fun trying to figure out how to make them look like bigger pictures than they were.

Roger was a big fan of the storyboarding that I learned at the American Film Institute. A lot of directors would give him little doodles, but he was very, very pleased when he saw a real storyboard that actually progressed the shooting. I would generate shot lists from the storyboards and Roger would go over them the night before and sometimes say, "You don't need this, you don't need that." Of course I shot whatever I wanted to, whatever I could, given the time and money, but Roger would be very much involved. Paul Bartel was my assistant on *Big Bad Mama*. He directed a picture for Roger and was three days behind schedule [so] Roger took his script, ripped out a handful of pages and said, "Now you're on schedule." These are the things that people talk about and joke about, but they're absolutely true. He was really keen, he'd sit in the editing room and in order to save time in editing he'd tell you where to cut. I had to play tricks with him in order to get a cut that I liked; very seldom would I win an argument. The things he taught me influenced everything I do in film, I can't credit him enough.

I love Bill Norton's Big Bad Mama *script.*

I went over the script with him but I didn't have much control over *Big Bad Mama* because of Roger and because of the fact that Angie Dickinson and Bill Shatner had script approval. Once a script was approved and a project was in motion, any changes were a big deal, especially with Roger. And at the time I wasn't that "into" trying to change scripts to make them my own, and I'm still not. If a script comes to me and I like it, the changes that I make are minimal. However, if I find some major flaw, I'll work with the writer and see if it can be corrected.

Do you think film schools should teach their students how to deal with producers that rip pages out of scripts and won't let directors edit the movie the way they want to?

Well, in my opinion I went to the best film school there is, the American Film Institute. At the time, this was 1970, we had everybody in the industry available to us, we could talk with anybody, everybody would respond. If I wanted to talk to Alfred Hitchcock I called him up on the phone. I mean, I'd bump into Lee Marvin in the library, I'd see Sam Peckinpah in the bathroom, it was unbelievable. All the instructors were excellent, the equipment was top-of-the-line and we could do anything we wanted, we had an unlimited budget. When I did a short horror picture called *The Tell-Tale Heart* [1971], based on the Edgar Allan Poe story, I made a budget—that was part of the learning experience—but I never kept to it because I could get anything I needed for free, equipment or people. The only governing factor was time. I had Sam Jaffe, Alex Cord, a lot of great actors and they were committed to a certain time frame so that kept things in check.

Who impressed you the most when you were at the AFI?
Gregory Peck, Charlton Heston, George Seaton and George Stevens Sr.—they impressed me the most because I spent the most time with them. They were my mentors, they were the guys who literally came once every week or ten days or whatever and sat down with me to critique my work, share their insights and tell me stories. I had a great time with these people, they were incredible.

How did you get involved with An Eye for an Eye?
I was doing a picture with Tom Laughlin, the guy who did *Billy Jack* [1971]. I prepared, cast and almost shot *Billy Jack Goes to Washington* [1977] and then Tom took it over. Frank Capra Jr. was the line producer, production manager, that's how I met Frank. When Frank went over to Avco Embassy, he came to me with *An Eye for an Eye*, introduced me to Chuck and we hit it off. Chuck, because he was so into teaching and promoting the martial arts at that time, had his own team, his own people. I just came in, put together a crew and worked on the script a little bit. Bob Remy, the head of Avco Embassy, was also a friend of mine from Universal, so everything went very smoothly. It was an amazing bunch of people and such a pleasant experience that Chuck and I said that we'd do another picture afterwards.

Was the Lone Wolf McQuade *script written for Chuck?*
No, the script fell into my lap from a writer called B.J. Nelson. It wasn't called *Lone Wolf McQuade* originally, it was called something with *Texas Ranger* in it, *Lone Wolf Texas Ranger*, something like that. It's actually based on a real character who was still alive at the time. I really liked it because it was unusual, a modern western, and I thought it would be a great vehicle for Chuck. When we were making *An Eye for an Eye* he had said to me that he wanted to do something more in the line of a John Wayne picture. So I had this thing in my mind that this guy wanted

Will they never learn? Professor Toru Tanaka tries his luck against Chuck Norris in Steve Carver's *An Eye for an Eye* (1981).

to be like John Wayne but he had this blonde nice-guy-next-door appearance, and I thought, "We gotta mess it up some." I got a lot of promises from him that he would grow a beard and he would drink beer and do all these things, burp, you name it, to make himself real rough. But at the time of shooting I had to fight with him to get him to do all this stuff because he said he had all these kids looking up to him as a martial artist, and he didn't want to let them down and play a character that may not be a good role model. So the whole design of the Lone Wolf character came from those arguments—a rough and dirty, but straightforward and honest guy. *Lone Wolf McQuade* was turned down by every major studio—even Orion turned it down. The only reason they did it was because another picture fell through and they had some money. They called two weeks after they refused it and said okay. This is how they get made.

The opening is so good.

Well, I liked Sergio Leone a lot, I love all the Italian westerns. The titles, the big close-up shots, were designed in imitation of the spaghetti westerns, particularly *Once Upon a Time in the West* [1968], my favourite Leone picture. But the pace had to be different because of the American market, especially at that time. The opening sequence was shot in El Paso, right on the border—we could throw a stone into Mexico from where we shot it.

David Carradine was someone you worked with a lot.
I met him on *Fast Charlie, the Moonbeam Rider* which Roger was making for Universal. The script, about a cross-country motorcycle race in 1929, was originally meant for Steve McQueen, but McQueen wasn't doing it for whatever reason. I had to meet Walter Mirisch and get okayed and all that stuff but, unlike *Capone*, it wasn't really a studio-over-my-shoulder-type picture. David was late coming to the production so I didn't meet him till I went on location in Oklahoma. I was nervous to meet him because I'd heard a lot about him—that he was on drugs and all this sort of stuff. Even [Martin] Scorsese, who did *Boxcar Bertha* [1972] with David, told me some stories, and I thought, "Oh my God, this guy is a real loon. He's gonna jump on me, beat me to death or something." Anyway, maybe a week before we started shooting, he walks in, sits across from me, barefoot, picking his toes, and whatever he was picking he was eating, and he was just looking at me like, "What do you want me to do?" and I'm thinking, "This is David Carradine?!" I was so surprised and he was so fantastic to work with, the sweetest guy and a consummate professional. I did six pictures with David and he became one of my best friends. If you look at the films that I've done, you'll see there are certain actors that I've worked with many times and this is because they are so professional, so loyal, so down-to-earth, and those are the type of people that I like being around, that I like working with, especially under pressure. On *Fast Charlie, the Moonbeam Rider* there was a scene in a bar where he was supposed to go in and order a baloney sandwich and take a couple of bites out of it. At the end of every take, David would run outside and go out into the woods. I'm scratching my head thinking, "What's he doing? Is he doing drugs?" So I followed him out and I saw him sticking his finger down his throat, throwing up. When I asked him what was wrong, he said he was a vegetarian, he didn't eat meat. I said, "Why didn't you tell me? I would've had the prop man

make you a tuna fish sandwich!" and he just said that it wasn't a big deal. That's how David was.

L.Q. Jones and R.G. Armstrong are always good value.
They're great. These are the two greatest guys around. I wanted them in every film, they're like my entourage. These are the type of guys, you tell them to jump off a building and they say, "What floor?"

Would you ever commit to work on a film with actors you didn't get along with?
Well, unfortunately, the first television film I did, I don't want to go into detail because there's litigation on it, but there was an actor on it who kept coming in drunk, and he was well in enough with CBS that he made a phone call and said that I was harassing him on set. Maybe I was harassing him, he was harassing me, he was drunk, you can't work with somebody that's drunk. I yelled and screamed and I walked off the show and that got me blackballed at CBS for years until I did *Oceans of Fire* for them and got back in their good graces. If I don't like an actor, if I can't fire them, why work? I'm out there to have fun, I'm out there to make a picture that's commercial, I'm out there to work with people and be professional. If I can't do that, and I can't make the picture that they're asking me to make, that I'd like to make, that I committed to make, why do it? Which maybe isn't a very practical attitude now because pictures are hard to come by, but in the past there were pictures being offered all over the place and if I went into a meeting and they said, "We're going to have a say in all the rushes and tell you what to cut," forget that, who needs that?

Is working on studio movies less fun than it used to be?
Yeah, it's different now. Because the film is pre-sold, and because the actor has a following and is worth X-amount of dollars at the box office, the actor has tremendous power—even actors that are coming up, that did two pictures or a television show. The studio will stand behind them because they're a bunch of yes-people and the director doesn't have a leg to stand on. If the director has won lots of awards and made a lot of commercially successful pictures, then maybe there's a middle ground somewhere; but most directors I know, who have worked during my time, a lot of guys that I've mentored and so on, they're having a really tough time just coping. They hate the job and that's a shame.

Howard Browne, who wrote Capone, *was an interesting guy.*

Howard Browne was great, he was a reporter in Chicago. The script was written around footage that Roger Corman had shot for other pictures—another example of Roger trying to make a cheap picture. It was like a novel, a lot of factual information. Howard was a very factual, to-the-point writer, but not very good with dialogue, so other writers came in. He visited the set once and I had a really good conversation with him in regards to what Capone was actually like, tremendous background. Unfortunately Ben Gazzara didn't take advantage of it and was hard to work with on the set. It's hard to explain but sometimes when a picture gets shot, the script gets lost in translation. I'll tell you an old adage that I believe in: If you have a good script, you can make a good picture or a bad picture. If you have a great script, you can make a good picture or a great picture, but you can still make a bad picture! The only way you can make a great picture is if you have a great script. The script is everything. I mean, you can have glowing moments of character development and beautiful shots and this and that but it can only go so far, you have to have content and that's where the script comes in.

Do you have a preference for making action movies?

Absolutely, making an action picture is great. You're out there like a kid blowing things up. Every time I see an explosion, I start to feel a little jittery! And there's a lot of choreography and a lot of art in doing the stunts. There's a lot of timing, there's a lot of selling something to the audience that doesn't really happen, fights with no connecting of punches and so on. In *Oceans of Fire* I had a bar fight with Ray "Boom Boom" Mancini and Ken Norton—two world champion boxers—and Lyle Alzado, a professional football player. All the Mexican stunt guys knew and respected them and they all said, "Don't fake it, hit me," so they pummeled these Mexican stunt people, knocked them to the floor and almost out, and they were so honored that these great athletes took them down, they got up after every shot and said, "That was great!" So stunt work is really fun to do, though inevitably things go wrong sometimes. When I was doing *Bulletproof* with Gary Busey we had a prop helicopter loaded with explosives that was suspended from another helicopter by what's known as a pelican hook. It was supposed to drop on cue and blow up in the air, but the hook bent, and they couldn't release the prop helicopter. Everyone turned to me and said, "What do we do?" I wanted the shot, but the helicopter had started to go into what's known as auto-gyrating, where it starts swinging around in circles, which is very dangerous. It could have taken the other helicopter down, and it would have come down on the crew, so I told them to blow the damn thing. It detached after we blew it and luckily the other helicopter—which was twice the size of the one they were dropping—was able to escape the explosion. On *Drum* Kenny Norton was shot accidentally by John Colicos because Colicos didn't hear the cue. On *Capone* Ben Gazzara pulled his machine gun trigger when everyone was out of position. Cars were blown up, bullet hits were all over the place and a whole bunch of extras almost got injured. On *Fast Charlie, the Moonbeam Rider* David was riding his motorcycle through a field and a biplane was supposed to come down and strafe him, which it did many times, but there was one time where I could have sworn that the plane's wheel hit him. I radioed him in the field and asked if he was okay, and David said he was fine, the plane never touched him, but when he came back there were plane tire marks on his helmet! I couldn't believe it. I mean, it could have took his head off! Another time some careless assistant poured gas all over David's bike when he was filling the tank, and as he was flying through this big shot with a whole bunch of action and shooting, there was an explosion. David was a ball of fire and everybody ran over to him with fire extinguishers. We put out the fire and David just walked away and said, "That was fun." What I'm getting at is that with stunts and special effects, it's precarious, but I like the danger element.

But would you do it yourself?

When I ask Chuck Norris to do a double flying kick or something like that, I know he can do it. When I ask another actor to let Chuck come flying at him, potentially decimating his face if he misses, I look at the actor and I basically tell them I'd do it—but of course I wouldn't! On *Capone* there was a scene where Harry Guardino was supposed to be shot. The special effects man was a super guy by the name of Roger George whose face had been burned in an accident while he was working on *Badlands* [1973]. I'm telling Harry, "Look, this bullet hit won't hurt you, this effect won't hurt you. Here, talk to my special effects guy," and [George] walks up and Harry looks at him and he's got all these scars! It took a while to calm Harry down and get him to do it.

Is the relationship between actors and directors sometimes difficult?
Sometimes they cop an attitude: "What's he telling me?" "What does he know?" all that sort of stuff, and you have to win them over. A lot of times I learn things. I'll tell an actor to do something and he'll say, "Let me try it this way" and I say to myself, "What a waste of time and money"; but when I look at the take, hey, it's pretty good, sometimes it's better than my way. Sometimes you're too quick to judge an actor, write things off as ego, as an overreaction, but really what it is, is passion. You have to make a lot of split decisions as far as saying yes and no on the set. There's a lot of things I wish I hadn't had to say to actors and there's some things I wish I had said. It's a tough, tough business.

How do you go about winning them over?
I have passion for what I do, I have excitement, enthusiasm, I believe in it and I do the best job I possibly can, and they have to respect that. It may not be up to their standards, it may not be exactly what they expected, but in the end they come to me and I get the hugs and kisses and tears. I get Ben Gazzara hugging me and kissing me and telling me how much he enjoyed working with me after giving me hell! It's a weird industry, an industry based on relationships that sometimes are real and sometimes aren't, and it's hard to tell.

Michael Preece
Director

Director Michael Preece started his career in script continuity. One of the first movies he worked on was *The Great Locomotive Chase* (1956), an exciting and jarringly tough-minded Disney western helmed by Francis D. Lyon.

His subsequent assignments included a batch of movies starring Marlon Brando, including the notoriously troubled and tardy *Mutiny on the Bounty* (1962), and a bigger batch in the action category. He worked with Anthony Mann on *Men in War* (1957) and *Cimarron* (1960), Sam Peckinpah on *The Getaway* (1972), Richard Fleischer on *The Don Is Dead* (1973), Andrew V. McLaglen on *Mitchell* (1975), and Tom Gries on *Breakheart Pass* (1976). With teachers like that, it's no wonder so much of his directorial work has action appeal.

In the 1970s the studios shifted meat-and-potatoes action production to the small screen. Preece was part of that shift. He learned his directing skills in action features, but put them into practice in action television: Quinn Martin's *The Streets of San Francisco* (1972-77), *Dog and Cat* (1977), the Robert Conrad Bond riff *A Man Called Sloane* (1979-80), *Freebie and the Bean* (1980-81), *T.J. Hooker* (1982-85), Stephen J. Cannell's *Hunter* (1984-91), Dean Hargrove's *Jake and the Fatman* (1987-92) and a hugely impressive seventy-episode stint on *Walker, Texas Ranger* (1993-2000) with Chuck Norris.

You were originally a script supervisor.

I started in 1955 at Disney. It was a summer job that I got because my mother was a business manager for the Script Clerks Guild, as it was called at the time. I was trained by a guy named Ted Schulz, on a movie called *Davy Crockett and the River Pirates* [1956]. They were paying $165 a week, which was a lot of money back then. The business was so good at the time that after that, they sent me to Georgia on a movie called

Michael Preece • Director

The Great Locomotive Chase with Fess Parker. They asked me if I'd like to be the script guy on the second unit. I didn't know what I was doing but I took the job! After that I just kept working and I did it for twenty years.

Including on two films with Anthony Mann.

Anthony Mann was kind of a street guy, a little bit vulgar. He would get on the big crane to do a shot and start swearing, but he didn't know he was doing it. He'd say, "Move those fuckin' extras" and a welfare worker would come up and say, "Mr. Mann, if you don't stop swearing, I'm going to take the children away from the set" and he'd say, "I didn't realize I *was* fuckin' swearing." He was a character, but he knew what he was doing. He took a year to make *El Cid* [1961] but he could also make *Men in War* in something like 24 days, a real short schedule.

Can you explain what a script supervisor does?

It's continuity on the set. If an actor walks through a door with something in their right hand, a script supervisor makes sure that when they shoot [that scene's next shot] three months later, it's still in their right hand. You also cued the actors their dialogue, kept notes for the editor about what lens was used, why you didn't print a take, all kinds of little details. Today it's much easier because of video, but in those days they relied very much on the script supervisor. It used to be mostly women that did it, the director's secretary would go on the set and keep notes for the director and that's how the job evolved. Around 1936 or so they wanted to get organized, brought in my mother, who happened to be friends with a script clerk, wrote up some bylaws and formed a guild. After Disney I worked for Desilu on series like *The Whirlybirds* [1956-59] and *The Sheriff of Cochise* [1956-60]. Then I went over to MGM and worked on some movies, starting on one called *The Subterraneans* [1960] with Leslie Caron.

And don't forget George Peppard!

He was a good guy, I liked him, we were young and ... he liked to chase girls.

Hey, who doesn't?

I worked with him again on *How the West Was Won* (1962) with ... everybody! Everybody was in that, but George Peppard and Debbie

Reynolds were the backbone of the movie, they were the characters that ran all the way through. So I was kinda friendly with George, never seen him since, but at that time we hung out together and went to the swimming pool on Sundays. As script supervisor you get to know the actors better than almost any other crew member because they're always calling you over to run lines with them, which is how I got to know Brando.

What did you work with Brando on?

I worked a little on *One-Eyed Jacks* [1961] and got to know him. He liked me, we were kinda friends, so he asked for me on *Mutiny on the Bounty* [1962] and another movie called *Morituri* [1965].

So what's your take on the Mutiny on the Bounty *saga?*

If you were the producer or the director, it was a miserable experience. If you were a crew member, it was a memorable and great experience. Brando was very funny and easy to work with but I'm glad I wasn't the director or producer 'cause he was kind of a bad boy.

In what way?

Before we started shooting Brando went to the studio and said he wanted to switch parts. He didn't want to play Fletcher Christian anymore. He wanted to play the part that Richard Harris ended up playing, the one who instigated the mutiny. Of course they said no and it made Brando kind of angry, he argued and although he didn't do it on purpose, he delayed things. They fired the director, Sir Carol Reed, and replaced him with Lewis Milestone, who was a famous director but—I hate to say it—was old and not well enough to take over a project like that. They'd scheduled it for sixty days and we went three hundred and ninety days or something like that. It was a mess but it was a good job to have because it was two years of employment and they couldn't fire me because I had all the notes!

What was Brando like as a director on One-Eyed Jacks?

I didn't work on it that long so I can't really judge whether he was a good director. He was good with the actors, he tried to trick them into leaving the acting alone and just playing the part as they were. But from my point of view he also over-directed: He was trying to get everybody to do it the way he would, not to act like him but have the same emotions as him. Karl Malden could do that, he understood Brando, but some of the other actors were incapable of it. I worked with a lot of directors and the best ones don't do it that way. If you cast well, you can just let them get on with it. Peckinpah wouldn't say anything to his cast about acting. If he cast them, they were what he wanted. Like they say, casting is everything.

You worked with some good directors on the series I Spy.

The best directors on *I Spy* were Dick Sarafian and Paul Wendkos, I thought they did a very good job. Wendkos gave a better performance behind the camera than the actors, he was very excitable and dramatic, which doesn't really work because you don't see it on screen. Sarafian was an interesting guy, more low-key, and I enjoyed working with him. We had a lot of directors on *I Spy* but most of the episodes were directed by Earl Bellamy and Christian Nyby. They got it done and the actors and locations took care of the rest. The chemistry between [Robert] Culp and [Bill] Cosby worked and we shot in Hong Kong, Tokyo, Mexico, Italy, Spain, all over the world. I looked at the directors more critically on *I Spy* because by then I wanted to direct so bad!

Action movies don't come much better than The Getaway.

Peckinpah was great, I admired him. He drank too much and he'd hire guys who liked to drink and party with him—people like Jason Robards, not that he wasn't a great actor. But [Peckinpah] was fast. When it came to staging, he was like a television director, he could stage a scene with twelve actors in three minutes, he was wonderful at that. But he also had a very bad temper. Every time I'd see somebody make a stupid mistake, I'd cringe and think, "Oh my God, Peckinpah's going to fire him" and sure enough he would. There's a scene in *The Getaway* where Steve McQueen drops into a manhole through a hole in the floor of a van. Now they had an unlimited budget on *The Getaway* but when they brought us the van, the hole was too small, you could barely fit through it, and it had jagged edges. I saw it before Sam did and thought, "Oh boy, a movie star has to climb through that? Sam's not gonna like this!"

How would you compare the way Peckinpah worked to the way Tom Gries worked on Breakheart Pass?

Tom was a delight. I worked with him a lot, he was a great guy and a good writer and director. Tom was friends with everybody and knew everyone's name, whereas Sam was kind of gruff with people. They were contemporaries, they both worked on *Route 66* [1960–64] and a few series like that. Tom directed Sam's girlfriend, a beautiful Mexican actress, in an episode of *I Spy* and of course Sam came on the set and was telling Tom, "No, no, have her do that again!"

What did working with Peckinpah and Gries teach you about directing?
Don't drink! But then Tom Gries was a health nut, he played tennis and ran and took care of himself and he died much younger than Sam, who drank and did everything wrong.

Did you get to know Steve McQueen and Charles Bronson?
I didn't like Steve McQueen much but I loved Charlie. To become a movie star, coming from where he did…. Charlie Bronson was a miracle. A lot of people didn't like him because he was curt, but I thought he was great. I'd done a couple of television shows with him and when he walked on the set of *Breakheart Pass* he looked at me and said, "Jeez, I thought you'd be directing by now."

It wasn't long after.
Right. In fact, that was almost the last film I worked on.

Your first directing job was on The Streets of San Francisco.
I started off as the sound guy on that, for one season. There were a lot of car scenes in that show but the director was too old to lie down in the back seat and the mixer got tired of hiding in the trunk, so when we did them it was just me, Karl Malden and Michael Douglas. We'd have three cameras, one on the hood and one on each side. Michael was always driving, Karl was in the front passenger seat and I'd be in the back seat with my script. I'd hit the slate, turn on the sound panel, duck down and say, "Action." I'd ask them to do lines again if it was necessary and all the time we'd keep rolling so we didn't waste film, didn't have to stop and re-light. We'd come back and I'd say, "We got your scene." We were in the car so much that Karl and Michael starting saying, "You direct half the show, you should be a director." A guy named Billy Hale was also pushing for me to direct, he'd done a lot of movies of the week at Universal—*Murder in Texas* [1981] was a good one. One day Quinn Martin and the producer John Wilder came on the set; I walked over to their limo as they were leaving and said, "Excuse me, Quinn, but I'd like

Michael Douglas, Michael Preece and Meg Foster shooting a 1975 episode of *The Streets of San Francisco* titled "Trail of Terror" (courtesy Michael Preece).

to..." and he said, "Don't ask, I know what you want" and two weeks later I was on the list to direct.

You had a lot of experience, but were you nervous?

I was scared to death. My wife, who was a hair stylist on the show, shot a little film of me saying, "Action" and wandering around—it's three minutes long and I must've buttoned and unbuttoned the top button of my shirt twenty-five times. But I was lucky, it had a great cast, Michael and Karl of course, but also James Woods and Meg Foster, and it worked well. After that I did an episode of *Sara* [1976], a show starring Brenda Vaccaro who was dating Michael at the time. Then suddenly I was under contract at Universal, on their terms. If a director got sick, or got fired, they'd send me down to take over. I did second units and all kinds of stuff and got a lot of experience.

You worked on the short-lived cop show Dog and Cat.

Kim Basinger was a brand new actress, she was just a kid, twenty-one or something, and she was a little pudgy so we had to hide her butt whenever she walked away from the camera, which is funny because a few years later she had the best body around! Every once in a while you get somebody really good in a show and think, "Jeez, I'll be amazed if they don't become a movie star" and the funny thing is, often they don't. A few years later Kim did and when I'd run into her I'd say, "Have you done anything since *Dog and Cat*?" Lou Antonio was also very good, he was a director as well and whenever we'd get a little behind Lou would suggest I do this or that, do the scene in one shot or something so we could all get home. Larry Gordon produced the series and Walter Hill wrote it; that's how I got the job on *Dog and Cat*, because I was friends with Walter Hill, who wrote *The Getaway*.

Was Walter Hill on the set during the shooting of The Getaway?

Not one day, he said he'd never go on a set where they were shooting his script unless he was directing. Very smart guy. He was a trainee assistant director on *I Spy*, he was yelled at and belittled and he said it was great fun. Later he was doing a movie with Culp and Cosby called *Hickey & Boggs* [1972] and they had no idea, they didn't remember him and he never told them who he was. He was an AD or second AD on *Gunsmoke* [1955–75] and I was acting in it. He came over to me and gave me some direction and I said, "Oh, you're gonna be a director, you're good," and he became a great director.

You acted in a couple of things. Were you interested in pursuing acting as a career?

No, I just did it for money. I went to acting school for a while, but I realized it was easier to remember dialogue as a script supervisor than it was as an actor. As a script supervisor I could never understand when actors blew a line. I remember Dean Martin said to me, "It's easy for you, you've got it in front of you, *you* can read it."

You're in the Burt Reynolds movie Skullduggery *[1970]*.

I met my wife on that movie, it was shot in Jamaica. Originally Richard Wilson was the director but he got fired after something like a week's shooting. Then they brought in Gordon Douglas, fired him too, and a stuntman ended up directing it. It was an interesting project but it would've gone way over budget 'cause they kept firing the directors.

What can you tell us about the Quinn Martin series A Man Called Sloane?

The pilot starred Robert Logan but they didn't want him for the series and got Robert Conrad. I see Robert once in a while, he lives near me and he's fine now, but back then he had a reputation for being a pain in the neck. They had a meeting and Conrad said, "I know I have a bad reputation but I'm a changed man" and they went with him. First day of shooting he was supposed to be there at seven, seven-thirty, but he didn't show. We got an establishing shot, I staged a scene, which is not a good thing to do without your star, and he still hadn't arrived. Ten-fifteen, I remember it like it was yesterday, I looked down the street and there was Robert Conrad in a complete sweatsuit with a towel around his neck, running towards us in front of a Winnebago. He said, "Sorry I'm late, but I had a lot of things going on this morning" and went and took a shower because he was wringing wet with sweat and he was supposed to wear a suit in the scene. Eleven-fifteen he came out and said, "Oh, and by the way, I'm on Johnny Carson tonight and I have to leave at four-thirty" and he had like a ten-page scene to do! But we did it, and this is where a little bit of script continuity experience helps, because we shot all his stuff as fast as we could, all his close-ups, then when he left we went back and did everybody else's close-ups for the day, including Robert Culp's, who was the guest star. That was Robert Conrad on his first day after saying, "I'm a changed man," but you know, he was a good guy! But whether it was insecurity or whatever, he had an ego that just would not quit, and after three or four episodes I went to the producers and said, "I can't take this. Let somebody else have the problems," and soon after that they were cancelled.

Would the director have a say in casting and locations on a show like A Man Called Sloane?

Locations, yeah. Casting, Tom Palmer was the casting man on that show and I never had a problem with anyone he cast. Quinn Martin had the final say for all casting on his shows. He had his favorite actors and a lot of the time you'd get them. Virgil Vogel, who was quite a well-known television director, used to say that he never got involved with casting because if he did, he wouldn't have anyone to blame!

I hope you're not going to tell me that T.J. Hooker *star William Shatner was difficult.*

No, Shatner was great, I liked him and he was very easy to get along with, I do have a funny story about him, though. We were shooting in downtown Los Angeles where there are a lot of homeless people. We were doing tow shots, a truck was towing the police car with, again, three cameras attached to it and the actors inside. We pulled up and while they were reloading the camera, Shatner went over to talk to a homeless man. After a while he came back and asked if any of us had a ten dollar bill. Now this was my first episode on *T.J. Hooker* and I said, "Yeah, here, I got one" and gave him ten dollars. So he walked over and gave the guy the money, and the guy hugged him and thanked him and then I realized—Shatner got all the credit and it was my money! I'd wondered why everybody else had turned their heads and pretended to be real busy when he'd asked for ten dollars. Two weeks later he did it again and I pretended to be real busy too!

Fred Dryer and Stepfanie Kramer made a great pair on Hunter.

I did one episode, Fred Dryer and I hit it off, and we're still friends today. Fred was very powerful on the show and I think he just said, "Keep him around." We were doing an episode once, it was something like four o clock in the afternoon and we had one scene left to shoot. It was an office scene with Fred, Bruce Davison and Stepfanie. Fred had all the dialogue and he was having a lot of trouble remembering it, he couldn't get it out. I suggested that when the boss asked Fred what happened, he should turn to Stepfanie and say, "You tell it." Stepfanie was great with dialogue, she could remember anything, and she went through something like four pages in one take. I said to Fred, "Steve McQueen, Charlie Bronson, Clint Eastwood, they don't say anything, they just do it all with looks" and Fred said, "That's what I'm gonna do."

How would you compare working with Quinn Martin, Stephen J. Cannell and Aaron Spelling?

Aaron Spelling I hardly knew at all. He never interfered or came on the set on any of the shows. He was involved in *I Spy* but was never around, it was all Sheldon Leonard. Stephen Cannell never came on the set. He'd go to dailies at lunchtime and I'd sneak in, stand at the back of the projection room and listen to his remarks, but I never spoke to him.

He showed up at a party that the cast and crew of *Hunter* were having, I was out in the parking lot talking to an assistant prop man and Stephen walked by and said hello and afterwards the prop man turned to me and said, "He doesn't know who you are, does he?" And I'd directed like thirty-five episodes for him! So he didn't know what I looked like, but he knew that I got the job done. The only one I knew was Quinn. People have told me that they worked for Quinn Martin for ten years and never met him. He never came on the set, or seldom ever, but I knew him quite well. He liked me and gave me a break, he said, "If you stay with me, I'll make you a rich man"—loved that statement. I was doing *Barnaby Jones* [1973–80] for Quinn and he took me off that to work on *A Man Called Sloane*. Later he apologized for that and said, "That was a bad move, you coulda made more money!"

You certainly stayed with Walker, Texas Ranger *for a long time.*

Chuck Norris was ideal to work with. I think I did eight or nine years on *Walker, Texas Ranger* and I never had a cross word with him. He was always on time, looked good, stayed in shape, and as an actor he really improved. Sheree Wilson helped him a lot and he got better and better. He was very cooperative and tried harder than anyone I've ever worked with to know his lines and do it right. I looked forward to going to work every day. He doesn't have a great sense of humor but he's a nice man!

What are the qualities needed to get the job done as a director?

You have to know what you're doing because you have sixty people on a set waiting for you to say, "Okay, put the camera here." You gotta be able to tell them what your idea is and you can't change your mind, even if you're wrong. You gotta think it out ahead of time but you also have to have an open mind and be inventive, especially in television. You have to be able to change directions constantly and roll with the punches. If you're shooting outside and it starts raining, you put 'em under an umbrella! You have to be the boss, because on the set you are, but you should listen to everyone from the assistant director to the cameraman. Get on their good side and they'll try to make you look good.

Gary Conway
Director

Like his contemporaries Simon Wincer and Richard Franklin, Gary Conway began his career making cop shows for Hector and Dorothy Crawford's Crawford Productions.

An Australian equivalent of Britain's Euston Films, Crawford Productions made action television that outclassed many a big screen effort in energy, scripting, and acting talent.

The Crawford shows boasted the most impressive roster of macho leading men Australia has ever produced: Gerard Kennedy, Terence Donovan, Mike Preston, Dennis Grosvenor and Peter Adams, to name but a few.

Their leading ladies, like Lynda Stoner, Victoria Quilter and Pamela Stephenson, were far too disruptively glamorous for the timid mainstream of the Australian film industry to ever accommodate.

Conway directed episodes of all the Crawford classics: *Homicide* (1964–77), *Division 4* (1969–75), *Matlock Police* (1971–76), featuring the Australian-born Hollywood veteran Michael Pate, *Ryan* (1973), a private eye series created by American writer-producer Mort Fine, *Bluey* (1976–77) starring king-size comedian Lucky Grills, and *Cop Shop* (1977–82), created by the talented Terry Stapleton.

For the Grundy Organisation, Crawford Productions' main rival for Aussie airtime, Conway directed "The Massage Girl Murders," the first episode of the hard-edged *Bellamy* (1981), and multiple episodes of *Prisoner* (1979–86), a hugely popular "women in prison" series with a great cast that included Val Lehman and Maggie Kirkpatrick, two powerhouse performers in the roles of their lives.

How did you get involved with Crawford Productions?

I started in the print room. You'd work nine to five being a messenger boy and printing things off, that sort of stuff, but they used to have an acting and radio school in Collins Street, and you'd do shifts there as well. The school had three separate studios, one for television, two for radio, and you had to operate the quarter-inch tape machines, fire the camera up, turn the lights on. You were the general dogsbody but you were learning how to operate the equipment. They had acting for television, acting for radio, radio announcing, and there was a children's class on Saturday that we all used to dread. The parents used to sit in this little green room, mostly knitting, and talking about how wonderful their daughters were and what awards they'd won—there was lots of one-upmanship. During my first year there, I was in the control room with the tutor of a radio class and the sound was all muffled. I couldn't work out what was wrong, I'm a new boy, I'm nervous and it's summer so I'm perspiring like a pig. Eventually I had to ring Ian Crawford at home, to find out what was going on, and I discovered the microphone I'd plugged in was in the cupboard! Well, I sorted that out, went to another class—which was audio, all I had to do was push a record button—and I just plonked in the chair and the tutor said, "My God, boy, you stink!"

You must've come good because they kept you on and made you a director!
When they started *Homicide*, they made David Lee the director and me the assistant director, though in those days you were called the unit manager. I assisted him for a couple of years and then he got married. The pilot had been directed by Ian Jones, who also wrote it, so we all assumed that he'd come back and direct while David was away on his honeymoon. Ian was a very talented guy, he wrote a lot of episodes of *Homicide* and as each show started, they'd usually get Ian to start it off for the first few weeks. I got a call on location to go see Hector [Crawford] and I thought, "Oh my God, what have I done? I'm sacked." I get there and he says, "David's getting married on Saturday fella" and I said, "Yes, Mr. Crawford" and he said, "Well, we need a director" and I said, "Uh huh" and he said, "Well, you're *it*" and I went, "Me?!" Crawford's were fantastic in that they'd give anyone a go, they'd throw you in the deep end and just see how you went. Alan Arnold, the D.P., was a fantastic guy who'd been around film for years and I was sure he'd be able to help me out on crossing the line and suggesting shots and everything

else. But when we turned up at the location on the first day he wasn't there, his wife was sick, and his assistant became the cameraman. He was no help whatsoever because he was stoned twenty-four hours a day so anything I suggested, he said, "Oh man, that's fantastic!"

The first scene was the Homicide detectives looking for a body in Studley Park. I contrived this really beautiful shot with the body in some bushes in the foreground, and the Homicide people stumbling around in the background, which was a criminal mistake because I gave away to the audience where the body was at the beginning of a two-minute scene. It was like a pantomime, I'm sure the audience were going, "It's under the bush!" I hadn't thought about the drama of the thing; you don't let the audience get ahead of your heroes. I did that for four weeks and that included one episode where we got to the edit room and the editor said, "This will not cut" and went to Hector and told him so. Hector said, "Stop being a drama queen and make it cut" and I thought, "Go Hector!" After that I went back to being an assistant for a while, and because I was thinking, "I'm above this now" kept on stuffing up! About six months later they gave me another go, one episode, and then gradually David and I started alternating. It was a fantastic time. There was no film and television school, you just learned on the job. Overtime was a word that hadn't been invented, you'd work until you finished, some nights you'd go to midnight, two a.m. You'd have a crew drink in the bus or the caravan every night, and you'd still be there at seven the next morning bright and breezy going, "Ooh, what's going to happen today?"

How big were the crews on the Crawford shows?

When we started *Homicide* it was like a four- or five-man crew: There was a cameraman, a clapper loader, a guy with a fi-cord (a little battery-operated tape recorder that you could do a wild track with), a unit manager and that was it. There was no lighting, we put the wardrobe and the props in the boot of the police car and off we went! With *Division 4* we were doing sync sound so it was a bit bigger, but it still would've been only eight or nine people. Once you start recording sound, you need a recordist and a boom operator. Later on we got a few lights and a lighting person involved as well. It was like doing second unit today, which I love, 'cause these days crews are so big and, although everybody's got Motorolas, communication is not very good; whereas if there's only half a dozen of you, it's easy to get together and say, "Let's do the two-shot" and everybody knows.

I assume the schedules were very tight.
From day one you'd chase your ass shooting, you'd never get enough time. I can remember doing an interior car shot outside the Royal Oak Hotel in Bridge Road Richmond. It was starting to get dark so we got a loan of a bed lamp from inside the hotel, ran a cable out of the pub, clamped the lamp on the window and lit the shot with it. That was an early *Homicide* and because it was black-and-white you didn't have to worry about color temperature or anything. Another time we were doing a two-shot of the detectives in the car in Toorak Road; again, it was getting dark, so we parked our station wagon, our camera car, on the wrong side of the road facing the actors' car. Then we turned the headlights on high-beam and encouraged people walking past to come and sit on the tailgate so the nose of the car would tilt up and light the actors. You did those sorts of things all the time because you had no equipment, you didn't have any lighting. You improvised. You did tracking shots by putting the cameraman on a motor-mower, or if you saw a forklift truck at a factory nearby, and you wanted to do a nice elevation, you'd go and say, "Have you got ten minutes?" and they'd all be into it 'cause they were excited there was television being made in Melbourne. You got fantastic cooperation from everyone. In those days you didn't send letters off weeks ahead and get them to sign contracts, you just walked in and said, "Would you mind?"

We got fantastic cooperation from the police. Originally if we wanted police cars we'd get them from the police and use real cops in the show. Then when Crawford's started doing more than one show, they started getting cars from Ford or Holden and dressing them up themselves. There was a period when Crawford's had their own little police force, with three police cars, a police station wagon, and when *Matlock Police* was running, two motorbikes, 'cause Paul Cronin rode a motor bike on that. It was a handy way of getting to work in the morning if you were in a hurry—people would give way to you left, right and center!

Were the car chases done in a catch-as-catch-can manner as well?
We didn't have stunt people, we used to do it all ourselves. Either the actors drove them or, if we needed extra shots, I'd go out with Hector

Crawford's chauffeur and the two of us would shoot them. That changed after there was an accident during the filming of a *Matlock Police* episode. An assistant cameraman was killed and from then on stunt people got involved.

Were there many professional stuntmen in Australia at the time?
No, I don't think there were many around. There wasn't even much feature film production in those days, so there might not have even been any. If there were, they were few and far between.

Where was Division 4 *filmed?*
It was originally going to be based in St. Kilda police station and I think it was going to be called *Saints and Sinners*, but Channel Nine didn't like the idea. The main location was an old police station, which has since been demolished, in Montague Street, Port Melbourne. It was supposed to be set in an inner city suburb, so we used Port Melbourne, South Melbourne, mainly I suppose because they were convenient to Crawford's. We filmed in factories, little single-fronted houses, it depended on the story. But with *Division 4* you tended to stick to the inner suburbs whereas with *Homicide* we'd do a lot of stuff out in the country, because homicides happen everywhere, more so than robberies and those sorts of things. In the early days of *Division 4* the location stuff was shot on film and the studio stuff was on tape. You didn't shoot the whole episode in one week, you did the location stuff, they cut it and put music to it, then the studio stuff was usually scripted so as there'd be someone saying, "Let's go and investigate" and you'd cut, they'd roll the location film, and the cast would scamper over to another set for the next scene. The bizarre thing was that initially one director did the location stuff and another did the studio. I think that was because Dorothy Crawford didn't think the location directors could cope with studio, because switching three cameras was a totally different technique to shooting with a single camera. So after you'd done location for, say, twelve months, they'd put you in the studio for twelve months. They'd slowly train you and eventually they'd let you go out and do a whole episode.

What were the challenges of shooting with video in the 1970s?
I think things had improved by *Division 4*, but on *Homicide* they used

to record from commercial break to commercial break 'cause editing video tape in those days was a really big deal. I think you had to paint a solution on the two-inch tape and that would show up the fields, then you'd cut it with a razor blade, making sure you didn't go over a field because the picture wouldn't lock up if you did. You might almost get to a commercial break and one of the actors would dry and you'd have to go back and start again. So courtroom scenes in early *Homicide* episodes were really funny, we'd end up with the prosecutor or the defense counsel leading the witness, saying, "Is it not true ..." and you'd see the actor go, "Oh yeah, that's right, that's what I should have said!"

Did you work on Hunter *[1967–68]?*

I did because when you were at Crawford's you might do a year on *Homicide* and then you might go to *Hunter* or *Matlock Police*—you swapped around a bit, you didn't tend to do just the one show all the time. Ian Jones wrote quite a few episodes of *Hunter*. It starred Tony Ward but Gerard Kennedy...

As Kragg!

He was the baddie, but eventually they did some research and discovered that the audience thought that Tony Ward's character Hunter was boring as bat shit and that Kragg was the one. So they made Kragg a goodie, and this was after he'd killed about fifty people in all walks of life! But the audience just accepted it and they kept on going.

What can you tell us about working with Kennedy and Terence Donovan on Division 4*?*

Gerard Kennedy was funny, he constantly got lost going to location, it would always be "What a stupid bloody place to pick, who picked this location?" So on his birthday the crew bought him a Melways street directory! But he had an amazing memory, he'd turn up and it was blatantly obvious he hadn't read the script. He had what must've been one of the first battery-operated shavers and he'd read through the script while he was shaving and then say, "Okay, good," and he'd do the scene and spit out all his dialogue. It used to fascinate us because some actors have a hell of a time remembering lines. Terence Donovan was known as Boobs ... Boobs Donovan.

Why?

I'm not quite sure. Well, he did have big boobs whenever he was doing anything with his shirt off. But he was also the jester, he was always pulling jokes. One time we were doing a long lens shot of someone being followed, they're walking towards the camera and a car pulls up in the background and Terry gets out. It was a complicated shot with lots of focus pulls and I don't know how many takes we did. Eventually we're doing a take that's going beautifully and I'm thinking, "Thank Christ, we've got it," and Terry stops, pulls his shoe off, pretends it's a bloody phone and starts talking into it! They all got along really well, there were no prima donnas. That was one of the good things about Crawford's, there was no chance for anyone to become a "star."

How do you deal with prima donnas, with difficult actors, when you do come across them?

You usually compromise, get half of what you want just for the sake of getting it done.

How did the change from black-and-white to color television affect the way you worked?

They were quite clever because they'd started making *Division 4* in color twelve months before the change-over, so they then had a bank of stuff ready. They fitted out this really clapped-out old caravan as a control room and they used to park it in the loading bay. I missed the transition to color, I was living in England at the time, but when I got back it was all up and running.

What were you doing in England?

I was there for almost three years and my plan was to try and get work in the industry. But this was in the '70s, they'd just come out of the three-day week, and there was huge unemployment. It was the old thing that you couldn't get a job without a ticket and you couldn't get a ticket without a job. I only ever got into the union office once. The guy I spoke to opened a filing cabinet, pointed to a load of files with red stickers on them and said, "See all these? They're all members of our union that are unemployed. Why do I need to add another one to the list?" I could have worked at the BBC but not in London, it would've been in the regionals. I was something like twenty-eight years old and wanted to live it up in London so I ended up working as a technical clerk. The only shooting I did over there was for a two-hour *Homicide* special. Just after I left for England, they were talking about doing some movies. They never got to do them, I don't know what happened, but they did do some two-hour specials. Bud Tingwell wanted to go back home to sell his house and they've gone, "Ah, here's an opportunity, we can shoot some stuff in London." So they got in touch with me and I shot the London elements, but they hadn't even completed the script. They'd written a couple of scenes but there were also notes saying, "We think Bud's going to be checking out musical stores. Can you do a montage of him looking in some windows and get him to walk past Trafalgar Square? We're not sure why yet but we'll work it out."

To let everyone know you were in London.

Yeah! And that was difficult because in London, even in those days, you had to get what they called a tripod permit to shoot anywhere in the city. This meant you had to make an application, you had to draw a map, you had to specify how long you were gonna be there and how many crew members there were. So we did a lot of undercover stuff, shooting from people's doorways. We were gonna do a big sequence at Buckingham Palace but the police kept on turning up and we had to keep jumping in the car and driving around the block, waiting for them to leave.

Bud Tingwell was such a great talent. He was in there with Richard Burton and James Mason in The Desert Rats *[1953] and he more than held his own.*

He was just a fantastic guy, lovely, and I was so upset when he died. He'd always arrive at the set half an hour early and sit down and arrange things in his character's office in the way he thought they should be. He could be frustrating as an actor because his theory was that an actor's job is to do what's on the page, so if you said to him, "Bud, that line doesn't work. How about we just cut it?" he'd say, "No, no, I must be doing it wrong. Give me another go." He would fight tooth and nail to keep every word that was on the page, and you had to eventually say, "Bud, for Christ's sake, it doesn't work! Get rid of it!"

Were there any restrictions put on Crawford's by the networks, regarding subject matter or levels of violence?

No, there were no real restrictions. *Homicide* was quite violent. It wasn't like CSI programs now where you're seeing great detail, but there were murders and blood and fights were open slather. I think that's because they were all on at an eight-thirty time slot where you were fairly free in that area. Look at some of the stuff in *Prisoner*; they wouldn't be game to touch it these days.

Ryan was obviously aimed at the international market.

Rod Mulinar, who played the lead, was a naughty boy, always up to mischief. There was an episode that I think Simon Wincer directed, where he had to drive his Charger into a lake. They only wanted it in a couple of feet but he took off at such a pace that the whole thing ended up floating, it was out in the middle of the lake and Hector wasn't happy! *Ryan* was running the same time as *Homicide* and when Channel Seven pulled the plug on *Ryan*, Hector thought the crew was so good that he didn't sack them, he kept them all on and they started making two episodes of *Homicide* a week: *Homicide Blue* and *Homicide Green*. I really respected Hector for that. The cast was fantastic because they'd be doing a scene from one episode, be thrown into a cab, taken to a new location, and do a scene from another episode.

How much did Hector Crawford involve himself in the shows?

Hector had a good sense of what would work and what wouldn't, he was very knowledgeable in picking an audience, and it's just a pity there aren't a few of them around these days. I get the impression these days that all the networks are run by accountants and finance people. They don't understand entertainment; some of the things you see that start up, you just think, "My God, who thought this had legs?" and sure enough, four or five weeks later, it disappears. Dorothy was the one who had a big say in how the shows went and what storylines they used. Whenever you went into a script meeting, before your backside hit the chair, her first question was always, "Who do we care about in this script?" I just think that's so important in everything, no matter what sort of drama it is, you need to care about someone. You never saw Hector at script meetings, you never got to know him that well, he was the figurehead. He was handy if you wanted to do a chase down Swanston Street though, 'cause he was usually good mates with the Lord Mayor!

Do you think it's true that Crawford's was punished by the television networks because they were campaigning for stronger local content rules?

Well, I've heard it, who knows how accurate it is, but it makes sense because Ted Hamilton and, I think, Terry Donovan were working on the "Make it Australian" campaign and they used the Crawford telex machine to send off information. The word is that the networks got onto that and thought it was Crawford's actually doing the push, which I don't think was true. All three networks cancelled their shows within days of each other, which I can't believe was a coincidence. It gave the impression that the networks were going, "Hey Mr. Crawford, get back in your box."

Do you think the Australian film industry could have used a few Hector Crawfords?

Yes. We were treated as "Ughh, they're the people who do television," but if you look at any production these days there'll be a large number of people that learned at Crawford's. You were trained to work efficiently, there was no mucking around, you had to get the episode shot within the six days, if it rained, stiff shit, somehow you got it done. The cast was also trained in doing things quickly, flying by the seat of their pants, and I often think that actors give their best performance when they don't think about it. The more they analyze it, the less real it is. I do like actors to query things; at least then you know that they've thought about it, that they've read it! I remember we were doing a scene one day on *Prisoner* and it was obvious that Sheila Florance had no bloody idea of what she was doing. I said, "Sheila, have you read this?" she said, "No I haven't." I said, "Why?" and she said, "Scripts depress me these days"! I had no comeback to that.

The Crawford's shows had a big impact on Australian popular culture, unlike most Australian movies.

Yeah, most of the features that were made in those days were dogs and even today with *Neighbours* [1985–] we have more viewers in England in a day than big-time American directors get for a movie in a week.

Bluey sold to the U.K. as well.

Gerda Nicholson, who played the policewoman, was a lovely lady, she was fantastic. Because he was a comedian, Lucky always wanted to add joke lines. He went to Hector and asked him if he could and Hector, stupidly, said it was okay. Well, some of the things he used to suggest were just not appropriate for the sequence and when you told him that, he'd say, "Hector said it was all right"! John Dierdrich played his offsider and the set that they had for his character was supposedly ultra-modern with a lounge suite made from big cut blocks of foam. Lucky was so big that whenever he sat on it, he'd sink to the floor, he was like a beached whale struggling to get back up. So the grips came up with a device, using a plank and a brick, so that when the time came they could sort of eject him out. Sometimes they'd be a little too enthusiastic and he'd be launched out like a rocket and go flying across the room.

He was in a rush to solve a crime!

And they kept on scripting chase scenes! We used to be worried that Lucky was gonna have a heart attack because he'd be puffing and panting and his face would go red. We shot the last episode out at a hotel in Heidelberg. It was a night shoot and we had some lights in the bar. One of the lighting guys kept on going inside to check the lights, or have a beer more likely, and he couldn't wait to tell me that when he was in there, this old codger had asked him, "Who's that gray-haired old cunt out there giving all the orders?" So Georgie Greenhill, who was in the art department at the time, printed up a t-shirt with a drawing of me on it and **G.H.O.C.** written underneath it. It was hanging on the line at home one day when my mother visited and she went, "What does that mean?" and I thought, "Oh my God" and I went, "Oh, Gray-Haired Old.... Conway!"

Alvin Rakoff
Director

Canadian-born, U.K.-based director Alvin Rakoff made his name in television. He specialized in intimate teleplays, but could also turn his hand to brisk thick-ears like the Harry Alan Towers–produced crime series *Dial 999* (1958).

His big screen career began with *Passport to Shame* (1959) and *Treasure of San Teresa* (1959), two British star vehicles for Eddie "Lemmy Caution" Constantine, France's favorite American tough guy. These were followed by *On Friday at Eleven* (1960), a Rod Steiger heist movie based on a novel by crime writer James Hadley Chase.

He directed "The Ex-King of Diamonds," an episode of *The Saint* (1962–69) that paired Roger Moore with American import Stuart Damon. It served as a model, with its chalk and cheese playboys, dolly-in-distress and chic surrounds, for Moore and producer Robert S. Baker's next television project, *The Persuaders!* (1971–72).

Working again with the team from *The Saint*, Rakoff made the witty, zippy *Crossplot* (1969), an ITC-scaled *North by Northwest* with Moore and Belgian charm-fest Claudie Lange on the run in swinging London—and swinging Bedfordshire too.

How did you get involved with Passport to Shame *and* Treasure of San Teresa?

I was getting quite a reputation as a television director, a few of us were, but it was very hard for a television director to break into movies. I can't emphasize enough how difficult it was. I was a little reluctant to do *Passport to Shame*, an exploitation film about prostitution, but I decided losers can't be choosers. Eddie [Constantine] had to give his approval of me, and he did.

Were they conceived as vehicles to break Eddie into the English-speaking market?

Very much so. Eddie was already a big star in France and Germany, so much so that when we were in Germany making *Treasure of San Teresa* it was really difficult because he'd get mobbed by fans, like a pop star. One of the reasons Eddie wanted to do this, while I think of it, is that he was determined to get in with the New Wave, he wanted to do a picture where he wore a black leather jacket.

Was this a stated aim?
Yes, it was! He said it to me. Because of course as Lemmy Caution he was always immaculately turned-out in a suit, shirt and tie, trilby. He wanted to get with the Albert Finneys and the New Wave.

He ultimately did, working with Godard and Fassbinder.
The New Wave that came along had all seen his earlier low-budget films and respected him, which is quite right, they should have done. Eddie and I got on well when we were making *Passport to Shame* so when the next movie came up he asked for me as director. *Treasure of San Teresa* was filmed in Germany, some of it in France, some of it in the U.K. We were in the extremes of Germany, north of Hamburg, and we were so cold that we'd take turns at who would take their gloved hands out of their pockets and turn the script pages to see what the hell was next. Both *Treasure of San Teresa* and *Passport to Shame* would have been four- to five-week shoots, tough, but coming from live television, where you're shooting a ninety-minute film and you've got two days in the studio to do it, four to five weeks seemed quite grand.

Live television must have been exciting.
Exciting and very, very difficult. You'd plan the studio rather like a chessboard, you move everything around and everyone knows their allocation. We rehearsed two days and then you did it live, multiple sets, cameras running from one set to another, from one studio to another. Of course we'd rehearse the actors for three to four weeks before that so that they knew what they're doing.

How much rehearsal do you like when you're making a feature?
On a film, it depends on the script, but most scripts are visual rather than verbal and there's no point discussing the visuals. So a day or two to sit around, read, get to know each other.

What do you advise shooting first? Simple stuff, or something meaty?

Simple stuff, definitely. It's a great mistake to go into the bedroom scene immediately. The actors are human beings and they haven't related to each other. Don't do the father versus son heavy drama, you need gestation time for the actors' thoughts. And for the crew, it takes time to meld everyone into a unit.

Everybody comments on the dance-dream sequence in Passport to Shame.

I hated doing it! When I've lectured to younger directors, I've told them that all dream sequences should be banned! It's a bad writing prop that you use to get certain facts over and, really, they're useless. Find another way out of it, because it's a weakness in a script. I don't care which film it is, even if there's a lot of money. *Passport to Shame* was very, very low-budget, unbelievably low considering the fact we had some very good U.K. stars in it—Diana Dors, Herbert Lom, as well as Eddie coming over from France.

And you've got Christopher Lee in Treasure of San Teresa, *they're dream casts. Would you agree that an instinct for casting is an indispensable tool for a good director?*

That's true whether you're directing for film, theater, television or the local concert hall. You've got to go with instinct because sometimes you'll find a beginner and you'll give them their first big job. I gave Sean Connery his first leading role, in a television play I did in the U.K. called *Requiem for a Heavyweight* [1957], written by Rod Serling. Sean used to "walk on" for me, as an extra, and it was just instinct that made me cast him in a lead. There was another small-part actor who was always bugging me to walk on who was also in that show, Michael Caine. Years later when they made *The Man Who Would Be King* [1975] together, the billing on the posters was "Connery and Caine together for the first time." I kept shaking my head and saying, "That ain't true! They were together for me in 1957."

Have you ever made any major casting mistakes?

I sure have. Remember, I'm a Canadian, right, I arrived here in a country where I didn't know any actors. There were no casting directors when I started in television, the director did all his own casting. One was bound to make mistakes; but then, strangely, it wasn't so much in the early stages that I made mistakes, it was later on.

How did you deal with it?

Usually fire the person. If it's not going to be what you want and if there's no way of getting it, you've got to be brutal. Sometimes you can make it work without that extreme measure, but basically if you've made a mistake like that, what you should do is bite the bullet, speak to the actor as a human being and say, "I'm sorry but it's really no good for you and it's no good for me and you won't look good in it anyway so I think you should go" and they usually go. Being fired is part of the routine of show business, it only happens in 1 or 2 percent of cases. I've been fired myself a couple of times!

An actor who I assume would be very different from Constantine in approach is Rod Steiger, who you worked with on the James Hadley Chase story On Friday at Eleven.

When they ordered a round of shots, they didn't know what they were getting themselves into. Rod Steiger in Alvin Rakoff's *On Friday at Eleven* (1960).

That was the second time I worked with Rod Steiger. What happened was, again, there was an American television play written by Rod Serling called "A Town Has Turned to Dust" [1960]; Rod Steiger had done it in America and these were the days when there were no tapes so if you wanted to reproduce the show, you had to do it again. So it was brought to England, and the BBC asked me to do it and both Rod Steiger and his wife at that time, Claire Bloom, said it was better than the American version. Then he was offered this German-American co-production, essentially German-based, called *On Friday at Eleven*, and he asked that I direct it. I got along with Rod very well, as much as one can with a full-blooded method actor.

And how did Rod's full-blooded method-ness impact on the making of the film?

Well, you had to sort of stand aside, let the steam come out of the kettle. Totally different actor than Eddie. Rod could say a sentence in twenty different ways whereas with Eddie you'd be lucky if you got two or three. Huge difference in their style of acting.

Was Crossplot *star Roger Moore as charming off screen as he is on?*

Definitely, one of the most affable people one could meet, and I understand he still is. That was just one of those jobs that fell into my plate. Robert S. Baker, who produced *The Saint*, asked me to do it and the only thing I asked of him was that I do an episode of *The Saint* first so that I'd get to know Roger and get to know the crew that we were going to use.

The writer Leigh Vance was very talented, with some great British B-movie scripts to his name.

He emigrated to L.A. and joined the Hollywood circle, mainly wrote television series. John Kruse worked on the *Crossplot* script as well. We brought in several other screenwriters to sort of help it along.

Crossplot *is very much in Robert S. Baker's signature style. Did he stress certain qualities that he wanted you to emphasize?*

No, he wasn't that sort of producer. He was the sort of producer who set up a picture, gave it to the director and that was that. The only thing I would have preferred is more control of the editing; he was one of these producers who liked the film to be assembled as we were going

Masters of the Shoot-'Em-Up

along. I find that difficult because you're thinking of today and tomorrow and suddenly you've got to look back at yesterday. I've always preferred, and it's only happened to me once or twice in my life, that there's no assembling of any footage. We know we got the stuff, it's in there somewhere, and you assemble three days after the shooting stops, so you've got two days to go get drunk, and then sit down with the editor and start editing it then. If I'd become a big-name director I would have insisted on it throughout my career. With *Treasure of San Teresa* I in fact arrived at the studio after shooting to do the editing and was told by the man at the gate that he'd been told not to let me in, that the producers had decided they didn't want me around when they were editing it!

Had you had previous trouble with these producers?

Probably, but I don't remember! But I'm not a weak director and I probably put my oar in several times. I never got in to edit a foot of that. But of course what happened was, the editor would ring me late at night and say, "What did you have in mind here?"

Did you start trying to protect yourself from unscrupulous producers after that?

Not possible, not if you're a jobbing professional director. If a job comes along, you don't say, "I shouldn't work with this producer." I was raised on the mean streets of Toronto and I didn't have that sort of money in the bank. A lot of people, because of commercial television, had the money in their pocket from doing commercials but I wasn't in that position. I was very jealous of those directors who could decide what they were going to do and stick to it, who had the foresight to say, "I'm not just going to be a jobbing director." If you can orchestrate your life so you could do that, then you'll be happier. Once you've learned, but just make sure you've learned because learning to direct takes years and years, I don't think you learn it at school, I don't care what school you go to. I think to deal with all the various aspects of directing for film takes years of doing it. If you stick with it, and you learn, then stick to your guns and stay with your vision.

With all the people involved in making a movie, and all the complications, how much of your original vision would you say you got onto the screen with these films?

With *On Friday at Eleven*, quite a bit of it, because the Germans were in awe of the auteur thing and had great respect for the director. But usually I was either barred or shoved to one side or producers wanted to get the material out quickly. I was involved in the editing when I made *The Comedy Man* [1964] with Kenny More, who was a wonderful actor to work with, but then the editor got tired, one replaced another, and the distributors came along and re-cut the party scene, which broke my heart. It could have been a great scene but it was re-cut and it doesn't build the way I wanted it to build, they hit the climaxes at the wrong spots. But again, one had little or no say in those days. Any instance where I produced and directed, I could follow my visualization through to the end. Most producers can't produce. I always think of a producer as, when it's raining, the producer is the guy standing with the umbrella over the director's head—but most producers that I worked with didn't know what an umbrella was, or couldn't find one.

Or locked you outside the studio gates in the rain.

And while I was out there went and found a cold hose pipe and shoved it down the back of my neck!

Robert M. Lewis
Director

Robert M. Lewis came to directing via the editing room. His editing background is evident in the confidence and economy of his work on *The Alpha Caper* (1973), a television heist movie featuring Henry Fonda, Larry Hagman, Leonard Nimoy and James McEachin, the brilliant, charismatic star of *Tenafly* (1973–74).

Lewis helmed several other action telefeatures including *Pray for the Wildcats* (1974), the "skyjacked beauty queens" crowd-teaser *The Night They Took Miss Beautiful* (1977), *S+H+E: Security Hazards Expert* (1980), a lady super-spy story starring Cornelia Sharpe and written in part by Bond scripter Richard Maibaum, and the Australian-shot *No Room to Run* (1982).

He also directed episodes of Aaron Spelling's "hippie cop" hit *The Mod Squad* (1968–72), *McMillan and Wife* (1971–77), *Kung Fu* (1972–75), *Griff* (1973–74), a private eye show starring Lorne Greene and created by Larry Cohen, *Harry-O* (1974–76) and *Serpico* (1976–77), the spin-off series with David Birney in Pacino's beard.

The first thing I want to ask you about is The Night They Took Miss Beautiful.

Oh God, it was a terrible film!

Hey, beauty queens, skyjacking, chemical weapons, what more could anybody want?!

It was very, very high-rated, but a terrible movie. By that time I was already a very successful television movie director and I didn't wanna do it. It was an awful script and it had Stella Stevens, Sheree North, Miss Germany...

Stella Stevens and Sheree North are a big plus!

Well, I like Stella Stevens a lot, as a person, we made another movie together and her performance was fine, but that's not why she was hired for *The Night They Took Miss Beautiful*! It was so bad that it was the only movie of mine where I didn't attend the screening, I hated it that much.

So how did you get involved with it?
Do you know the film *Ring of Passion* (1978)?

About the Joe Louis-Max Schmeling fight.
Right. Originally it was called *Rehearsal for Armageddon*, a much better title. I really wanted to do that so I made a deal: If they let me do *Rehearsal for Armageddon*, I'd do their piece of shit as well. So here's what happened, *Ring of Passion* gets an audience of one, nobody ever saw it and I can't even get a copy of it, but it was actually pretty good; *The Night They Took Miss Beautiful* was a gigantic hit, I think it was the highest rated television movie of the season, and it was the worst!

Chuck Connors is in it. He was pretty cool.
My wife worked in costuming on *The Night They Took Miss Beautiful* and the only thing I can remember about Chuck Connors is that he was talking about her and said, "Not much to look at, but boy, what a great pair of legs."

Maybe I've gone off him now! You started as an editor, didn't you?
My first job in Hollywood was at Allied Artists, I was an apprentice assistant film editor on a William Wyler picture called *Friendly Persuasion* [1956], so I started off my career working with one of the ten greatest film directors of all time. It was an extraordinarily lucky break because in those days most people started off working in the mail room. I was on *Friendly Persuasion* for nearly a year, which was spectacular because even then everything in Hollywood was freelance. There was no such thing, except in rare circumstances, as a studio employee, almost everyone worked from job to job. I was working for a wonderful film editor named Robert Swink, he'd done a lot of work for William Wyler, films like *Roman Holiday* [1953], and he was so good to me I can't tell you. He let me edit scenes and, honestly, I didn't know anything. I mean, I'm a graduate of UCLA film school but back then college didn't really teach you that stuff. If you were gonna learn anything, you did it on your own. After *Friendly Persuasion* I got a job as an apprentice editor on *The Pride and the Passion* [1957], an absolutely dreadful Stanley Kramer movie

with Frank Sinatra, Cary Grant and Sophia Loren. It was probably as bad a movie as I ever worked on. The first cut was five hours long and after we'd run it for Kramer he shut everything down with an eye to re-writing and re-shooting, because he didn't have a movie and he knew it. Being the aggressive kid I was, I went to him before I left the studio and told him I had some ideas about how he could fix the story. He said, "Sure, just write 'em down." So I spent a couple of days writing, gave him my ideas, and off I went. Some months later the production was reconstituted but I wasn't rehired. I was working on another film at the studio where they were re-shooting and I happened to run into Kramer. He said, "Oh yeah, I meant to tell you, I used all your ideas in the rewrite," and I said to myself, "Yeah, but you never asked me back." The end result was still a perfectly dreadful movie.

How hands-on were Wyler and Kramer in the editing room?

I don't know how Stanley Kramer worked with his editor but William Wyler was not hands-on at all, not like a lot of directors today. Willie would make sure that Bob got his notes during production, make sure he knew his preferences for takes, but he trusted Bob and once he started cutting he'd leave him alone. I don't think Wyler saw *Friendly Persuasion* until it was completely put together, but he may have looked at scenes when I wasn't there, I wasn't privy to everything that went on. I was just a kid who got excited about having lunch with Gary Cooper!

Did you work with Robert Swink again?

He asked me to work as an assistant on the George Stevens film *The Diary of Anne Frank* [1959], but the union turned me down. Everything was unionized at that time and to get a job in editorial you had to be accepted into the union. You started off as what was called a group three member, after four years you became a group two and in four more years you became a group one. Until you became a group one member, you couldn't be a film editor. You could be an effects editor or a music editor but not a film editor. By that time I'd been promoted from an apprentice to an assistant editor, but I was a group three assistant, and that meant that if there was a group two assistant who wasn't working and wasn't drunk, unemployable, they got the job, not me. And that's exactly what happened, there was a group two assistant available, and it was Hal Ashby! So I was looking for a job and the only job in editorial that was available to me at that time was in television, on a series called *The Real McCoys* [1957–63] with Walter Brennan and Richard Crenna. I started when they'd just shot episode seven and I left after episode 224, six years later. I came onto it as an assistant editor, ended up as post-production supervisor responsible for all the mixing, and was one of the first people, if not the first person, to work with Charley Douglass's artificial laugh machine. The series was made by Danny Thomas and Sheldon Leonard and after it ended I continued working for them. By then I was eligible to edit and worked as an editor on *The Andy Griffith Show* [1960–68], *Gomer Pyle, U.S.M.C.* [1964–70], *I Spy* [1965–68] and *That Girl* [1966–71]. Then Danny and Sheldon ended their partnership, I don't know why, maybe they just got so bloody rich they didn't need each other any more! And after that, Danny found this slender writer named Aaron Spelling and I went from series to series with them.

Which led to The Mod Squad.

They were looking for someone to edit the pilot and my name came up. The guy who ran the editorial department for Thomas and Spelling spat on the floor when he handed me the script, he said, "This is the worst piece of crap I ever read in my entire life. Wanna do it?" and I said, "Sure I wanna do it!" Aaron knew I could do things like *Accidental Family* [1967–68], but he wasn't sure I could do a tough cop show, so he got me to cut some tests they'd shot with the kids, to show him what I could do. They were good, I was a good editor, but I think what really got me the job was that I grew my hair! I had a Marine haircut at the time and I thought, "If I'm gonna cut a hippie show, I should look like a hippie" and grew it into an Afro. It was a stupid idea, a hippie is so far away from what I am, but I think it convinced Aaron! The pilot was directed by Lee Katzin who did a wonderful job on a truly awful script. I did a very good job editing it, and the series became a monster hit. There were really two versions of *The Mod Squad*, because there were two producers, Tony Barrett and Harve Bennett, and they hated each other. There was the "Barrett" version and the "Bennett" version. I edited ten or twelve shows in the first season and most of them were for Harve Bennett.

What was the difference between the two?

The Bennett episodes were better. Tony Barrett was an oldtime writer and he did shoot-'em-up action shows. Harve Bennett was an executive from ABC and was trying to do important stories. Harve Bennett hired a lady story editor, which was very unusual for an action show at the time. Her name was Rita Lakin and she had written, I dunno, half the episodes of *Peyton Place* [1964–69]. I directed a show that she wrote for the second series called "In This Corner—Sol Albert" and we ended up getting married, but that's another story!

How did you make the transition from editing to directing on The Mod Squad?

At the end of my first year as an editor I asked Harve Bennett for a chance to direct and he said yes. It was as easy as that. They had problems getting me approved by Aaron, who said, "Directors are a dime a dozen, a good editor is hard to replace," but Harve Bennett's contract was up for renewal and he actually had a clause put in it that guaranteed me one show as a director. I was so nervous about doing it I insisted on editing it as well. One show became 17 and when Harve moved from *The Mod Squad* to Universal I went with him. I directed about five episodes of *McMillan and Wife*, a thing called *Griff*...

Oh, you've gotta tell me about Griff.

That was Steve Bochco, it was his series. It didn't last very long but Steve and I are still friends. Strangely, when you consider all the series he made, I only directed one other thing he wrote, a television movie he didn't get credit on. We have bigger connections, we owned an apartment building together!

Which one of your movies did Bochco write?

The Alpha Caper, a great, fun movie that played overseas as a feature for a long time.

With Henry Fonda and that great cast.

Harve Bennett told me that Fonda was going to play the lead but wanted to meet me first. I was taken to his enormous Bel Air house and we sat and chatted for a while. He had no objections to me and I think he just wanted to put a face on me. When we left, the production manager of the film told me something that turned out to be very important. Fonda had just finished a movie called *Sometimes a Great Notion* [1971] and Richard Colla was directing it until Fonda had him fired for asking

Top: Lorne Greene, the under-lensed Barbara "99" Feldon and Mark Miller in "Death by Prescription," a 1973 episode of the Universal Television detective series *Griff*, directed by Robert M. Lewis. *Bottom:* And the winner of the 1973 "Mr. Urbane America" competition is ... James McEachin, Leonard Nimoy, Larry Hagman and Henry Fonda in *The Alpha Caper* (a.k.a. *Inside Job*), a Universal telefeature directed by Robert M. Lewis.

him to stage his own movements in a scene. It's easy to get insecure when you work with big stars, particularly when you're a young director. You tend to want to give them whatever they want because you think, "Who am I to tell them what to do? They're a star!" But Fonda just wanted to do his lines and let the director tell him where to come in, where to go, when to stand and to sit, he didn't want to block scenes. Compare that to people like Al Pacino or Dustin Hoffman, all they wanna do is block the scene! Or James Dean who didn't let the director do *anything* on *Rebel Without a Cause* [1955]. Fonda just wanted to come in, do his job and go home. He was very prepared, knew his part and knew exactly what he was doing. If he had trouble with a line, it meant there was something wrong with it and we changed it, but that happened very seldom. We had a great relationship and I have very fond memories of him. I found that the old movie stars who came to television, like Rock Hudson and Henry Fonda, were really good guys to work with. The kids who were suddenly thrust into stardom were awful to work with, awful, and as a general rule the male stars were easier to work with than the female stars! The only male stars I ever had any trouble with were George Peppard and David Carradine—I was actually fired off *Kung Fu* because I couldn't get along with Carradine. He was so stoned all the time that he'd fall asleep in the middle of the set. Great situation!

What's the key to a fast and efficient shoot?
A fast and efficient crew, a cameraman who gets along with the director so the two of them are not constantly fighting, and a star who turns up! That's what makes a good shoot and that's the reason why Steven Spielberg has used the same editor, the same composer, and only a couple of different cameramen for every movie for the last thirty years! When you find people you can work with, you stick with them because it's hard to create that connection, technical and emotional, between the director and the crew. I used the same film editor on sixteen movies, and we talked shorthand.

Did you trust your editor to put the film together or did you sit in?
No, I trusted him, if it was Les Green, I absolutely trusted him. I saw the dailies and we talked about the day's work each day and if he had a problem he told me and if I had a problem I told him. But I never stood

behind him for the first cut, never. First of all, editors hate that and secondly I didn't feel the need to do it. I trusted him, that's what you want.

I'm extra-interested in No Room to Run *because it was filmed in Australia.*

The Australian reviews for that were awful. We re-adjusted Sydney in terms of where things were and the literal Australian reviewers couldn't stand that.

Hadn't they ever seen a movie before?

I met my current and spectacular wife on that movie and that was more important to me than anything else about it. She doubled for Paula Prentiss. She wasn't really a stuntwoman but she was the only person available who was physically similar. When I was in Australia, the film industry was very primitive, it was hard to get a crew and there were only something like two cameramen who were at the level we needed. The cameraman we used was very good, as was the camera operator, but the grips, gaffers and electricians were just not experienced. The whole set-up was poor, it was very early for this kind of production, an action movie, they're difficult, dangerous and slow to make and it was a difficult shoot. The stunt people were very careless and that made me crazy! I prided myself that in all the years I'd been shooting stunts and action, nobody had ever got hurt, but we came very close in Australia because the stunt men were not professional.

So why was it shot in Australia?

It was put together by a guy who ran the off network productions at 20th Century-Fox. They were trying to make movies that would play overseas as features and he had a deal in Australia to make four or five of them. He wanted Rita Lakin, who I was still married to at that time, to write a pilot he was looking to do called *The Last Bride of Salem* [1974] and she agreed to do it if he'd let me direct one of his Australian movies. Rita also came over to Australia and worked with George Kirgo and Joe Gantman on the script, but we never fundamentally solved the problems. I mean, it was okay but it wasn't breathtaking.

How much do you involve yourself with script?

Totally, completely, and I've written a couple of scripts as well. I co-wrote, directed and produced a very good television thing called *Dead*

Reckoning [1990]. Cliff Robertson was in it and it was a very big hit. It was shot on the water in Canada during storms, very hard to do; we were trying to shoot on water and match rain! I wrote a script for Roger Corman called *Don't Sleep Alone* [1999]. Roger and I were friends for years, he bought the script but I didn't direct it. He wanted me to do it but he didn't hire union directors.

How much of the film is yours?

None of it, the title! It was a disgustingly good gothic horror script and they turned it into a sex movie. I think they paid me more for the script than they spent on the film!

Richard Maibaum was the perfect writer for...

Oh my God, you're gonna ask me about *S+H+E*! You're really picking all the crap.

People love these films!

Proof that you can be unhappy even when you're standing next to Anita Ekberg. Robert M. Lewis on the set of the Bond-inspired telefeature *S+H+E: Security Hazards Expert* (1980) (courtesy Robert M. Lewis).

I know they do. Okay, why did I do *S+H+E*? Because it was three months in Rome on somebody else's money! Maibaum was kind of an old guy by then, his script was awful and I think I had almost nothing to do with him. My ex-wife did the rewrite and off we went.

With Anita Ekberg!
Anita Ekberg was very difficult, she wouldn't show up, she'd just disappear. The executive producer was a guy named Marty Bregman who had a big track record—*Serpico* [1973], *Dog Day Afternoon* [1975]. I said, "She's crazy, she's really making my life crazy," and Bregman's response was, "Fire her." I said, "Are you kidding! We've shot film on her," and he said, "I don't care, fire her." That's the feature sensibility. In television you don't fire anybody unless they're dying on the set or so drunk you can't find them. So I fired her and then rehired her when she promised to be a good girl, and she was. She totally shaped up and was perfect for the rest of the shoot.

That's the secret!
That's the secret if you can do it, but try to do it with Al Pacino! You're the one who gets fired. See, the problem was that she felt it was a terrible comedown and she only took the job because she needed the money. It was the same with Omar Sharif, he didn't take the job because he thought it was the greatest script he ever saw, or because he wanted to go to Rome—he was in Rome all the time. He took it because he needed the money, and that's always a problem. He was also an enormously difficult person, but not on the set, not with me. He was very punctual, always knew his lines and his work habits were never a problem. The problem was, he did take one and Cornelia Sharpe needed thirty takes so they hated each other. She was a model for a perfume company, very, very pretty, but not an experienced actress. I got an acting coach for her, but it really didn't help.

How do you work around that?
You go crazy!

Jeff Kanew
Director

Is Jeff Kanew's *Eddie Macon's Run* (1983) the last studio film in the 1970s–'80s "good ol' boy" cycle? The string of rural action movies that started with the classic *White Lightning* (1973) reached their box office peak with *Smokey and the Bandit* (1977) and included surprise smashes like Phil Karlson's *Walking Tall* (1973), the low-budget Roger Corman drive-in movie *Thunder and Lightning* (1977) and very low-budget Earl Owensby drive-in movies like *Buckstone County Prison* (1978).

Eddie Macon's Run is linked to these movies by its rural setting, chase plot, outlaw hero, title—evoking as it does Max Baer's enormously successful *Macon County Line* (1973)—and most of all by its star, John Schneider.

The good ol' boy formula of bad sheriffs, moon-runners, country music, hot cars and hot women (in denim shorts) was brought to the small screen with *The Dukes of Hazzard* (1979–85), a huge hit that made its two leads, Schneider and Tom Wopat, household names. *Eddie Macon's Run* was Schneider's shot at becoming a movie star and Kirk Douglas was on hand to show him how it's done.

Before he started directing, Kanew produced movie trailers (with great success) and worked as an editor (ditto). Other films he helmed that fall within the scope of this book are the Woody Strode–narrated documentary *Black Rodeo* (1972)—the title says it all—and *Tough Guys* (1986), a Disney crime comedy that reteamed Douglas with his *Gunfight at the O.K. Corral* (1957) co-star Burt Lancaster.

You started your career making trailers.

I was going to college, trying to be a rock star and cutting a lot of classes. I got suspended from college but fortunately one of my neighbors from when I was growing up was an executive at United Artists and he offered me a job there as an office boy. I ended up the gofer for the trailer department and I realized I had an affinity for it; as a songwriter and a musician, I connected with cutting to music, and I started focusing on that, developing skills in that area. Eventually I went out on my own and started a little trailer company and lo and behold I got lucky. There was this little movie with no big stars in it that Embassy Pictures had. They thought that because I was young, I'd know how to sell it, so they hired me to do the trailer. The movie was *The Graduate* [1967] and all of a sudden I was "the kid who did the trailer for *The Graduate*" and work started to come to me. I spent twelve years as a pretty big deal movie trailer maker in New York and ended up doing something like five hundred trailers.

Did you ever think, "This movie is no good, I'm going to deliberately misrepresent it and make it look better"?

That's your job. Ideally I tried to show the movie for what it was whenever possible, but sometimes you know that if you do that, you're shooting yourself and the film company in the foot. If it's not any good, your job is to disguise it by stealing all the fruit and presenting that. But really, the audience somehow smells it out most of the time.

Did producing trailers influence the way you make films?

Yes. Brevity is the soul of wit! I have an impatience about letting things linger, which is maybe not the right pace to have in your head for all films. I had to fight it on *Natural Enemies* [1979], my first film. It was a long, talky, grim drama, so I couldn't keep that nervous trailer-y pace, but in all the other stuff I've done I've tried to keep things moving, dropping scenes if they slowed things down. A producer that I worked with on *Revenge of the Nerds* [1984] introduced me to the process of pre-screening a film for audiences, tightening and tightening it, before even showing it to the studio. After that I made it a practice on all my films to have a number of screenings, taking comments and trying to feel where the audience was getting itchy or antsy. I don't think Terrence Mallick does that sort of thing!

Pre-screening must be nerve-wracking.

It's horrible because you're showing people material you're not sure about. There were times when the films played well and that was exciting, but generally the minute you hand someone a comment card, asking what they liked and didn't like, they become an instant movie critic. The way I tried to deal with that was by getting my little nucleus of crew together and reading them all the worst cards out loud. We laughed about it and that took the sting out. Of course we did listen and reshape, if there was a consensus about something.

What if it was a consensus that you didn't agree with?

Sometimes I'd overrule the jury, but if we had ten screenings and something came up over and over again, I'd have to concede, even though it was often painful. I took my favorite scenes out of several of my movies and since they weren't hits anyway I feel like I should've left them in because at least I'd be happy when I watched it.

Eddie Macon's Run *originated with you, didn't it? You optioned the book.*

I read the book and really liked the story. It's about a man in trouble who loves his family and goes through hell and high water to get back to them. I optioned the book and wrote the screenplay but I didn't really have the connections to get it made. I'd already made *Natural Enemies*, but that was a little independent film that played for a week and disappeared off the face of the earth. I did have one friend who was a big-time producer and he was nice enough to volunteer to help me with it, but then my agent at William Morris convinced me to switch over from him to Marty Bregman, another producer, who somehow, with a sleight of hand, became the owner of the project and my boss. The first thing he did was tell me that the script was all wrong because of this, that and the other thing. The book was about a man in his thirties who's lived a tough life and has a wife and two kids, but Marty Bregman decided to offer the part to John Schneider from *The Dukes of Hazzard*, who was at that point nineteen or twenty years old. I said, "That's wrong for the character. The character needs to have lived a bit before he goes to jail so that we can feel his loss. He's not just a kid in punishment school." But Bregman said, "Yeah, well, get on a plane to Atlanta and if John Schneider approves you, you'll direct the movie with him." That's a little bit how it is in the world of studio projects, the director's not exactly an auteur until he's had hits. So I played ball and John Schneider approved me and the next thing that happened was we had to pick an actor to play his adversary. I was interested in someone like Gene Hackman or Peter Boyle, a character type, but Martin Bregman said, "No, we're offering it to Kirk Douglas. Go out and meet him and if he approves you,

you'll be directing the movie with him." So I flew to L.A. and I met with Kirk and luckily for me he'd seen and liked my first film, depressing though it was, and I was okay in his book. We've been very close friends ever since, even though I was awestruck by his experience and very intimidated by him at the beginning.

Intimidated?

Kirk gets very involved, he likes to give the director notes about the script, his character, the other characters. He sent me a very long memo with all these different notes and I being inexperienced and being the writer and director thought I had to defend the script. I had a meeting with him on his first night on location. I'd shot that day and was tired and defensive and started going through his list of notes explaining why each note didn't work for me. I'd gone through six or seven out of maybe fifty notes when he stopped me and said, "You know, I've done a few movies and I might not be right all the time, but I'm not wrong all the time either. Why don't you get the fuck out of my hotel room." He threw me out and I thought, "Hmmm. This is going to be an interesting experience." The next morning his driver came to my room and told me that Kirk wanted me to ride out to the location with him. On the way there, Kirk said, "Look, I respect your film, I like your script, but you're inexperienced so I'll just tell ya, it's your job to make the actors feel that you're listening to them, even if you're not," and I thought, "That's a good note," and we proceeded to do the day's work. He was playing a tough cop and in the first scene we did, he had to interrogate a woman. He suggested he play it as a seduction and again, not being too bright, I said, "No, it's not a seduction, it's an interrogation." I thought he meant it literally. He said "No"—he didn't say "No, you idiot" but that's what he meant. He said, "No, I don't mean I'm going to literally seduce her, I mean I'm going to get the information in a quiet way, rather than bully her." He told me about the scene in the movie *Champion* [1949] where he threatened the actress Marilyn Maxwell. The director wanted him to play it very tough but he said, "I'm playing a boxer, I don't have to be tough with a woman, I can be quiet and it will be more threatening." He showed me how he read the line, very sweetly, and he was right, it was so much better. We worked well together from that day on and he taught me a lot: about production, about working with actors…

Still got it. A sixty-something Kirk Douglas in Universal's *Eddie Macon's Run* (1983), directed by Jeff Kanew.

Is it easier to be objective when you're directing someone else's script?

Yes and I much prefer that. I try hard not to be the writer any more, that way I don't have to defend things just because I wrote them. When an actor questions something, I can just look at it and say, "You know, you're right," as opposed to being embarrassed because I got it wrong or didn't see it that way. Now I'm much more the conductor and much less the composer and for me, as a director, that helps.

John Schneider was a young television star, Kirk Douglas was a Hollywood veteran. Were there any differences in their approach to their work?

Kirk had developed his style and skills over a long period of time. John had mostly just done the one television series and it didn't really tax his inner life too much. When it came to real, dramatic moments, his approach was, "I'll just say the line and then I'll run out the door." He didn't want to do too much emotional homework. Kirk thought John was a little green and needed to reach inside himself a little more and there was a bit of tension about that. He'd take me aside and say, "I got a gun in his face and he's still smiling at me!" and I'd say, "John, this man is a killer, I think you'd be a little more frightened here." He didn't mind making the change, but he didn't really see why because in television if you look good, you *are* good. But it never became a hostile thing, everybody got along well. And as far as the results, I thought John did well enough and Kirk did very well, but I have trouble judging.

Do your memories of making a film, the experiences, the relationships, override your ability to look at it as a piece of work?

Well, first of all you have all your sense memories about the process of making it so it's hard to be completely objective, and also, in that particular case, it's not my version of the movie. My big skill and strength up to that point had been editing. I'd cut *Ordinary People* [1980] and lots of other stuff, but the first time Marty Bregman saw the movie he stopped it after ten minutes and said, "This is terrible. We need a new editor." I pointed out that editing was the one area I had credentials in and his response was, "I don't care." We had a big battle over that and ended up with an agreement that we'd screen my version and his version to different audiences on the same evening, and see which one got the best response. Well, even though my version was longer, the audience thought his was. He'd taken out too much of the emotional connective tissue because he thought it was boring. My scores were better on the cards, my audience liked the movie better, so he fired me! The movie was re-finished without me. I was not involved in any of the premieres, which were minimal, and the first time I saw it in a theater was in Europe. I was in New York and decided I wanted to see my film, but it wasn't playing anywhere that I knew of in the U.S. It was playing in Paris, though, so on a whim I got on a plane, went to Paris and watched the film in four different theaters in one day. They were mostly empty and I got so depressed I flew back home the next day, but it was all part of my education!

Was it a big leap going from a small-scale drama like Natural Enemies *to an action film like* Eddie Macon's Run?

You're making the movie in your head all the time, you're seeing it broken down into shots, so when you're writing an action sequence you have an image of it and it's just a question of trying to duplicate that while you're filming, with the help of the stunt coordinator and crew. It was certainly on-the-job training for me but I did have an idea what I was going for and I felt like I accomplished it. I remember one shot where the camera was mounted on the bumper of a car so the street was rushing underneath—I took that from *The French Connection* [1971]. That's what directing is a lot of the time, imitating what you've seen in other movies.

As the director of Black Rodeo, *were you responsible for the rodeo element in* Eddie Macon's Run?

No, that was in the book. *Black Rodeo*, that's a different story. In 1971 I was at the peak of my career as a trailer-maker, but I was already starting to get itchy about wanting to make a film and was writing a script about an escaped slave who becomes a gunfighter. I always felt like the trailer-makers were the guys who made the menus and the directors were the chefs, and I wanted to be a chef. Someone told me that there was going to be a black rodeo in New York and I thought, "Wow, I bet an audience would like to see that" and put aside my script, which probably wouldn't have been made because *The Legend of Nigger Charley* [1972] came out that same year. So I tracked down the people who were putting on the rodeo and they agreed that I could film it for a couple of days. I got Muhammad Ali to come down and participate, we shared an attorney, and he was really great, the best part of the movie. I'm a New York person and originally I was not too thrilled to be filming in Harlem because in those days it had a reputation as a kind of scary place; but it wasn't, not in the time we spent up there. It was the least scary place I'd ever been to.

As a New York person, how did you find shooting in Texas for Eddie Macon's Run?

Shooting in Texas was ... different. Kirk was a little bit unhappy because all the extras were taller than him! We went there because we needed a desert location and it rained so much that by the time we started shooting it was completely covered in greenery and flowers.

Did you learn anything on your first feature that served you well on Eddie Macon's Run?

You learn every time. The main thing I learned on *Natural Enemies* was chapter one of what I learned on *Eddie Macon's Run*, which was how to deal with actors. I was really clueless on my first picture. If a take was good I'd say, "That's great" and move on, which was absolutely wrong. Actors need an audience, and on a film the director is their audience. They need praise and validation and I learned that the hard way. So I was better with the actors on *Eddie Macon's Run* and by the time I made my third film, *Revenge of the Nerds*, I was very good because Kirk had taught me so much.

Revenge of the Nerds *was a big hit.*

Yes, that was a big surprise to everybody. The head of the studio hated the movie and tried to bury it in a hundred rather than a thousand theaters. He didn't like it because he was exactly like the people that picked on the nerds, he thought they were ugly and shouldn't be winners. But the public somehow found it and supported it and it wouldn't die; and from that point on, for quite a number of years, I was on a roll. Suddenly people thought I knew what I was doing whereas before that, it was, "Who's this guy? Why should we hire him? Why should we listen to him?"

On Tough Guys *you worked with Kirk Douglas and Burt Lancaster. How would you compare the two of them?*

By the time we got to *Tough Guys*, Kirk and I had a relationship in place that Burt and I didn't have. Burt felt my loyalty was to Kirk and therefore he was not that open to me and working with him was difficult. Kirk and Burt had done five or six movies together and they were extremely competitive. They had a bond but there was also a lot of friction, it was a love-hate thing. Burt was very professional and I thought he was very good in the movie, he was great at being Burt Lancaster, that's for sure, but his attitude was, "Let's just shoot the script and go

Kirk Douglas and Jeff Kanew on the set of Touchstone's *Tough Guys* (1986), a gangster *Ride the High Country* (1962) with the giggles (courtesy Jeff Kanew).

home" whereas Kirk loved to make suggestions and improvise. There's a scene in the film where Kirk is on top of a train, Charles Durning is in a helicopter chasing him, and Kirk moons the helicopter. That wasn't in the script. Kirk called me up one Sunday and suggested it. He got the idea from a Chicago Bears quarterback who'd mooned a helicopter as it flew over the Super Bowl training camp. I said, "Kirk, it's a Disney movie. I don't think they're gonna want to see your bare ass." I also pointed out that Burt, who saw himself as a very dignified guy, wouldn't go for it either and Kirk said, "We'll do it when Burt's not around!" So we shot it and I thought it was really good and kept it. Later, when we screened the film for some college newspaper editors, one of them raised his hand and told me I should be shot for making a superstar like Kirk Douglas bare his ass in a movie and I said, "Well, it was Kirk's idea!" Next time I saw Burt, I told him the story and he said, "I agree, you should be shot!"

When The Expendables *[2010] came out, a mate of mine said, "It's just* Tough Guys*."*

Yeah, but that one would be called *Very Tough Guys* ... with plastic surgery!

Paul Annett
Director

Although he's best known for the one-of-a-kind werewolf whodunit *The Beast Must Die* (1974), there was no shortage of action-related bits and pieces to discuss with director Paul Annett.

He rubbed shoulders with Bond alumni Harry Saltzman and Guy Hamilton when he made the promotional documentary *The Battle for The Battle of Britain* (1969), and was on the spot at the Eon offices when *On Her Majesty's Secret Service* (1969) was in production.

He helmed standout episodes of the British crime-action series *Fraud Squad* (1969–70), starring Patrick O'Connell and Joanna Van Gyseghem, and *New Scotland Yard* (1972–74) starring John Woodvine and John Carlisle. On an episode of the latter he was first paired with Billy Murray, an actor whose facility for playing smooth hardcases has made him a Brit-grit icon. Annett and Murray teamed up again on the crime teleplay *Grass* (1982) and on numerous episodes of the soap opera *Eastenders* (1985–).

He also directed two episodes of the series *Spy Trap* (1972–75) with Tom Adams, an impressive action lead who was often touted as a potential James Bond and spent the 1960s and '70s playing variations on the theme: as super-spy Charles Vine in *Licensed to Kill* (1965), *Where the Bullets Fly* (1966) and *O.K. Yevtushenko* (1968), in Peter Graham Scott's stylish and muscular *Subterfuge* (1968) and in *Spy Trap*. David Warbeck, another Bond contender, also appeared in a handful of *Spy Trap* episodes, giving the series a certain frisson for Bondologists (or weirdos) like myself.

How did you get your start in television and movies?

There was a vacancy in the camera department and I went in and fibbed and said, "Oh yes, photography is my life, I love it," and I got the job. I was a camera assistant, then a cameraman, and I absolutely hated it. I was on contract and it was like a job, going in every day, but I did it for about eight years and it was very useful because I learned a lot. My break into directing came when I was working as the promotions director at ATV, doing all the trailers and publicity. It was a great time to do it because I got to meet and interview people like Richard Burton and Elizabeth Taylor, Liberace, Sammy Davis Jr., Tom Jones and Peter Sellers. One of the producers at ATV, a lady called Josephine Douglas, introduced me to her husband at a New Year's Eve party and he hired me to make a promotional film for United Artists about the making of *The Battle of Britain*. They'd put something like seventeen million dollars into the movie, which in those days was an awful lot of money, and suddenly remembered that America wasn't in the war at the time of the Battle of Britain and most Americans didn't know much about it. It was shown widely, was very successful, and was a wonderful thing for me.

What can you tell us about producer Harry Saltzman?
Saltzman was a Jack Warner or a Goldwyn sort of character, very impressive, strong, a bit scary, which he needed to be to deal with United Artists and all the other companies he was working with. He and "Cubby" Broccoli were still doing the Bonds and were auditioning for the one with your countryman, George Lazenby.

A great man!
I saw his screen tests and thought, "They can't be choosing him," but they did. And when they were shooting I remember great dramas going on because they were in Switzerland and there wasn't any snow! They had this fantastic office in a beautiful mansion in Audley Square, Mayfair. Down in the basement they had screening rooms and I used to go and watch the rushes of the films they were making, like *Goodbye, Mr. Chips* [1969] with Peter O'Toole and Petula Clark. The screening rooms had these heavy doors and one time I opened them wide and came out and Brigitte Bardot was on the other side! I very nearly squashed her essentials behind this soundproof door! I think we screened my film down there 'cause that's where we cut it. My producer was quite smart and suggested we do a little dub on it even though it was only a rough cut. (People always say they'll be able to imagine what it'll be like when it's finished but they can't.) So we did a rough dub, put all the aircraft noises in, and showed the film. The screening room was full, all these people

from UA, a lot of Americans. At the end there was complete silence until Harry Saltzman turned to me and said, "I like it, kid" and suddenly all these other guys starting saying, "Yeah, we like it, we like it!" And then Harry said, "I'm gonna give you a present, kid, I'm gonna give you Michael Caine." I was about to say, "Can I have Laurence Olivier?" but I thought, "No, shut up, take Michael Caine." We shot some footage of him in Carnaby Street and I got to know him quite well. He kept coming back and doing more for us, but it was the late 1960s so each time he did, his hair was longer!

Director Guy Hamilton and cinematographer Freddie Young—any memories of them?

Guy Hamilton was at that time a highly successful feature director. We got on okay and I did an interview with him, but I didn't have that much to do with him and I think he wanted it that way. He was the way I might've been if I'd been directing the feature and I'd seen some young smartass guy going all over the place and getting the best angles. I was able to do that because I'd been a cameraman, I knew where to put the camera—not that Guy didn't but he was obviously more restricted because he had a much bigger camera! Freddie Young had a great aura about him, he had his own car with a driver who'd drive him wherever the camera was. His crew seemed in awe of him. I always found him very approachable, a really lovely man, with such a fascinating history in the cinema. We were doing a big sequence, it was meant to be the Normandy landing. It was a huge wide-angle with a small amount of crafts in it, about half a dozen landing barges, and he took the time to come over and explain that it was a matte shot and that there'd be thousands more ships put in. He cared that much.

You did a lot of work on the series Fraud Squad.

I started on that in 1969, when I was but a child of course! I had friends at ATV who'd always wanted me to direct for them, but the program controller never chose me, he didn't like me for some reason, perhaps I was too bumptious. I got my own back though because after I did *The Battle for The Battle of Britain* they were doing *Fraud Squad* and hired me to work on it—at about four times the salary that I would have got had I still been under contract! In the first series I was only free to do about two or three of them, but in the next series they asked me to do every other one, which was like eight of the thirteen. It was pretty exhausting, but it was a wonderful experience. I met some incredible actors and writers and worked with some really good people. The producer Nicholas Palmer, who sadly is no longer with us, was a great supporter of mine, a great friend, and I did an awful lot of stuff for him after that.

Fraud Squad star Patrick O'Connell was a good actor.
"Paddy" O'Connell was a dear man, a very charming man, still is. I think he always felt a bit miffed because Edward Woodward, who was doing *Callan* [1967-72] at the time, got a car every day and he didn't. *Fraud Squad* was number one in the ratings almost every week but *Callan* was considered a more important show. He had so many lines to learn and so much to do and I always felt sorry for him. He worked extremely hard, was very conscientious, always knew his lines, did what you asked of him and contributed bits and pieces. Joanna Van Gyseghem was his co-star and she was smashing to work with. I still know her and I had her in *Eastenders* [1985-] about two or three years ago. Michael Gambon was in the very first *Fraud Squad* I did. He'd just done a Scottish series called *The Borderers* [1968-70] but was still unknown. We became quite friendly and I got him onto a series I did for Yorkshire television called *Kate* [1970-72] with Phyllis Calvert, an old British movie actress who was still quite big. Then I got him in *The Beast Must Die*. They didn't want him in that, they said, "Who is this guy?" and I said, "He's a terrific actor and he's also great fun." Sometimes that happens, you meet an actor you admire and get on well with and you bring them into other things you do. Of course now he's one of the leading actors in the world.

Coming from a technical background, did you find dealing with actors difficult at all?
No, I'd done a lot of acting as a child, even some early television, appearing on ghastly youth programs when I was about 16. I was really bucking to become a director for a long time and used to go off and do things in the theater which I loved to do, which I still do. So when I started directing and working with actors it wasn't new to me, I'd been around the block a bit and I always got on well with actors. Actors are very insecure and want you to love them, but they're always actors,

they're never really your friend, they can't be because they're always moving from job to job. My dear friend, the late director Charles Jarrott, said that towards the end of making *Mary Queen of Scots* [1971] with Glenda Jackson and Vanessa Redgrave, he got the sense that they felt he was reneging on them by finishing the picture, that it was like the end of a love affair. They need to be loved, they need to be cosseted and they need to be looked after. They also need to be disciplined because some of them can be a complete pain, usually new ones who've only done one or two things.

I've never worked with a star who's been trouble, ever, and I've worked with Joan Collins and all sorts of people. They're never trouble because if they've agreed to do the thing, it means they trust you to look after them, to present them to their best possible advantage, and you owe it to them to do that. You should know their character as well as they do and let them have their head, and they should do their homework and work out what they want to bring to the scene. A certain amount of apparent freedom is needed, but you must have a plan in place in the back of your mind, you must know how you wish to present the scene. I did a thing with Francesca Annis and she was wonderful, you'd tell her what you wanted her to do and she'd do it, but she'd always add to it, bring something of her own to it.

Was there anything about directing that threw you when you started?
Not really, because as a cameraman you worked with a lot of directors who weren't terribly good at the technical side of things and if you had ambitions to be a director, you more or less did the shows for them. Visually, anyway. You used to get a lot of older directors who couldn't get jobs in movies any more so they'd come into television to be confronted by multi cameras and you'd have to help them work it all out.

Were there any directors you worked with who did impress you?
Yeah, there was a lovely guy called Quentin Lawrence. I went to a lecture he did once, when I was about 18 or 19, and I rarely went to lectures. It was all about the basics of television, two-shots, over-the-shoulders, eye-lines, which of course everybody ignores now, everybody crosses the line all the time! I learned a lot from him, he was a lovely, charming man and a real character. Curiously enough, he was the aerial director on *The Battle of Britain* when I turned up. By then his great days had

passed, though. And something must have happened because suddenly he was gone and Guy Hamilton was doing the whole thing himself.

You directed some episodes of the series New Scotland Yard.

That was for what was then called London Weekend Television. One of the first ones I did had Dennis Waterman, who was quite big at the time. It starred John Woodvine and John Carlisle as two inspectors. They were all interesting stories, all set around London and the Home Counties. I knew John Carlisle from when I was a cameraman on the series *Emergency-Ward Ten* [1957–67]. His character was quite sadistic, he was always being kind of unpleasant whereas John Woodvine's character was much more straightforward. John Woodvine was a bit depressive, I think—he used to get in a state about things and you can see that in his performance. He's a very thinking, slow-speaking, ponderous person, but very good, and a very handsome man too.

Spy Trap *is something of a lost series.*

Spy Trap was one of the first things I did for the BBC. I did a big *Play for Today* [1970–84] and then they asked me if I'd go and do this *Spy Trap* thing. It was quite popular, there were some interesting scripts and I worked with some good actors on it. It starred Paul Daneman, who was a terrific actor and very nice to work with, and Tom Adams who I also knew from *Emergency-Ward Ten*. Paul Daneman was mainly a theater actor, he was a bit like Peter Cushing in that they both had brilliantly blue eyes and they knew it. Color television had really just started and they'd both wear something blue and near their faces to compliment their eyes. Tom Adams was always auditioning for James Bond, but never got it! Tom was a technician too, he knew what I was doing with the camera. I was quite smart with the camera considering the restrictions. I knew what to do with it and how to achieve the best results. I'd do things like pan him with a long lens through out-of-focus heads, and he used to enjoy it because stuff like that didn't really happen in those days.

How much leeway did you have in that area? Were you ever told, "That's too avant-garde for Spy Trap*"?*

They weren't that smart! Because I had the advantage of having been a cameraman, I could fool everybody, I could do these things and they wouldn't actually notice. Producers are usually not technical people, their main concern was that you got it done on time. On *New Scotland Yard* I had a wonderful designer called Brian Bagge and together we'd try to make things look like they had bigger production values than they really did. We did this big prison sequence and, with three or four hours to record it, we did glass shots and things that nobody had really done. As long as you worked it out with the designer, you could slip things like that in without the producer being aware that you were up to visual mischief.

The episode you're referring to has Billy Murray in the cast.
   That was the first time I worked with him and we became very good friends. I did another crime thing with him for London Weekend, a play called *The Grass* which was really good. It was him and Judy Geeson, a lovely actress, and they were terrific. He's got my video tape of it, he asked me if he could borrow it to make a copy and the rotten bugger has never sent it back! It's quite a historical piece because we had huge wide angles of the London docks before they were redeveloped. He's a lovely, easy person to work with, I've never had a cross word with Billy. He's very disciplined and he's also a technician—he knows what I'm doing, respects my technical knowledge and I can always tell him the effect that I'm after. With some actors, if you tell them that it freaks them out and that's all they can think about, they can't think about their performance; Billy can combine both.

So how did you avoid freaking actors out with technical instructions? Did you let them work out their moves first, before you decided on the camera set-ups?
   In the old days, you had so little time that you had to work it all out in advance. The actors would have to go to a certain position, do a head turn, do this, that and the other. There was very little filming, you were mostly working in the studio with sets, and there were only certain angles you could do. You had three hours to record in and you didn't have the time to put in and light a fourth wall. If you're filming in real buildings, which you usually are today, it's easier to let an actor have their head. Once they've settled on what they think is right, you can maybe amend it here and there, but if you impose too much on an experienced actor they'll feel restricted, they'll feel that they can't give the

performance as much as they'd like to. If an actor is very experienced, they'll know, they'll have an innate sense of the technicalities of the effects you're after and they'll build that into what they do. As a director you need to learn who can do it, who can't, who needs discipline and who can be allowed freedom.

I love the look of these shows, the mix of film and video.
Do you? It still freaks me out when I see things like *Poldark* [1975–77], that mixture of the studio stuff and all that marvelous filming down in Cornwall. The audience obviously never noticed it, but I would've loved to have done the whole thing on film, or all on video like today. The combination of the two always bothered me. In those days you got more clarity and color from video than you ever wanted, more definition somehow, whereas the 16mm, I don't even think it was Super 16, would be much fuzzier. You had one or two days of filming outside, shooting all the getting in and out of cars, the running about and fights, and the rest of it was done in the studio on video. *Spy Trap* was done in Birmingham and they were less experienced than they were at Television Centre in London; they wouldn't have a second tape lined up and you could wait an hour while they did it. It was terribly restrictive, but that's where I was very fortunate in that the technical side was never a problem to me. I'd done those eight years as a cameraman and had learned how to do it, how to shoot things quickly and efficiently, where to put my cameras so that I wouldn't be shooting one into the other, all of that.

I'm always amazed when crews tell me about directors who come on the set, don't know where to put the camera and take half a day thinking it through. I've always said that any script I was handed, I could shoot within about five minutes, I could get it done. That isn't vanity, it's true. A lot of people used to screw up because they didn't have that knowledge, they came from theater or somewhere else. Quite often in those days theater directors would come in, especially on all the big Shakespeare stuff, and if you look at the credits there'll be a "director" who'd work with the actors, and a "technical director" who'd sort out where to put the cameras and all the technical stuff. Obviously they'd have an idea what they wanted, but they didn't do the whole thing by themselves because it was very tough.

What sort of shooting schedules did you have on shows like Spy Trap?

It was incredibly tight. When I think about it now and look at the shows on DVD, I don't know how we did it, but we did, right up to the 1980s. You'd rehearse for ten days, during which time you had to work all the moves out. You had to do a camera script of every single shot which was typed up and given to everybody in the crew. You'd then do run-throughs and indicate the cuts to the crew because you'd be cutting it live with a vision mixer, you couldn't go back and patch things over like you can today. The first day in the studio you'd rehearse on camera. On the second day you'd rehearse in the morning, then in the afternoon you'd have three, possibly three and a half hours to record—that's with moving sets and costume changes. There was a lot of pressure and the whole team had to work extremely hard.

Were there any differences in how Fraud Squad, Spy Trap *and* New Scotland Yard *were produced? Any differences in how the producers worked?*

Well, yes, producers are people … sometimes; I've been a producer, I know. The secret of being a good producer is to hire the correct writer, work with them and get the script right, hire a director who knows their job, and let them get on with it. If a producer starts sitting on me and telling me what to do, it doesn't work so well, but they rarely want to do that because they don't know anything about the technical side of things and time is too much of the essence, every second is costing them money. I worked as a producer and director on *Eastenders* and if an actor started asking you questions on that, you were dead in the water, because time is money and money is everything, and that's horrible, and that's why I don't do it any more.

How did working on The Beast Must Die *differ to working on* Fraud Squad *or* Spy Trap?

It was completely different. I was very comfortable in television, I knew all the people around me, all the crew and the actors. In television you're supported by a massive structure, or you used to be when you were with the big companies, whereas when you do a film you're out on your own, and it's real money—you've got a guy sitting in a hut paying people with cash at the end of the day. The screenplay was not terribly good so I rewrote it with Scot Finch, a dear friend of mine who's passed away now. He brought the idea of *The Wild Geese* [1977] to Euan Lloyd and worked with for him for a long time. *The Beast Must Die* was done at Shepperton Studios, for Amicus, in 1973. In that year there were only eight films made in England, everybody who worked in pictures was free and needed work, so I had the pick of everyone, people like John Stoll the art director and Jack Hildyard—it was like using a sledgehammer to crack a walnut! Whatever anyone thinks of the picture, it looks beautiful and that's because Jack was a brilliant lighting man. I kind of camera-scripted the whole thing, I knew exactly what I wanted visually all the way through it, and I wanted to make it look as elegant as possible. Jack Hildyard wasn't somebody who'd say, "Oh, you can't possibly do that," he wasn't a prima donna, he'd just do it and light it beautifully. All the interiors were beautiful, he'd do things and I'd look at them and think, "My goodness, they're like paintings on the wall." I loved shooting the film but it was a fairly rugged experience, there was horrendous

Paul Annett (left) and cinematographer Jack Hildyard on the set of the British horror favorite *The Beast Must Die* **(1974) (courtesy Paul Annett).**

pressure from certain people who just didn't want me there, wanted some of their old cronies—that's what happens when you make your first film. There was an associate producer on it who wanted to bring in people he knew. Some of them, like Jack, were brilliant choices and I was very fortunate to have those people to learn from. Others were not so great, they were absolutely horrible. There was one man in particular who said to me, "I want to be doing your job and I'm going to see how difficult I can be." Well, when you get someone saying that to you on the start of your first feature film, it's a bit tricky!

Bruce Kessler
Director

For most of us, a career as a professional race car driver would be enough achievement for one life. We'd go home and polish our laurels. For Bruce Kessler it was just the beginning. He helped himself to a career in movies and television as well, and what a career it was.

He started off as an assistant script supervisor in the company of Billy Wilder, turned heads with his groundbreaking short *The Sound of Speed* (1962), then spent several years working for Howard Hawks. Collaborations with John Frankenheimer and Arthur Penn were followed by several impressive forays into feature directing such as *Angels from Hell* (1968), a biker movie for larger-than-life B-movie producer Joe Solomon, and *Killers Three* (1968), a *Bonnie and Clyde* (1967)–inspired period action movie for AIP. From there he moved into television, bringing energy and dynamism to episodes of *It Takes a Thief* (1968–70), *Adam-12* (1968–75), *Baretta* (1975–78), *The Rockford Files* (1974–80), *Switch* (1975–78), *Freebie and the Bean* (1980–81), *McClain's Law* (1981–82), *The Fall Guy* (1981–86) and *The A-Team* (1983–87). Simply told stories about heroic professionals, with action, humor and male camaraderie given equal footage. If Howard Hawks had been starting his career in the 1960s and '70s, they would've fit him like a glove.

You started your career working with Billy Wilder.
I started as an apprentice script supervisor with Billy and the Mirisch Company on *The Apartment* (1960). Billy was a very important influence on me and he was also the one who told me that I'd be a director. When I did become one, I had to unlearn habits that I'd picked up from him, like cutting-in-camera. When I started, I didn't know enough to do that. One of the reasons that Billy could do it was that he had Doane Harrison, who used to be in charge of editing at Paramount, as his associate producer. He would always be around to give Billy advice.

Did Howard Hawks hire you because he'd seen The Sound of Speed?

Howard Hawks felt that most of the writers he worked with lived in apartments in Greenwich Village and did not understand life and death, but that people who did things like I had done in my previous life did. He heard about me when I was making *The Sound of Speed* and came out to watch me shoot. After that, he invited me to his home and asked me to come and work for him. I worked on *Man's Favorite Sport?* (1964) and *Red Line 7000* (1965). I drove for all the actors in *Red Line 7000*, I just put on a different helmet and different coveralls. I did the over-the-shoulder and process shots. The actors couldn't do it because it was beyond their reaction time.

How would you compare Wilder and Hawks?

Both were masters of their craft, two of our great directors. Billy Wilder wrote all of his films, usually with one other writer. Hawks had many writers on his films and contributed to all of them himself, but never took credit. Howard did not have the kind of sardonic humor that Billy had, he looked at a story from a different perspective, which I think every director does.

The Sound of Speed *must have been an influence on John Frankenheimer's* Grand Prix *(1966).*

Grand Prix has a very similar opening and a very similar end scene to *The Sound of Speed*. John Frankenheimer had seen *The Sound of Speed* and wanted to know how I made those shots. I explained it to him and laid out the photography, with the idea that I was going to be the second unit director. I also gave him the book *The Cruel Sport* by Robert Daley, and pointed out the Phil Hill story. I said, "I think this is the story that you want to do," and that's basically what *Grand Prix* was. Nobody had ever seen anything like *The Sound of Speed*, nobody had ever seen action done like that, they were astounded and they didn't know how I did it. The reviews in some of the magazines considered it a kind of *Red Balloon* (1956) of action pictures, it was so different for its time. Billy Wilder had looked at the story and made some suggestions, particularly in regards to the opening. He said to me, "This is the last time you'll work for yourself. After this, you'll be working for other people," and he was right.

One of the movies you ended up working on was Bonnie and Clyde.

I created, directed and photographed the chase in *Bonnie and Clyde*. Not a lot of people outside of the industry know that. Arthur Penn and I were having lunch and he asked me to do it. I was not in favor of doing it until I went over to hear the music by Flatt and Scruggs. Only one of them was there because the other one was sick. He played along while Charles Strouse, who was the music supervisor, played the piano. The minute I heard the music I got the idea, I thought, "Why would they go down a road if they just wanted to get out of town?" I thought we should do "cowboys and Indians" instead and Arthur bought that immediately. I suggested that he shoot it but he told me that I should do it instead. I shot it in one day and Arthur didn't even come down. Dede Allen, the editor, told me that she'd assembled it from my script notes exactly the way that I'd written it, and nobody changed a thing, from her first cut of the sequence. That had never happened to her before. Both Arthur and Warren [Beatty] liked it exactly the way that I saw it in my mind, the way I thought it should be cut.

Killers Three *was similar to* Bonnie and Clyde *in period and setting.*

I rewrote most of that myself, much to the dissatisfaction of Larry Gordon who was the rewrite guy back at the studio. I didn't want to shoot the script as it was written and I'd made a deal with Diane Varsi that I'd change it. It was kind of an interesting show, they chopped it up and did this and that with it but I do like the film. I shot it in seventeen or eighteen days with no dolly, no nothing, I shot it on sticks. The ending of the film was quite moving. I wrote the entire scene without dialogue, except for the little boy saying, "When are we going to California?" Dick Clark, who was in the film and was also the producer, loved that scene and when I saw the film with real audiences they loved it too. They cried, which surprised me because I hadn't realized it would affect them so strongly.

Did working in movies prepare you for working in series television? What were the differences?

The main difference is that a film becomes part of you, even if it's a low-budget film. No matter how a picture turns out, it takes a lot out of you. You're on it so long and you invest so much of yourself in it, so much of your time and energy trying to create something. Then they change the title, or recut it, and that can be very hurtful. In television they want you to contribute, that's why they hire you, they hope you'll bring something to it, but they still want it to be whatever the series is, they want it to fit the established format. You're making it for them and you don't put as much of yourself into it.

Did you ever finish a film and think, at least for a period, "That's enough, no more"?

Yeah, I had enough of making features and concentrated on television. I liked making films but I didn't want to wait around. I shot a lot of television shows I liked but then it started getting repetitious for me and I was ready to stop. When I retired from television I was sixty-two. I had a minor heart problem and I was ready to stop. I was ready to quit being a relief pitcher in the World Series, coming in to save the day.

Can you explain that?

I was quite often a problem solver, I was known as that in the industry. When a show wasn't working, they'd ask me to come in and find out what the problems were, and try to straighten them out. There were scenes that Stephen J. Cannell wrote that hadn't been usable when other directors had shot them. Things like, for instance, somebody in a dark room holding his shoe and making people think it's a gun. He'd give those scenes to me and I'd make them work.

Did anything you did in television become a part of you the way your features did?

Some things suited me better than others. There were a number of shows where I could tell the sorts of stories I liked to tell. Equally there were shows I turned down because I wasn't comfortable with that kind of work. I liked doing *The Rockford Files* because I liked working with Jim [Garner]. *McCloud* [1970–77] was very much my sense of humor and I guess Dennis [Weaver] was very comfortable with me. I shot a lot of those including the show where he rides the horse down Fifth Avenue. I shot an episode of *Kolchak: The Night Stalker* [1974–75] that was written by David Chase, the guy who created *The Sopranos* [1999–2007], who I'd worked with before. I liked that and it was highly acclaimed.

What about The Two-Five *[1978], the cop show pilot you shot with Don Johnson?*

I liked the pilot but it didn't get picked up, which was the best thing that ever happened to Don Johnson because he got *Miami Vice* [1985-89] and that went on forever. But I thought it was a good show and it had a guy called Joe Bennett in it that I liked. Why shows sell or don't sell is something I've never understood. Today, television is better than films. Cable shows can hire any talent they want and the really good talent will work for the television price. I only wish I could be shooting now. In my time there were a lot of things that they wouldn't let you do, ideas I had that were just not acceptable.

Can television directors tell which of their peers shot a show just by looking at it?

A lot of us can, yes. In my day I could tell who directed a show, and movies.

Any directors in particular whose work you could always spot?

There were directors that I was always very fond of. Billy Wilder and Hawks naturally ... John Frankenheimer, brilliant director. Some that I worked with when they were in television, like Dick Donner.

Richard Donner's television work always stood out. Why do you think that was?

He knew what he wanted and he knew how to get it, and of course when he moved into features his *Lethal Weapon* movies were wonderful. He's an innovator and he has a great feel for what he does.

I really like Jack Webb's work. Any memories of him from when you worked on Adam-12?

Very quiet man, never spoke to me. He'd sit at a card table and watch me when I worked on the set; and he always dressed in a suit, which was very unusual at that time.

Did the stuntmen you worked with in television know about your auto racing background?

Yeah, I would imagine most of them did because it was very soon after the end of my racing career. They were certainly aware of it when we did driving sequences because if they couldn't do what had to be done, I'd have to take over. If we were running out of time, the crew would say, "Go do it yourself, boss," and that's what I would do. I'd jump in the car and make the shot.

Were you allowed to do that?

The director has the final word on the set. He can do any job he likes.

Joseph Scanlan
Director

Joseph Scanlan is a highly successful television director. Sci-fi, sitcoms, kiddie shows, soaps, he's done it all. He occasionally worked in the action sphere, most pivotally with *Our Man Flint: Dead on Target* (1977), the television pilot spin-off from the cinema hits *Our Man Flint* (1966) and *In Like Flint* (1967), both starring James Coburn as super-spy Derek Flint. Small screen Flint was played by Ray Danton, who'd earlier headlined numerous European spy movies like *Codename: Jaguar* (1965), *Secret Agent Super Dragon* (1966) and *Lucky the Inscrutable* (1967). Despite Scanlan's talent and Danton's rightness for the role, *Our Man Flint: Dead on Target* did not become a series. The public's enthusiasm for the super-spy genre—Bond notwithstanding—had peaked and drastically waned in the days of *The Man from U.N.C.L.E.* (1964-68). The Anthony Franciosa series *Matt Helm* (1975-76), another 1970s attempt to revive the cycle, was likewise under-loved.

Scanlan also gave us *Spenser: The Judas Goat* (1994) and *Spenser: A Savage Place* (1995), two telefeatures starring Robert Urich. Both were based on Robert B. Parker's *Spenser* private eye novels. *The Judas Goat*, the fifth book in the series, with Spenser and his badass offsider Hawk hunting terrorists in London, Copenhagen and Montreal, is a particularly fine effort.

How did you get involved with Our Man Flint: Dead on Target?
In other words, you want the story of my life?

As much as you can give me until you get bored.
That is so, so long ago. I was living in Toronto at the time, I was a freelance director, I knew the producer from doing some series work for him and he offered me the job. I didn't start on the creative side of things, I started as a salesman at a small television station in California, then did little jobs on the set like gofer and that sort of stuff. I didn't

really do any serious directing till my late twenties, early thirties, so I was a late starter. I started directing in soap operas a hundred years ago in New York and that experience gave me my first and most valuable experience dealing with actors. Prior to that I had done a few documentaries that were sort of successful, but the soap operas were my first dramatic efforts, and they helped me in two ways: one, they taught me how to understand and deal with actors, which is a challenge in itself, and two, they taught me how to stage scenes, because on a soap opera you dealt with three cameras and you had to stage it with each of the three cameras in mind, set your shots and then go into the control room and shoot the thing. You had to work so fast in staging and blocking and actor communication, and because of that experience I went, surprisingly quickly, into drama, night time, prime time, television drama in Toronto. I lived in Toronto for twelve years, I got a lot of work and that was 100 percent down to word of mouth: A producer I worked for liked me and hired me again, some other guy asked him what I was like and hired me too.

What were the other differences between shooting in America and shooting in Canada in the 1970s?

I found both sets of crews to be equally efficient and talented. American crews had far more experience, but Canadian crews, especially in the '70s when they were just beginning to burgeon, were very cooperative and willing to learn and listen to you. In those days everybody was on a learning curve. There weren't more than two crews in Toronto at any one time; if you came in there with three pictures, you couldn't do the third 'cause there'd be no crew. Toronto allowed me to be a bit of a big fish in a small pond.

When I moved back to the U.S., to California, it was mainly because I wanted to be a big fish in a big pond and I got to be, not a big fish, but a medium to large one, and that's where you really needed an agent. I've had some very good agents over the years so I didn't have to sell myself or take any meetings until somebody was really interested in me and I could go for a meeting having read the script. The irony is that I must've done more work in Canada after I moved back to the States than I did when I was living in Toronto, because they thought, "He's in L.A. now, he must really be a hotshot" so almost all of the dozen or so large films

I did, I did in Canada. I didn't do one movie in the United States, even though I was living in L.A. I became known as an actor's director, and I really was. I could communicate with them. The most important thing I learned from working with actors is to listen to them. You have to be smart enough to know that they may have an idea that's better than your own. You have to have the courage to use their ideas when they're good, and to tell them when their ideas are lousy. So much of directing television drama is based on that.

What was Ray Danton like to work with?
Generally speaking I've had no problems with actors, I've been lucky, but there have been a few exceptions and Ray Danton on *Our Man Flint: Dead on Target* was one of them. He was a halfway decent actor, but he was difficult. He was very hard to communicate with. He did what you asked him but you never got a sense that he understood what the scene was all about. He was very disrespectful to some of his fellow actors, particularly the leading lady who came to me in tears one day because he was so rough on her.

Bill Devane and I did *Knots Landing* [1979–93] together and he was tough, but not in a mean way and I ended up loving him. I was on that show, freelance, for probably four or five years, I directed a ton of 'em. I can remember the first day I worked with him, I'd heard that he really tested directors and we're doing a scene and I said, "Bill, you go stand over there" and he said, "Why?" The most difficult question a director will get from an actor is, "Why?" and, boy, you better know why! I said, "Bill, I dunno, but you gotta stand somewhere," he says, "Okay" and we got off to a pretty good start, because you cannot bullshit these people, not the smart ones, and it's been my experience that most actors are very, very smart people. You can't pretend you know something you don't or come up with some phony answer, you've got to make them part of your team, or join their team. One time I was doing a film and an actress asked me, "Why?" and I said, "You know, I don't know" and I didn't! And she loved me from that day on because, my gosh, finally a director who doesn't have the answer to every question, because none of us do, we just pretend to. Directing is a whole exercise in human relations, and that's what I love so much about it. I got Keenan Wynn as a guest star on a series I was doing, he was a big star and I thought, "Jesus,

I hope I'm good enough to handle this." Well, we did a take and I said, "Keenan, that was dead on" and he said, "No, no, please, don't say that, don't say that, I won't be able to do it again!" He was totally, totally insecure, humble as a new actor, surprised the hell out of me.

What are the essentials of staging and blocking a scene?

Everyone has their own approach. One of my closest friends would block everything using schematics and drawings and camera angles and lens size. When he got to the set he'd say, "You go there, you cross here, you stand there," which is why a lot of actors didn't like him. When I came to the set I'd say, "Okay, here's the scene, let's just run it," the actors would say, "Well, where should we go?" and I'd say, "I dunno, lemme see what you do with it." So right away I've got them on my side because I'm not telling them what to do and I'm open to using their ideas, and when I do suggest something they're more than willing to try it. As they were moving around I'd be blocking it in my head and figuring out what I needed, whether I was going to start the scene in a wide shot or a close-up, how many pages I could do with a single shot—I love doing as many pages as I can with a single shot, the camera keeps moving, going in and out of focus, it's much more dramatic that way. I did a little bit of Off-Broadway directing in my early years and I look at a film set as a proscenium, I always have and always will.

How involved were you in the development of the scripts you shot?

It wasn't until I'd been in the business ten or fifteen years that I started taking a more critical look at scripts. Up until then I was just glad to have the work and I'd do whatever the script told me to. As I became more experienced, I developed a clearer understanding of the meaning of each scene, how to interpret it and how to enhance it; I began to recognize where there were beats in a scene and where I could add them. Sometimes what's on paper is so brilliant you can't hurt it, and sometimes you can and do hurt it! As I matured and became a writer myself, I began to notice structural problems in scripts as well, I came to understand the three-act concept and things of that nature, and ended up writing about fifteen screenplays. I only sold two of them but that's not a bad record considering the marketplace. Over the years I worked with some really good writers and the thing that you find with most writers is that they don't know how we get stuff on film. Their ideas are brought to life on the screen by your choice of shots, performance and attitude. One time, I can't remember what the show was but we were stuck, just stuck, so I called for the writer who was becoming a friend of mine. When he arrived on the stage, you would've thought he'd just stepped onto the moon, he looked about as out of place and as scared as you can imagine. We rehearsed the scene for him, I asked him what he thought we should do to make it work and he said, "I might have written it but I don't know how to make it happen!"

Was Robert B. Parker actively involved in the Spenser movies you made?

No. I met Parker once on a plane, and I guess I told him I was doing one of the Spenser movies. I didn't write any of the scripts although I did have to rewrite some of the scenes because one of the writers didn't really know Spenser or Parker as well as I did. I'd already done one of them and I loved his books, I think I read them all. The Spenser series was wonderful because Robert Urich *was* Spenser, no doubt about it, nobody could have played that character the way Bob Urich did. He was a treat to work with and it was a totally, totally happy set, great producers, great cooperation.

What about wardrobe and props? Did you exert an influence over things like that?

If you're directing a movie, whether it's a television movie or a feature film, you are deeply involved in every single aspect of it. Not so much with makeup or hair, that's its own thing, and if some actor came out with makeup and hair that I didn't like I'd have a hell of a job getting it changed. But I would always check the wardrobe department, they'd offer me some options and I'd suggest that this or that would work. Location managing is very important, you've got to have a good location manager. My location manager would pick four or five places for me to look at and when I went to those places, I had to know right away what would and what wouldn't work from a staging and camera angle point of view. I learned that in my documentary days because when you make a documentary you just fly, you arrive at locations you've never seen before and within twenty minutes you're filming. You need to know where the camera should go, where it has to go, and you have to be really fast. My relationship with the DP was always pretty solid, they could tell that I sorta knew what I was talking about—I'd gone to film school and

Masters of the Shoot-'Em-Up

Tough guys wear sports jackets. Crime fiction legend Robert B. Parker (left) meets action TV legend Robert Urich, the actor who played his detective creation Spenser in the Warner Bros. series *Spenser: For Hire* (1985–88) and in numerous television movies. Two of them were directed by Joseph Scanlan.

I'd developed a pretty good eye by walking the streets of New York taking stills. Aside from the DP, the most important person on the crew is your assistant director. Some assistant directors work for you and some of them work for the producers and you gotta be careful which is which. I used to know a director who at the very start of a shoot would ask his first AD, "Are you on my side, or their side?" because if you get the wrong producer, or the wrong production manager, their side can be the enemy and they can shoot you down. That's how it was in Hollywood, it was quite a game, but not in Canada. There they had the English point of view, the director was the "Guvnor" and what he said went.

How did the production of television movies change between your making Our Man Flint: Dead on Target *and the Spenser movies?*

It sounds strange to say but from my point of view—interpreting a script, working with actors, staging, blocking, shooting—nothing changed. The material changed, the focus of stories changed, as time went on you began to get the odd DP who took forever to light a scene, and getting rid of them was always dodgy; cameras changed, lenses changed, I wouldn't know what to do with some of the cameras they've got now. I haven't directed in twelve years now and, boy, I miss it, and what I miss most is being dropped into the middle of something new. You'd go to one production meeting and hit the ground running: new cast, new crew, new production team, everyone with their scripts underlined for how it affected them, and you had to know what they all did, you had to respect every department, props, wardrobe, makeup or whatever. The biggest mistake I made was firing my agent before I had another one; boy, that is the biggest no-no in the business. I was about ready to quit anyway so it didn't make much difference but my advice is, "Don't ever look for an agent if you don't already have one!"

What do television directors learn that directors who work solely in the cinema might not?

Speed. I was going into a new show at Universal, we had a meeting and one of the producers said to the others, "I want you to know one thing, there are two kinds of directors, ones that are fast and ones that are good.... Joe is good and fast"—that was the greatest compliment, I'll never forget it. I was doing a television movie, I think it was at Disney, and at the same time the producers were also doing a big-time feature film. The people at the studio were looking at the dailies from both productions, and one of them complained to the front office that I wasn't doing enough takes. *Hello*! I always felt that I had the discretion and the knowledge to know when I had it, and if I had it at take two, that was the end, I wasn't about to sit there and indulge myself and drive the actors crazy by doing it again and again, which is the luxury of a feature. A feature director will do twenty-one takes then pick take one; in television you had to do six or eight pages a day. I would do twenty-five setups and the feature film guy would do five, 'cause he's doing five times as many takes as I do. His material is no better than mine, it's just that he's used to indulging actors who say, "Let me do it again, let me do it again."

Can you remember anything about the shoot of Our Man Flint: Dead on Target?

No I can't, I can't even remember a scene, we're talking forty years, that's a long bloody time! It was so long ago I even forget if the movie was any good or not!

Les Sheldon
Director

Les Sheldon worked on several of writer-producer Stephen J. Cannell's most successful shows: as a director on *The A-Team* (1983–87) and *Hunter* (1984–91), and as a director-producer on *Hardcastle and McCormick* (1983–86) and *Wiseguy* (1987–90), an atypical Cannell production due to its emphasis on drama over glossy bash-and-crash.

Sheldon started out as an assistant director learning his craft from some of the biggest names in the business. He worked on the Howard Hawks–helmed auto-racing drama *Red Line* 7000 (1965), the Robert Conrad super-spy western *The Wild Wild West* (1965–70), the Elvis western *Charro!* (1969), *The Organization* (1971), the last and best of Sidney Poitier's "Virgil Tibbs" detective movies, and *The Man Who Loved Cat Dancing* (1973), starring Burt Reynolds.

He also spent several years with Steve McQueen's production company Solar. Okay, he didn't work on *Bullitt* (1968)—something of a religion for those of us who live for herringbone sports jackets and terse cops-and-robbers stories—but he did work on *Le Mans* (1971) directed, for a while at least, by all-time action movie master John Sturges.

How did you get involved with Hardcastle and McCormick?
Odd story. I was at Universal on a kind of producing development deal. I knew a Superior Court judge in Los Angeles who was assistant DA on the Manson trial and some other really interesting trials, and from talking to him I got the idea to do a show about a retired judge who sits in on one last case in which the guy gets off on a technicality and the judge takes him under his wing and mentors him. So my agent looks at it and he calls me up and says, "Look, this is really a good concept but I have to tell you something: Steve Cannell is thinking about pitching a very similar idea, and the bottom line is he's going to get the go and you're not" because Steve was very successful with *The Rockford*

Files and all those series. Steve's show was much more action-oriented and the characters were a little different, but the premise was, by coincidence, pretty much the same. The next thing I know, my contract's up at Universal, they want to renew it but my agent says, "Let's see if we can get you a good series." Who was my first meeting with? Stephen Cannell, and what was the show? *Hardcastle and McCormick*! The stories were very good, dramatic and charming, and we were lucky enough to get two wonderful leads, Danny Kelly and Brian Keith, a huge star. Brian loved it because he was getting big money and he didn't have to do a lot of preparing, he just came in and played himself. Danny was a wonderful New York actor and Stephen would take advantage of his acting ability. Danny usually had a fire up his ass about something but that was because of his passion. He was great to work with and I love him to death. We did it for three years, won a lot of awards, and it was a really fun show. I was a creative producer, the supervising producer, and that's where I started doing a lot of directing.

What were your day-to-day responsibilities as supervising producer?

Working with directors who might be behind me or in front of me in prepping for the show, going out finding locations with them, casting the episode, getting them used to the characters, getting them familiar with all the elements of the show and that particular episode. Even if I was directing, I would do it at night with the following director.

Did Cannell ever lay out to you what he thought made a good action show?

Steve's philosophy was just to give the audience something entertaining, give them characters that are fun, we've got to stay within the rules but this is a fun ride, the bigger we can make it the better, throw it all in and we'll find a way to photograph it—and he brought that stuff in on a budget, to television, that's why he was so successful. Stephen was a big kid and had an ego as big as the Empire State Building, which was wonderful. When it came to pitching shows to networks, he'd kind of bullshit his way through, use his charm, and convince them that they better not turn it down because he had a meeting at CBS next week, which he didn't, but he could've, because he was very powerful—why? Because everything he said he'd do, he came through with. Steve and I were very, very close and after *Hardcastle and McCormick* I did *Wiseguy* for him for three years, as executive producer and director. That was a totally different show, very heavy drama. We were the first series ever to try what's called arcs, which means we would do six or seven episodes dealing with certain characters, at the end of that it would come to a conclusion of some sorts and we would start a new arc, with different vicious people. We had nothing but huge stars, we had Jerry Lewis, Kevin Spacey, Ray Sharkey, Annette Bening ... I mean, it goes on and on. I got to work with and direct all these wonderful actors—unbelievable. We won all kinds of awards, we were the most critically acclaimed show for three years in a row, we were named as one of the 100 best television shows in the history of television by *TV Guide*, and our ratings stunk!

How did you get your start in the business?

I studied acting, I studied writing, then I had an opportunity to go into film editing and I became an apprentice, an assistant editor. When I was twenty I got an opportunity to get into the Directors Guild and I worked mainly in features for a number of years. I started as a second assistant director, then I became a first assistant, and then I started directing second units. I worked with people like Howard Hawks, John Sturges, Richard Donner and Howard Zieff. They were all great directors and I learned so much from them.

What did you work on with Hawks?

It was right after I got into the Directors Guild. The picture was called *Red Line* 7000, with Jimmy Caan. I was hired as a second assistant director, so I watched him shoot the whole picture. Howard liked me and he asked me to go out and shoot some action chase stuff for him as well, so I did and he'd come out to the unit and check what I was doing.

You then worked with another American icon, Elvis on Charro!

I was assistant director on that. Elvis Presley was a wonderful actor and a great guy. Elvis always wanted to do a legitimate part, he was getting sick of tired of these little musical things, and on *Charro!* his acting chops really came out. You ever take a look at the movie he did with Michael Curtiz?

King Creole *[1958]. I love it.*

He was wonderful in that, wasn't he? Why? Because he had a great director with Curtiz.

Masters of the Shoot-'Em-Up

The director of Charro, *Charles Marquis Warren, did some great work.*

Charlie was a writer, he wasn't really a director. He was a very nice man, very easygoing, very precise, and Elvis got along with him fine. He didn't really know how to direct the actors but he was a lovely man.

Can you explain what your job entailed when you were working as an assistant director and directing second units?

When I was working as an AD for directors, I'd break down the script for them, set things up for them, get the scenes ready. By the time I'd worked my way up to first assistant I was also directing second units. As a second unit director I'd always have discussions with the first unit director about what he was looking for. He didn't give me set-ups but I was fully prepared, I knew what he'd like to get. But my passion was always directing and once I started directing second units, I knew that was where I was going. I'd gotten so much experience in working with actors and staging and I got it from the best. Every director I worked with knew that I wanted to direct and they would always emphasize what I do when I mentor young directors: Do it your way, use your vision, but make sure you know the basics of filmmaking so you can achieve your vision. If you copy how I do it, mine will always be better because you don't have my vision and I don't have yours. You could take a script, have four different directors do it and it's amazing how they'll look like different shows, feel like different shows, hit different emotions—they're all there, but you can't hit five of them, you've got to be swung towards one.

How did you end up working with Steve McQueen?

My best friend, Tommy Schmidt, who passed away very early, asked me to come in and be his assistant and direct second unit on this movie with Michael Douglas called *Adam at 6 A.M.* [1970]. Steve wasn't in it but his company, Solar Productions, produced it. Solar was run by Robert Relyea, the greatest executive that ever lived, just brilliant. Steve came down several times to Missouri where we shot it. We'd never met before but he was very nice to me, he thought I was really bright, and he kept me with him for four years, directing second units for Solar. I got incredible experience working with Steve, his acting abilities, his personality, his whole persona. Steve was a very strange guy but I got along with him great. I adored Steve, probably because he was a brilliant actor—he was from New York, he studied with Strasberg, he was the real fuckin' deal. Yeah he did action movies but think about what the action movies were: *The Magnificent Seven* [1960], *The Great Escape* [1963], all great character studies. *Bullitt* was 80 percent performance and 20 percent action. I worked on *Adam at 6 A.M.*, *The Reivers* [1969], *Le Mans* [1971] and one other one I can't remember right now. We were working on another movie called *Yucatan*, but it never got produced. It was written by the great writer Edward Anhalt and was an action story set in Mexico and based on true events. It was kind of like *The Treasure of the Sierra Madre* [1948] and really interesting, but they didn't trust Steve with it after he'd gone so over budget on *Le Mans* so they pulled it and then Solar folded.

Did John Sturges quit or get fired from Le Mans?

He got fired, and he kind of quit. Here's what happened: John had directed Steve in *The Magnificent Seven*, but he had trouble with him on *The Great Escape*. All of a sudden Steve put a border up and was doing whatever he wanted, so John fired him, had him replaced with somebody else—you don't fuck with John Sturges. I mean, he did *Bad Day at Black Rock* [1955], c'mon! The guy's a legend. Steve came back and apologized and was brilliant in the movie. Steve was difficult, Steve was very difficult, but difficult and talented go hand in hand, if you're creative about it, not just an asshole.

With *Le Mans* they came up with the idea to photograph the entire twenty-four hours of Le Mans, then shoot for seven months or so around it. I directed the second unit for John with all the Porsche crashes and the Ferrari crashes and all that. We had to go to London to meet with the Samuelsons at Panavision, to come up with the first electronic cameras that could function inside a car—nobody had used these electronic monitor cameras before. Everything you saw was real, it was a very dangerous film to make. The script had no story, it was all the pits, and still today, it's the best movie for pure car racing ever made. John was getting pressured to shoot a storyline, he was willing to do what CBS wanted and Steve didn't like that. Three-quarters of the way through the film, Steve said, "You know, I'm sick of this shit. It's been my life's ambition to do a race car movie and fuck CBS Films, that's what I'm doing. We're already three-quarters of the way, they can't stop me now." They weren't getting along and Steve was pretty primary in getting John fired. Bottom line is, knowing Steve as well as I did, this was his opportunity to flex his muscles and fire John. They brought in a director by the name of Lee Katzin to finish it off and demanded that another writer come in and add a storyline with a girl and a villain—they shot it all, but it fucked the movie up. Lee Katzin was not a bad director, he knew how to get things done quick and we were like $18,000,000 over budget, which was a lot of money then. But Lee had the biggest ego in the world. The very first day that Lee comes to the set, they go into a take and Lee tried to pull this "No, no, that's not the way I see it" stuff with Steve and wanted to go again. Steve McQueen didn't care how Lee Katzin saw it. Lee Katzin always wore a suit and a tie, with a cigarette, Lucky Strike, hanging out of his mouth. Steve McQueen walked behind the camera, virtually lifted Lee Katzin up off the ground by his tie and said, "Listen, you little prick, you just shut your fuckin' mouth. Say action and you'll be fine, if not, find your own way home because we ain't paying for a plane fare. Is that clear to you?" Lee said, "Very," and that was that.

You worked on The Organization.

I was assistant and second unit director on that. Before I went out and directed second unit, I always wanted to see the scene being shot with the actor, Mr. Poitier picked up on what I was doing and befriended me. He was wonderful to me and was one of the most brilliant actors I've ever seen work. The director Don Medford had some problems, he was not at his best. He was a very good director in television and got a wonderful opportunity with the Mirisch brothers to direct features but he fucked it up.

The film works, though. I like it.

Walter Mirisch, who was a wonderful man, would come in and keep things calm and, truthfully, Sidney was the leader and ended up kind of directing the film as far as keeping the set level and getting the performances right. He'd see there was a problem and go to Don and say, "Why don't we try this?" He was always very polite and Don would say, "Of course" because he wanted to stay friendly with Sidney. Sheree North, who's a wonderful actress, was so nervous, and Sidney would say, "Don, I'd like to try something. Would you mind if I gave Sheree a note?" and they'd go for another take and she was fine. Sidney had her back and that's why she came off so well.

What can you tell us about The Man Who Loved Cat Dancing?
I love that movie. There's one of the greatest fight scenes of all time in that, with Burt and Jack Warden. Burt was great. A lot of people wouldn't know this but he's very intense, very focused, and, man, can he act! He can do subtle little things, kind of reminds me of John Garfield. He never overplayed, it was just subtle little looks, the way he delivered the dialogue. He became the person he was playing. He was very underrated as an actor, he was wonderful with comedy but he was also fantastic with drama. How was he to work with as a person on the set? The best, I rank him right up there with Elvis.

And what about the director Richard C. Sarafian?
Dick was always a great director. Odd guy, difficult to work with, hard to understand sometimes, but really a wonderful director. I worked with Dick on *Mission: Impossible* [1966–72], he remembered me and wanted me as his assistant on *The Man Who Loved Cat Dancing*, and also pushed me as a second unit director. I did things for Dick that no other assistant director did, I was very creative. When he was staging scenes, I'd add things to it that he loved. His son Deren Sarafian is a brilliant director, a really wonderful action director.

What advice can you give about working with actors and getting the rhythm and pacing of scenes right?
You've got to come in with a vision but you also have to look at rehearsal or a take and see what they're doing with their character and pick up on things that they might not even know they're doing, maybe adjust it a little. You have to be more up on their part than they are, see what they're comfortable with and collaborate with them because actors are artists. Three different actors will play the same part three different ways; the important thing is that they give as much as they have playing that character. You must respect everyone and the way they work at all times, otherwise it becomes your way, and your way is very boring. Why do you have these wonderful artists around you like set designers and production designers and directors of photography if you can't

collaborate with them? Give them your thoughts and your vision and let them do their work to bring those ideas to life.

What are the other qualities you need to direct?

When I said, "Use your own vision but make sure you know the basics," I meant learn what film editors do, what the composer does, what the art director does, what the grips and electricians do, spend time with them and learn what all the equipment is used for. If you don't know those things, you can come up with the greatest idea in the world and they're going to look at you and say, "Fine, it's going to take seven hours to light." But if you know something about what they do, you can collaborate with them, you can come up with suggestions as to how you can cut the shot down and get the same scene. So you must learn something about what every person does on that set and give them their due respect, because I do not recall ever showing up on the set in the morning and it was just me! I really don't remember making *my* movie, I think there was about eighty people around me!

So is the possessory credit "A Film by" presumptuous?

Not the title, but the behavior on the set can be. "Listen, this is my fuckin' movie, I'm directing this show and I don't know what you guys are used to but this is how I'm gonna do it." No! Do it the way you want to do it but collaborate and communicate with the people who are making that film with you. If you don't have them, your vision doesn't mean shit.

Ron Satlof
Director

Ron Satlof began his career as an assistant to directors like Hugh A. Robinson on the interesting Afro-action melodrama *Melinda* (1972), Martin Scorsese on *Mean Streets* (1973) and Don Siegel on *Charley Varrick* (1973), a flat-out action classic, like most Siegel movies.

Satlof made his television directing debut with an episode of *Get Christie Love* (1974–75), a series loosely based on ex-cop Dorothy Uhnak's "Christie Opara" crime novels, and went on to helm episodes of *Hawaii Five-O* (1968–80), *Charlie's Angels* (1976–81) and *The Dukes of Hazzard* (1979–85).

He worked with *Cannon* (1971–76) star William Conrad on *Battles* (1980), *Nero Wolfe* (1981) and *Jake and the Fatman* (1987–92), with writer-producer Glen A. Larson on *McCloud* (1970–77), *Magnum PI* (1980–88) and *The Fall Guy* (1981–86), and with Larson's peer and rival Stephen J. Cannell on *Hardcastle and McCormick* (1983–86), *The A-Team* (1983–87) and *Hunter* (1984–91).

"Pros and Cons," one of his *A-Team* episodes, is a boxing-prison tale featuring a host of action movie favorites: William Smith, Clifton James, Paul Koslo, Red West and Ken Norton. Don't watch it, ladies, you'll grow a moustache.

Charley Varrick is one of Don Siegel's best.

Don Siegel was one of my heroes and I loved working with him, he was a wonderful guy. I was listed as second assistant director on *Charley Varrick* but I was actually first assistant and worked very closely with Don on strategizing each day's shoot. He had a very powerful, very muscular way of doing film and he was very knowledgeable and expert at what he did.

What did he do to make it muscular?

He did it visually, through surprises, doing the opposite of what you expected. When a guy took a punch and fell, Don would have him fall towards the camera rather than away from it. You didn't really see a hundred percent of what happened but you felt the impact. Later that style was adopted by a lot of premier stunt guys on shows I worked on like *The A-Team*. Another simple little trick of his had to do with screen direction: When you look at a scene and there's a person on screen left, one on screen right, and someone in the center, you expect, without necessarily knowing it consciously, that when you get to a close-up of the person on screen right, he's gonna look screen left; well, Don would sometimes surprise you by reversing that and you were thrown by it, you didn't know where you were. Script supervisors would go crazy but he knew what he was doing: He thought the scene was a little sleepy and he wanted to wake it up. He was a great action director who worked very well with stunt coordinators and got brilliant results, but he was also a great storyteller and worked very closely with the writers to make sure the script was really pointed—think of *Dirty Harry* [1971]. He had a very strong thematic sense and was attracted to stories where the little guy, the underdog, triumphs over adversity.

You also worked on Scorsese's Mean Streets.

Once again I was listed as second assistant director and once again I was really first assistant, and I was in it too! I play a bartender and have two or three lines. Although *Mean Streets* wasn't Marty's first film, I think he had a sense that it could be his breakthrough, that it could make his career, so he was a little nervous, wearing editor's gloves to keep from biting his nails. Martin Scorsese is the most exquisitely prepared director I've ever seen in my life: He had every shot in the film drawn on little file cards in his pocket, very nicely storyboarded. The film was made on paper before he shot anything so he was completely in control of absolutely every minute.

You didn't use storyboards on series television?

If you were going to shoot a very complex action scene, you might have a little chicken scratch–type storyboard, a visual reference for yourself, the cameraman and the crew, but nothing as complete as Marty's. He had every single shot in the entire picture storyboarded, and not by a storyboard artist, by him. You couldn't possibly do that for a seven-day television shoot, even if you wanted to. Say what you will about creativity, and the wonderful creative people who work in it, but television is an industrial process, you crank out 22 episodes of your show a year and it's an assembly line. People made shot-lists, that's pretty routine, and if you're really good you give your assistant director a shot-list at the start of the day. They're pretty appreciative when you do that.

How'd you get your start?

I got into a great program out in L.A. for training assistant directors, sponsored by the Directors Guild and the Producers Guild. I don't know what the process is these days but when it was starting back in the late 1960s they took people with college degrees and made them sit an exam to assess their IQ, spatial sense, psychology, all sorts of things; you then did an interview and if you were successful they took you into the program and assigned you to the studios as a trainee assistant director. You worked under the assistant directors who used you as a kind of gofer, but also taught you what they did. The studios got you for free, because you were paid by the program, and you got an education that was priceless. It came about because previously the only way you got to be an assistant director was through having a dad who was a producer or an uncle who was a unit production manager—through nepotism. Well, not every producer's son was smart, capable and full of the leadership qualities you need to be an assistant director—it was inbreeding and all that gets you is a family full of idiots. They had some good guys but they also had a lot of aging, inefficient, bumbling guys and a lot of people were worried about where the industry was going. The program was two years of crappy pay and being bossed around, sometimes by idiots, but when you finished you were a full-fledged assistant director. One of the lessons of the program was how to work under people you don't necessarily respect. Most of them were terrific, but there were some assholes and you learned how to keep your mouth shut when they ordered you in the wrong direction. Sometimes directors can be assholes too. They might be inexperienced and too arrogant to ask for help, and the assistant director's job is to be diplomatic and guide them through, not necessarily to teach them any lessons or contradict them when they're wrong.

Did you ever contradict any directors?

Once or twice, but I never gained anything from it. Every time I did

I got slapped down for it, so I stopped doing that pretty early on. There were a couple of times when the director was just so completely wrong that the crew wouldn't have respected me if I hadn't pointed it out. We're not talking about creative things, we're talking about things like shooting everything you need when you're lit in a certain direction, because turning around is a long process and part of the assistant director's job is to keep things on schedule.

Tell us about your involvement with Get Christie Love.

They were pretty much ready to cancel it, it wasn't getting ratings and they were having terrible trouble with the star, a gal from *Rowan & Martin's Laugh-In* [1968–73]. In the pilot she'd played a sexy, sassy policewoman who worked undercover, sometimes as a hooker. Then when they started the series she became a Jehovah's Witness and had a list of things she couldn't do: She couldn't be sexy, she couldn't be sassy and talk back to her boss, she couldn't do any of the stuff that made her attractive and interesting in the pilot. Whoever was producing the show wasn't able to handle that so ABC asked the studio if they had somebody on their lot who wanted to try and save the show. They offered it to Glen Larson and I don't know why he took it on because it was a pretty hopeless situation! I was working with him at the time, line-producing *McCloud*, and he came to me and said that if I'd line-produce *Get Christie Love* I could have a shot at directing as well. I'd been begging for a chance to direct so he knew he had me. Producing *McCloud* wasn't quite as hard as producing a weekly show. We were making a two-hour movie a month which, believe it or not, is a fair amount of time in television. So I didn't view it as a particularly overwhelming thing to take on a weekly show, but of course I didn't realize how difficult it was going to be to deal with this person. Essentially there was nothing she *could* do that would be interesting—she couldn't do any action, she couldn't do anything funny or dramatic, she went from being this dynamic, sexy character to a kind of doe in the headlights. I'm not knocking the religion, but it didn't work in the context of the show.

But you got to direct.

I did and it was a rough experience but we got through it! I'd already gotten an Academy Award nomination for a short I'd made but *Get Christie Love* was my first official DGA directing shot and that allowed me to put myself up for directing *McCloud*. Glen, who was executive producer, was able to talk Dennis Weaver into letting me direct on the basis that I'd done a good job on *Get Christie Love*. Dennis, who was a great gentleman, was happy with the first *McCloud* I directed and had no objections to me after that—but when I was preparing it he wasn't so sure and was ready to shoot me down at any moment. So I was working under some pressure on that one as well.

Teresa Graves and Harry Guardino in the 1974 pilot for *Get Christie Love*, a Universal Television take on Pam Grier and Tamara Dobson's super-chick Afro-action hits.

Why do you think Glen A. Larson has had such success in television?

He's one of the most fantastic, most creative writer-producers to ever work in television. He's a natural humorist and a natural storyteller. He'd been a songwriter, he was a member of a group called the Four Preps, they were a huge hit, and he wrote a lot of their songs. Then he started writing for television and Roy Huggins took him under his wing. Roy was a great mentor to a lot of people, including Stephen Cannell. Glen flourished under Roy and took off on his own very quickly. He had an almost instinctual sense of what was working at a particular moment: He could take the core idea of a popular film, do a variation on it using lots of elements that couldn't be copyrighted, and create a successful series. So *Alias Smith and Jones* (1971–73) was essentially *Butch Cassidy and the Sundance Kid* (1969), *Switch* (1975–78) was *The Sting* (1973), he didn't create *McCloud* but that was *Coogan's Bluff* (1968)—nobody would ever admit it but that was basically the basis for the character. It wasn't plagiarism, it's not like he thought, "I can steal that"; he thought, "Hey, that's opened up a genre here and I can capitalize on it in television." The producers of *Star Wars* [1977] sued over *Battlestar Galactica* [1978–80] and lost because it wasn't a copy, it just capitalized on the then-current popularity of that particular genre. He could write very fast and some of his scripts were downright masterpieces of the medium. I remember a *McCloud* he wrote about a hooker who killed men by painting them blue. He wrote it over a weekend, we shot it with the least preparation we'd ever had, and it was one of the best and funniest episodes we did. It came about because we were over-budget for the year but still had one more show to do, so we had to figure out a way to do it very cheaply, confining it to our home sets. The term for that professionally is a "bottle show." Well, *McCloud* was a two-hour show, and it's hard to make a two-hour bottle show that's fast and funny and full of action. We farmed out the job of writing the script to a couple of writers we had a lot of faith in, but they didn't really come up with anything. Then all of a sudden it was the week before we had to start shooting and we still didn't have a script. Glen said he'd take care of it, ran a couple of ideas past me, went home for the weekend and turned out a magnificent script that we practically shot word for word.

Were there any differences in how a Glen A. Larson show and a Stephen J. Cannell show were run?

They were both brilliant, very fast writers and they had an unspoken competition going. Sometimes when I'd sit down and have a drink with Stephen the conversation would drift around to Glen and he'd say things about him that weren't entirely complimentary, and vice versa when I'd have a drink with Glen. They both made millions and millions of dollars, but in the long run Stephen beat Glen in that part of the competition because Stephen had his own company. Glen ran quite a few shows at once at Universal and Fox but he never had his own company like Stephen did, with all those hundreds and hundreds of people working under him. They were equal talents but not equally organized, Cannell was better organized, he tended to meet his writing schedule more regularly and everything ran a bit more smoothly with him than it did with Glen. It was very hard to control budgets when Glen was around, he was constantly thinking up improvements to scenes, because he was brilliant and ideas would keep hitting him. He'd even run down to the stage with new pages for a scene you'd just shot! That's a tremendous talent and level of caring for the work, but it was also very inconvenient to me!

Ron Satlof • Director

The A-Team *is the definitive Stephen J. Cannell production.*

Most of what I did on that was in the first season, a little in the second. Those were the glory times in the sense that the show was an almost instant hit and all the actors were fun and easy to work with, unlike later when some of them became kind of troublesome. From a directorial

Ken Norton, George Peppard and Mr. T do time in "Pros and Cons," a 1983 episode of Universal Television's *The A-Team*, **directed by Ron Satlof.**

standpoint it was a really neat show to work on because it was a combination of action and humor. When you got dialogue in there, if it wasn't just exposition, it was funny, and the action was all over-the-top: They'd shoot 5,000 rounds and nobody got a scratch. It had a comic strip feel and that made it fun to work on. It was the usual television grind because there was a lot of action to get through, but it was a happy grind. Dwight Schulz, the guy that played Murdock, hadn't done much television, he came from the theater and he was a remarkable improviser, every scene he was in he did something unexpected, funny and out of left field, which was just what the character called for. We were rehearsing a scene one time and all of a sudden he jumped into somebody's lap! From a logistical standpoint, Stephen's production company was fabulous, the producers, unit production managers, prop and special effects people were sensationally good and well organized, and that was with something like three or four shows all coming out of the same offices. There are always bumps in the road in television but *The A-Team* ran so smoothly you would've thought it had been shooting for five years.

What are the most common "bumps in the road"?

Human error is one thing—somebody forgot to dig a hole, the wrong car turns up for a chase scene. These people are sensationally good, everything is double-checked and triple-checked but occasionally, rarely, something goes wrong—somebody wakes up on the wrong side of the bed, has a fight with their wife, it doesn't take much. Then there's weather, you get out there and the weather just won't cooperate, you get rained out and yes, you can move to a stage and do another scene, but you inevitably wait an hour or two to see if it'll clear up before you do. Then if it doesn't, you've got to get the whole company moved, get the actors you need to do the new scenes, and you've blown half your day. Everything is about schedule. Yes, quality matters, storytelling and directing and all those things, but what matters most is making the schedule because at the end of the day these companies want to make a profit. You can tolerate the occasional day over because you can make up for it with a bottle show, but you can't tolerate much more than that. You're shooting an episode in six or seven days and it's a real war. You're not fighting people so much, the people are very cooperative; it's schedules, weather, logistics. There was a time when Universal was looking for ways to save money and they put out a memo that all one-hour episodic television shows had to be shot in six days. Well, sometimes that's possible and sometimes it's fucking impossible. It put a tremendous amount of pressure on directors because you're not always in 100 percent control, sometimes an actor won't come to the set or a light blows out or some other act of God happens. They wound up paying so much overtime for the six days that they went back to doing seven.

What are your memories of working on Hawaii Five-O*?*
I don't like to speak ill of people I worked with! The guy who played McGarrett, what was his name?

The Lord, Jack Lord.
Yes, the Lord of Hawaii! I'd heard all these horror stories about how he ate directors for lunch and I was somewhat taken aback by how easy to work with he was. The only problem I had with him was that he was too friendly, he was too complimentary about my work, it wasn't that extraordinary! And each time I came back to do another one, I felt like he got more and more friendly to the point that he was telling me how to set up shots, where to put the camera, where to put the actors, how to move the camera. When I got there, the show had been going eight or nine years and he was certainly in full control, I had no argument with that and just went out there to do my job. His intentions were good, he wanted to have as much control as possible because he felt he was the guardian of the quality of the show, and to a large degree he was; but he also had a sadistic streak in him and tended to put down some of the regulars on the show. It was their livelihood so they learned to take it, just like I did when I was an assistant director, but it was pretty cruel.

Is dealing with difficult people part of a director's job?
The media love to hear about difficult people, everybody's heard the stories about druggies and troublemakers and people like Tony Franciosa who'd hole up in his trailer for hours with some kind of acting coach doing I'm not sure what, something to do with his psyche. But those people are so rare. I had a 45- or 50-year career and in all that time I only met four or five people like that, four or five people out of thousands

of hard-working, well-prepared and talented actors, writers, producers, directors.

You worked a lot with actor William Conrad, who'd done a lot of directing himself.

Acting, directing, budgeting, scheduling, there were really no aspects of the film business Bill Conrad didn't understand. I loved him, he was the world's greatest gentleman, a total pleasure to work with. I don't think I ever directed that one where he was a fat detective [*Cannon*], but I directed him in a pilot called *Battles*, in *Nero Wolfe* and in the pilot and several episodes of *Jake and the Fatman*.

He was pretty much a fat detective in those too!

Bill used cue cards, and he was brilliant at it, but it used to be disconcerting for some of the other actors, because he didn't want them around for his close-ups, he just planted his cue card guy in all the various spots he had to look. He'd say, "I get it done in one take, it's over, you make your schedule and it ain't gonna get any better if there's somebody feeding me lines off camera." I'd point out that it made the other actor feel strange and he'd say, "I know, but they'll get over it." He also wanted to do all his reactions at once, he wanted to do all his line readings and then about thirty seconds of reactions. I said, "Bill, please! That's gonna confuse the shit out of me, I'm not gonna know what the fuck is going on. Please react to what the other actors are saying when they say it." He compromised on that and thank God he did because the one time we did it his way, he read line after line in close-up then shut up and started giving all these different looks—surprise, concern, anger. It was so funny that I ruined the shot! I'm sure it worked for him but it drove me nuts, I just fell over laughing!

Jerome M. Siegel
Assistant Director

Assistant director Jerome M. Siegel worked with John Sturges on *The Magnificent Seven* (1960). That alone would earn him a place in this book, but it doesn't end there.

He also pitched in on *The Ambushers* (1968) and *The Wrecking Crew* (1969), two of Dean Martin's perversely lovable "Matt Helm" movies—think Bond in his cups plus showgirls.

Then there's *Dan August* (1970), the Quinn Martin cop show that starred Burt Reynolds, *Diamonds Are Forever* (1971), the Bond movie that nearly starred Burt Reynolds, *The Mechanic* (1972) with Charles Bronson, the World War II epic *Midway* (1976) with half the tough guy actors in Hollywood, and *Switch* (1975–78), a Glen A. Larson series starring Robert Wagner as good con man Pete Ryan and Eddie Albert as ex-cop Frank McBride. Though undoubtedly inspired by the success of *The Sting* (1973), *Switch* is otherwise an archetypal 1970s detective series. In *Switch*, crime is just a catalyst for adventure and romance. Wit, sartorial rightness and a macho Irish name are the makings of a man. Wagner's character lives above a bouzouki bar run by Charlie Callas. It's a blueprint for a perfect world.

The Magnificent Seven *is a pretty impressive movie to have on your CV.*

That was a unique experience; I don't think something like that will ever be able to be made again. John Sturges really did his homework and knew what he wanted. His focus was getting the script and casting right. The cast was incredible and he got along very well with them. Each of the actors was different, each had their own ways of doing things. He knew what they were capable of and that's what made it work, made the whole group gel. We were shooting out in the hills of Mexico, I don't remember where. It's set in Mexico and the cost made sense 'cause you had to build things.

Is the assistant director around for that part of a production, when they're constructing and dressing sets?

No, he's usually involved with scouting the location, making suggestions, but that's about it. As assistant director you start by breaking the script down, scheduling the script, working with the director to figure out how many days it'll take him to do each sequence. I always tried to do it from the beginning to the end rather than skipping around from scene to scene, sequence to sequence. That way you keep the flow of the film going. You don't get too much involved in casting, your job is really running the set. You've got to know the script, know the scenes, know a little bit about how the director's going to approach each sequence so you can get it done a little quicker, know what you're gonna do that day and make sure everything is ready for the next day. You need to be able to get along very well with the actors and the director and keep the crew moving so the director gets his work done, without putting so much pressure on him that he misses something.

What can you tell us about working on Dean Martin's Matt Helm movies?

They were fun, tongue-in-cheek. Dean was a terrific actor, brilliant with comedy and very easy to direct. He never rehearsed, he was a natural, he just came on and did it. He knew his words and knew just what he was doing every time. It was a hoot to work with him. I worked with two directors on those, Phil Karlson and Henry Levin, very good directors in that kind of genre film. They worked very simply, nothing fancy, they had an actor who they knew was gonna do what he was gonna do and they let him do it. Some directors are very good but never get that one big hit that you need to continue making high caliber films; when you make a very successful film, the road becomes much easier. Phil Karlson was maybe a step or so below John Sturges simply because of the product he made. I learned from both of them, just by watching how they worked things out, but I guess I learned a little more with Karlson because I was working directly with him rather than through the first assistant.

What other directors did you learn from?

Billy Wilder, I worked with him on *The Apartment* (1960) and *Irma La Douce* (1963). It was very easy to work with Billy because he knew exactly what he wanted and how he was going to shoot it before he got

Spy Devore. Dean Martin on the run in Columbia's *The Ambushers* (1968) (courtesy Phillipa Berry).

on the set. He knew in his mind how each sequence or scene was gonna edit because he worked very closely with an editor called Doane Harrison, who was also a producer. If the actors didn't get it right, he just kept going till they did. Usually they got it very quickly because of the actors he hired—Shirley MacLaine, Jack Lemmon ... they just had to make sure they said the words as he'd written them, that was a must. I was second assistant director on *The Children's Hour* (1961) and Willie Wyler was completely different, a whole different kind of director. He was prepared in a sense, but he wasn't as sure as Billy Wilder. Billy knew what he wanted and when he got it he walked away from it. Willie would do lots of different angles, different takes, and make the film in the editing room.

For my money, Diamonds Are Forever *is Connery's best Bond movie. How'd you get that job?*

Masters of the Shoot-'Em-Up

I was working for Quinn Martin at the Goldwyn studio, doing *Dan August* with Burt Reynolds. It was an easy show as far as I was concerned. Television series are kinda cut and dried, you just do whatever you can do to make it move along. Quinn Martin was a very good producer to work for, he was very accomplished and he had a very good company going, a good group of people. I was just finishing up the series and was at the studio when a United Artists executive I was friendly with introduced me to Guy Hamilton, the director of the Bond film, and that's how I got the job. Ironically they were considering Burt Reynolds to play Bond. Burt and I were kinda close towards the end of the series and he told me he was up for a big picture, but he didn't tell me which one. We talked about it later, when I got hired for the film and he didn't. He was kinda disappointed but the bottom line was, as it always has been, they wanted an Englishman to play the part. On *Diamonds Are Forever* I just did the American side of it, whatever they did here in America I did, the rest of it was done in England.

So you did the chase in Vegas?

We had the streets blocked off, we were running around in Vegas and it was crazy. "Cubby" Broccoli was a hands-on producer and was around every day of the shoot. He wasn't that involved in the day-to-day shooting, he had a line producer for that, but he was always there observing, and if you had a question he was there to answer it. And of course he loved Vegas! It was an exciting film to work on because it was the last one Sean Connery did. In those days an action film was an action film but a Bond film was something special just because of the Bond name and Sean Connery. Action films are all pretty much the same to work on, the main difference is that some directors are easier to deal with because they are more prepared. Guy Hamilton was very good. I don't think he's in the John Sturges class, but he was very good for those films.

What about Michael Winner, who you worked with on The Mechanic?

As far as the shoot goes, it was just another action movie. None of them are easy, but some are harder than others. There was some night shooting, some explosions, nothing exceptional. But it was a very tough film because Michael Winner was a very tough human being. He was tough on the cast and the crew. Not so much with Charles Bronson, but with everyone else he was very demanding and sometimes not too nice. He knew what he wanted and he wouldn't settle for less.

Did he alienate the crew?
Yep, to some extent he did. But the crews are very professional, they know what they have to do and they get it done, whether they like the director or not. Charlie was very easygoing, you knew what sort of character he was, what you were going to get. Charlie and I had done *The Magnificent Seven* and *Kid Galahad*, the Elvis Presley picture, so we knew each other and got along. Elvis was a gentleman, a huge talent and, again, very easy to get along with. Unfortunately he was too controlled by the Colonel who was always around. The Colonel had the boys around Elvis constantly to keep him humored, keep him going.

I'll hazard a guess that Switch *with Robert Wagner was a fun show to work on.*
That was a treat. I was hired by Universal to work on *The Six Million Dollar Man* [1974–78], which was a hoot, we laughed a lot on that. Then I guess they liked me because they kept me on, kept me working. I think we got seven days to do a one-hour show, and fourteen or fifteen days for a two-hour show like *McMillan and Wife* [1971–77]. They put me on *Switch* and it worked out great because I'd known R.J. [Wagner] for years and we got along famously. R.J. is one of the most terrific actors and one of the nicest people in the film business. He was easy to get along with, open to suggestions from other people and very good with the crew. Everybody liked him because he was one of the guys, you never thought he was above anything.

When you're attached to a series like Switch *for a long period of time, is part of the assistant director's job showing new directors the ropes?*
In episodic television, the executive producer or writer comes up with the idea, promotes it through the studio, sells it to the network and then usually backs off. The studio then hires one or two people to run the show and hire the actors, writers and directors. After the first couple of episodes, the style is built-in, the actors know their parts, and it all kind of falls in place, so the director's job is pretty much just to get it done properly. They come in with ideas but you show them the shortcuts, tell

Careful what you say, Ryan and McBride are on the case. Eddie Albert and Robert Wagner in Universal Television's *Switch* **(1975–78).**

them what the actors are like if they haven't worked with them before, and steer them towards the easiest way to get it done.

Midway features quite a lineup of action movie and television faces: Robert Mitchum, James Coburn, Christopher George, Glenn Corbett, Tom Selleck...

Midway was really Charlton Heston, it was his film, the other actors only worked a day or two at the most, just in vignettes really. To my mind Robert Mitchum was one of the great actors of all time. I did *Two for the Seesaw* [1962] with him as well, and in that he had to do two very long sequences of dialogue, something in the area of seventeen pages. And he knew every word of it, he had an amazing mind. He had other problems but as an actor, and as a human being, I thought he was terrific.

Was Midway *the toughest shoot you worked on?*

It was a big film with a big scope, we were out on an aircraft carrier for a week in the Gulf of Mexico with airplanes landing and all of that, lots of people involved and lots to do. But the toughest shoot was a film called *The Todd Killings* [1971]. It started out with Barry Shear directing, then the production manager quit, the first assistant quit, the writer-producer, if I remember correctly, took over directing, I became production manager and it just went on and on. It was a tough shoot and nobody ever seemed happy with it. The most enjoyable shoot was *West Side Story* [1961] which came right after *The Magnificent Seven*. I started on that with the interviews, stayed on through the rehearsals with the kids that were in the show in New York, was involved in production, post-production, even the scoring. Bob Relyea, the first assistant, taught me a lot and it was just the two of us, we did the whole show and we had things under control. Today you'd have six assistants doing a show like that.

But the films aren't as good!

Unfortunately, you're right.

Mike McStay
Actor

First there was *Murder Bag* (1956–59) then *Crime Sheet* (1959) then *No Hiding Place* (1959–66)—British cop shows starring Raymond Francis as a detective called Lockhart. Mike McStay came onto *No Hiding Place* in 1964. He did "charismatic tough guy" very well. A star was born.

A few years down the track, a pair of super-producers named Broccoli and Saltzman were looking for a "charismatic tough guy" type to build a super-spy movie around and Mike was more than in the running.

Mike didn't play Bond, but he did menace Bond, playing a villain in "The Gold Napoleon," a typically perfect episode of the Roger Moore-Tony Curtis series *The Persuaders!* (1971–72).

He appeared in episodes of classic crime and action shows like *Z-Cars* (1962–78), *The Avengers* (1961–69), *Paul Temple* (1969–71), *Jason King* (1971–72) and *The Sweeney* (1975–78), and in the mini-series *A Spy At Evening* (1981), based on a first-rate spy-fi novel of the same name by action television scripter Donald James.

His movie work includes Val Guest's *Jigsaw* (1962), *The Stick Up* (1977) with *Starsky and Hutch* (1975–79) star David Soul, and the Peter Yates–directed *Robbery* (1967) in which he took his place alongside Stanley Baker, James Booth, Clinton Greyn, William Marlowe, George Sewell, Glyn Edwards, Barry Foster, Frank Finlay and Patrick Jordan in the most impressive assembly of British leading men this side of a Euan Lloyd birthday bash.

Thanks for agreeing to talk to me, Mike.

Actors love talking about themselves, never miss an opportunity. What did Marlon Brando say? "An actor is a guy who, if you ain't talking about him, he ain't listening!"

You're from Essex, aren't you?

You know, I've never been asked that question before in my life, you've thrown me! It was actually London, North East four or something. I was brought up right next to Walthamstow dog track, I suppose Essex is not far away, but that doesn't mean to say that I'm an Essex boy or an Essex girl!

How did you get involved in acting?

I took it up at school. I guess I loved the idea of being up there showing off! We had some very good teachers who used to encourage school plays and give their time after school. I really hate to mention his name, but Derek Jacobi was in those plays. Of course, being older than him, I got the star parts! From then on it seemed like a natural progression. My first job, after University and National Service, was twice nightly in Peterborough playing the noble savage in *The Little Hut* and covered from head to foot in some brown stuff that ruined the landlady's sheets! Then I worked all the repertory theaters, some in Ireland and Wales, until I finally realized that there were an awful lot of good actors out there, a lot better than I was, and if I was ever going to get anywhere I had better head to London. I was, with as much modesty as I can muster, a good-looking lad, and I figured I was cut out for lead parts. I found a very good agent who started to push me a bit, I kept doing theater work and did a lot of bits and pieces on television. I was finally spotted by Muriel Cole, the casting lady for *No Hiding Place*, and from that came, I suppose, the best two and a half years of my life.

It must have been fun being a young television star in London in the 1960s.

The "Swinging Sixties" seemed to be limited to a very small area of London—if you weren't there you

A publicity shot of Mike McStay for the Redifussion series *No Hiding Place* (1959-66) (courtesy Mike McStay).

weren't swinging. It was down the Kings Road about as far as the World's End pub, and after that it was normal people! I don't think people in York and Doncaster and Cornwall were having quite the same time as we were! It was the height of everything, exciting things were happening in almost every sphere and it was all there for the taking. The big thing that happened to me, a boy with an Irish father and a very correct Yorkshire mother, was that I discovered that women like sex! That was something completely new to me. Before that I'd thought that if I thrust my filthy body on some woman, I was going to have to marry her pretty damn quick! There were no drugs around, a bit of pot, but alcohol was the drug of the day. We all drank too much and the frightening thing is, apart from Michael Caine, they're all dead and gone, all the so-called hellraisers and mini-hellraisers. That worries me a bit, but I'm still here, as I keep on telling my doctor! There was a lot of work around, there were so many theaters in and out of London, so many television companies making action series like *No Hiding Place* and *The Saint* [1962–69] with Roger Moore before he became Roger Moore. So many good actors were coming out of the woodwork, Albert Finney and Tom Courtenay, people who didn't speak proper English, coming out because the barriers had been broken through.

Johnny Briggs says in his autobiography that the pair of you were mobbed by girls like you were pop stars.

We were, and strangely enough it wasn't at all menacing. There was a great program called *Ready, Steady, Go!* [1963–66] that was shot at the same studio as *No Hiding Place*; bands like the Rolling Stones appeared on it and when they arrived, the girls were always waiting to tear them to pieces, which I thought was fun, but it terrified them! One lunch time there were 50 to 100 girls waiting outside the studio because it was rumored that the Beatles were going to appear that night. We went round the corner to our favorite pub and when we came back there was triple that number. I said to Johnny, "That's what I want, I want that" and Johnny very wisely said, "Yeah, but they [pop stars] can never do what we've just done, sneak into the pub and have a glass of beer and a sandwich. Everywhere they go, they've got that and that's not much fun." But when it did happen, it was fun, it was just a lot of girls screaming. One time we went down to Cardiff to open the Ideal Homes Exhibition. A girl threw herself at Johnny, he turned to talk to somebody else, and she hit a display of historical artifacts that they'd set up. Johnny and I were mates, but there was a lot of good-natured rivalry between us, so as everyone stood there aghast, staring at the 200 years of Welsh history that had smashed on the floor, I said, "Johnny, why did you do that?"

How long did you get to shoot an episode of No Hiding Place?

We did the location filming beforehand but once you were in studio, you had pretty much an hour to shoot fifty minutes or so, and there were unions to make sure you didn't go over, not without some discussion. It was as good as live, they didn't have their own editing studios so editing was very expensive and they couldn't afford it. It wasn't a disaster if it went wrong but it was going to be costly so mostly you tried to carry on. I can only remember two retakes in two and a half years. One was when Johnny threw some golf clubs into the corner and knocked the entire set over! Another was when an actor blew his lines and had the courage to swear badly; they had to stop and do a retake then, but I don't think he ever worked for us again. It was pretty pressurized, but we were young and adrenalin carried you through.

When Muriel Cole cast me, she asked me if I knew what I was getting myself into and of course I didn't. On the first series I did, we shot six episodes and then we had a week off and I virtually slept for the whole week, I was absolutely worn out. Monday and Tuesday you'd work from ten in the morning till ten at night. Monday morning was spent rehearsing the following week's episode, then you'd head off to the studios for camera rehearsals and camera runs. Tuesday we were in the studio all day, shooting would start around nine and it was in the can by ten. I took Wednesday morning off because I'd go out and paint the town on Tuesday night—you had to get out and have fun, otherwise the swinging sixties might come to an end! Wednesday afternoon, Thursday and Friday we worked until about five-thirty, Saturday the producer would come and put his oar in, and we'd do some filming. Sunday we'd film, possibly into the night. So we didn't get much time off and when we did, we made the best of it. I had the pleasure of working with William Holden once, on *The World of Suzie Wong* [1960], and he was renowned for his late night activities. They were paying him a great deal of money and the second assistant was detailed to keep an eye on him and make sure he didn't get into too much trouble. One night he followed him around until four in the morning and then lost him. He was telling them this when William Holden walked on set, looking great, lines learned, professional as ever. I saw this and I thought, "That's the way to live: Be professional, don't let your fun interfere with your work, but for God sakes have some fun or you'll end up having a nervous breakdown."

You worked with lots of great actors on No Hiding Place.

I'd always been star-struck, I grew up going to the cinema two or three times a week and I still, to this day, want to be Humphrey Bogart when I grow up. So what really humbled me, if I as an actor dare use that word, was that I found myself working with actors I'd watched in theater and film all my life, and my name was above the title! I couldn't get used to that because I revered these people. I try and do whatever I can for the Royal Theatrical Fund, which basically tries to look after actors who have fallen on hard times in their old age. When I first went to their annual Christmas party I saw a lot of actors I knew, people who were a lot older than me. They were in their best suits and looked pretty good, but to my horror I realized that they were the beneficiaries! They'd spent their lives in the theater, where no one gets rich, and hadn't had the opportunity to make the sort of money we were making on *No Hiding Place*. I was making so much money on *No Hiding Place* that I literally couldn't spend it, I used to keep it in a drawer in my bedroom. Tax demanded that you get through £60 a week, which sounds like a small sum today but back then you could have lunch for two at the Savoy and it wouldn't come to a fiver, even with a bottle of wine and a tip! So what I couldn't spend I used to bung in a drawer and when my parents asked if I could help them buy a retirement bungalow they were looking at, I found that I had thousands of pounds in there! Thank God the girls who came to my bedroom weren't trying that drawer!

Why did you leave No Hiding Place?

I'd had fun but it was time to move on. Ray Francis, who was the nominal star of the show, had script control and if Johnny was getting too popular he'd cut him out and give me his dialogue, and vice versa. I discovered this because a friend had written a script and showed it to me before Ray Francis got it. By the time we shot it, virtually all my scenes were gone. I told them I was ready to leave and they started upping my salary until they reached a figure that I thought was hysterically funny. Afterwards I went to the pub and a great friend of mine, another actor, asked me if I was doing another series. I told him that I thought I probably would and he said, "In that case, shut up, stop moaning, take the money and enjoy it." I thought that was a good point, pretty wise, and that's what I did. The producer was a man named Peter Willes; in many ways he was a superb producer. They gave him the show to get rid of him, it was diving down in the ratings, and he turned it around and put it back on top. But he was a shit, he had a mean streak, and when Johnny and I did eventually leave the show he announced that we'd been fired, which wasn't true and wasn't a very good thing to have on your CV.

What can you tell me about Robbery?

The day I started on *Robbery* coincided with a Liverpool-Spurs match, Spurs were my team and I had to give up tickets, so I wasn't very happy! We were doing my close-ups and Peter Yates said he'd changed his mind, he wanted to do Barry Foster's close-ups instead. While they changed the lighting he took me aside and said, "You've done a lot of television, haven't you?" I said, "Yes," and he said, "Well, may I just tell you that filming is different. Your face is going to be six foot high on the screen. If you raise an eyebrow by half an inch it shoots up a foot. Don't move your face, don't do the television acting." He then gave me the filthiest lines you can imagine and told me to walk around practicing them, saying them with all the hate I could muster and without moving a muscle on my face. He'd decided to change the shot just so he could give me some advice and I was more than grateful. He was a wonderful director and he was under immense pressure from Stanley Baker and Michael Deeley, who were the producers. I'm told that Stanley Baker could be, as an actor, a really wonderful guy to work with, but as a producer he was not the best and treated his fellow actors rather badly. Where you could save a penny, Stanley would save it and when I left we were still fighting about certain things. I met him a little later on in a television studio, I was talking to Sian Phillips and she said, "Oh, by the way, do you know Stanley Baker?" and introduced us. I said, "Yes, we've met," and to our eternal credit neither of us wanted to offer the other his hand. Every now and then you work with someone who stands out as not the

From left: Patrick Jordan, George Sewell, Stanley Baker, Mike McStay and William Marlowe on the set of *Robbery* **(1967) (courtesy Mike McStay).**

most pleasant person in the world and in my book Stanley was one of them. But I do love actors, they are the great pleasure of the job. I'm so old now that I sometimes think I'm going to have to stop, I'm bored with the prospect of going through it all again, working with young directors who are reinventing the wheel and you've heard it all before; but I still love the actors because actors will sit down and talk forever, they've always got a good story to tell. You know it's not the truth but they tell it so well!

What are you memories of taking on Roger Moore and Tony Curtis on The Persuaders?!

Tony Curtis was a very affable guy but, as you know, he got done bringing pot into the country and there was a lot of that floating around the set. In our one scuffle I was holding a gun and he had to grab my arm. We went for a take and the gun fell against his back and he started saying, "Somebody hit me, hey, man, somebody hit me." I looked around and thought, "Well, there's only me here, must've been me." He was so high that it made life a bit difficult, but again, he was pleasant enough. Roger Moore is one of the nicest people I've ever met, he was just one of the lads. He came into the dressing room one time and stood at the window, trying to get a little bit of sun on his chest, preserving the image. Equity had just published a survey that said the average actor's earnings were about a thousand pounds a year. Roger looked at this and said, "If I stopped working, that would drop to about ten pounds, wouldn't it?" We had a fight scene together and he didn't even need to rehearse it. On each take he came at me a different way and never touched me. It looked great and it was just so easy. We were doing a scene and Roger thought I should drive right up to him in a large car. They set it up and told me that I should actually touch his legs with the bumper. I didn't think that was a very good idea and suggested they get a stunt driver to do it. The stunt driver took the car out, drove it around a bit, and said the brakes were spongy, they didn't work, and I thought, "I have just been saved from some of the worst publicity in the world … the actor who killed Roger Moore!"

Perhaps if you had killed Roger Moore, you might have got a certain highly coveted role that you were in line for…
There'd been an article in the paper saying "One of these six actors will be the next James Bond" and I was one of them. I'd been through a fair selection process, the only thing I hadn't done was a film test. Then I got a phone call from a reporter who said they'd got a cable from the Far East somewhere, where they were location hunting for the next Bond film, saying, "Next James Bond is ex-policeman Michael McStay"—I assume that "ex-policeman" was a reference back to *No Hiding Place*. My agent had heard nothing about it, couldn't confirm it, but the press were certain and arrived at my house in force. Lots of photographs were taken, including one where I'm leaning across the bar with a bottle of vodka in my hand looking very menacing. Quite by chance I went to a party that night and got talking to a man named Steve Previn, who was Andre Previn's brother and one of the top producers in the business at the time. He said, "What's all this shit they're shooting about the new James Bond? Everyone knows that Sean Connery is going to do another

one." I said, "Are you sure about that, Steve?" and he said, "Yeah, they've offered him Scotland or something" and that ended my brief stint as James Bond! I didn't feel too disappointed. I was excited about doing it but at the same time it was just another job to me. I would have had no problems doing it, I was young and brash and doing well, but as I've gotten older I've realized that you've got to be a pretty good actor to be James Bond, it takes a lot of skill to throw away some of those lines! That said, I know that of the six people in line to be the next James Bond, I was the best of 'em!

Who were they?
Robert Powell, I think. An actor called George Innes, who would've been an unusual choice, he wasn't your conventional good-looking lad. Those are probably the only two I can recall.

Simon Oates?
Oh yes, Simon, he was a lovely lad. Yeah, he would've been pretty good, but from what I can gather it was always going to be Roger Moore. Whoever they chose, including me, would have been a one-film Bond, a delaying tactic until they could get him. There were so many good actors working in that time and, given the fact that it was the swinging sixties, I knew them all from the pubs and clubs. After I got *No Hiding Place* I found out that an amazing number of them had turned it down! They didn't want to earn all that money, become famous and have all that fun, it wasn't for them. I thought, "Really? Isn't that fascinating," especially since as far as I know there was never much doubt that the job was mine.

You appeared on The Avengers, Jason King, The Sweeney, *all of them action shows, but you wanted to be the romantic lead, didn't you?*
I wasn't an action hero, not like today where action heroes are people who hurl themselves all around the place with huge effects going on around them. I was just an average, slightly unfit guy. If I had to run to the other end of the street, I'd need to stop for a retake. It was the sixties, we had a lot of fun, you couldn't be fit as well! I hate to think what would have happened if I'd got James Bond, the first thing they would have done was to send to me to a gym. They tried that with *No Hiding Place*, I went there for a week and at the end of it I couldn't move a muscle. I

went to my local pub and an elderly lady sent a pint across to me—she told the barman that she'd never seen a young man so badly crippled in her life! Oh no, I wasn't fit, I wasn't an action hero, why didn't I get the girls? What's wrong? You tell me. I never, ever got the girl in anything at all. There was one *No Hiding Place* where they gave me a girlfriend and of course at the end of it she turned out to be the villain! That was Kate O'Mara, my wicked girlfriend, I'll never forgive her!

Well, you tried to steal John Thaw's bird on The Sweeney.

I remember her, she was tipped for big things but it didn't quite happen, which is often the way, especially with girls. It's a sad business for girls. That was the sequence in a night club, wasn't it? I'd been to that club before and couldn't stand the bloody place. I went there with Lionel Stander and it was so noisy I walked out and thought, "They'd have to pay me to go back there," and they did! That was the first day's work I'd done after the cancer business cropped up. At the end of it my old friend Dougie Camfield said he'd only given me the part to see if I could stand up for a day, because at that point everyone assumed I was dying. Letting everyone know you've had cancer is a bit of a dodgy move to make professionally!

You wrote the television series Pull the Other One *[1984] starring Michael Elphick.*

A wonderful, talented, self-destructive man. We had a lot of fun with him, but the drink, oh dear, the drink. It's got a lot of us. I've stopped writing now, but I've written a memoir, it'll never get published but my kids said, "Dad, write it down," so I have. Muriel Cole once said I was a very good actor but "inconsequential," I suppose because I didn't suffer enough, and two of my radio plays were rejected on the grounds that they were "irrelevant." So I've called my memoir *Inconsequential and Irrelevant* which is more or less how I'll be remembered!

Jeffrey Byron
Actor

Sci-fi fans know Jeffrey Byron for his starring role in *Metalstorm: The Destruction of Jared-Syn* (1983), a *Mad Max* (1979) knock-off directed by second generation B-movie hero Charles "Son of Albert" Band. Byron was still in his twenties when he made that movie but he was already an old hand.

His first screen appearance, at age eight, was in John Ford's *Donovan's Reef* (1963). A rowdy, good-natured action comedy starring John Wayne and Lee Marvin, *Donovan's Reef* is Ford in full "slapstick punch-up" mode. For my money it's his best movie—take that, conventional wisdom!

In the 1970s Byron worked with top directors like Bryan Forbes and Peter Bogdanovich, and took the lead in *The London Connection* (1979), a Disney spy-thriller made for American television but released in cinemas overseas.

The team behind *The London Connection* were action experts to a man: Gail Morgan Hickman, whose credits include *The Enforcer* (1976) and multiple episodes of *The Equalizer* (1985–89), contributed to the script; the director was Robert Clouse who gave us such indisputable action masterworks as the John D. MacDonald "Travis McGee" adaptation *Darker Than Amber* (1970), *Enter the Dragon* (1973) and the outrageously enjoyable *Blackbelt Jones* (1974); the supporting cast includes Roy Kinnear, Lee Montague, Nigel Davenport, Dudley Sutton, Burt Kwouk and Percy Herbert, veterans of countless British action movies and television series; and the score is by John Cameron, eminent jazzer-composer and music director on Gerry Anderson's *The Protectors* (1972–74).

Disney made a handful of small "s" spy movies like *Guns in the Heather* (1969) with Glenn Corbett, the colorful, stunt-filled *Condorman* (1981) and the Malta-set *Trenchcoat* (1983), a well-deserved star vehicle for the gutsy Margot Kidder; but *The London Connection* is the closest they got to out-and-out Bondery. *Herbie Goes to Monte Carlo* (1977) has spies in it too, but we'll class that as a footnote.

How did you get involved in The London Connection*?*
I'd just finished a film in the U.K. called *International Velvet* (1978) where I starred opposite Tatum O'Neal, Anthony Hopkins and Christopher Plummer. Disney was trying to cast this as a sort of young James Bond and they brought me in to screen test for the part. They had great plans for this project but unfortunately it didn't really turn out the way they anticipated. Originally they'd planned to follow *The London Connection* with *The Paris Connection* and *The Rome Connection* and so on and so forth. It was made for television, for *The Wonderful World of Disney* [1968–79], which I believe was on at seven o'clock in the evening on NBC; but they were looking for a slightly more mature audience and decided, in their infinite wisdom, to air it at eight o' clock instead. Well, unbeknownst to us, there was a television movie on ABC that night called *The Jericho Mile* [1979], which got like the highest rating in the history of television! It just wiped us out, so unfortunately *The London Connection* was a one-off—despite that I had a great time!

Robert Clouse was a perfect choice to direct it.
We all revered him because we knew he'd directed Bruce Lee in *Enter the Dragon*. By the time he directed *The London Connection* he was a bit older but he was a very nice guy, and really understood what he wanted in the project. At the time I was very interested in the martial arts and, having studied karate for two years, had a minor background in it. I mentioned to him that I could do some back kicks and side kicks and things like that and he was very keen for me to try it in the movie. It wasn't scripted at all but they choreographed the scenes and we pulled it off.

The cast is full of great British character actors.
All of them were great. Roy Kinnear was a legend, Nigel Davenport was a legend, they were all consummate pros, knew their stuff, were prepared, lovely to be around, no egos, it was lots of fun. I was maybe 21 going on 22 and still a little green behind the ears. It was basically my film, I was in every scene, and that was really exciting for me. It was all

Masters of the Shoot-'Em-Up

An American spy in London. Director Robert Clouse and Jeffrey Byron on location during the making of the Disney spy-thriller *The London Connection* **(1979).**

shot in England, shooting on real locations in London, which is probably still my favorite city in the world. Some of the interiors were done at Pinewood, which of course was legendary for James Bond. They were shooting *Superman* [1978] there at the time so I got to meet Christopher Reeve, which was really fun. The only scene that wasn't shot in England was the opening, that was shot on the back lot of Disney Studios—I'm opening up a safe with a black mask on, then I go onto the roof, jump on a ladder and a helicopter takes me away, 60, 70 feet in the air. I did that, I did virtually every stunt on my own. There might have been one or two where they had to have somebody double me for safety reasons, but they allowed me to do almost everything. I was fairly athletic at that time in my life and it was a very physical part. I was running, jumping, shooting and climbing and it was a lot of fun. Of all the work I've done over the years, it was certainly one of the highlights.

Was working for Disney different in any way from working for other studios?

The head of the studio at that time was a fellow called Ron Miller, who I believe was married to Walt Disney's daughter. I'd screen-tested and they'd pretty much determined that I was going to play the part but before they officially offered it to me, I had to meet with him in his office. He was kind of trying to keep the Disney "code" intact, so I was asked a lot of questions to find out whether I was wholesome enough and fit the Disney brand. Whatever I said apparently worked 'cause I got the part!

Donovan's Reef *is such a great film.*

Well, I have great memories of that. The director was my godfather so that kind of helped in getting the part! My mother, Anna Lee, was quite a famous British actress and had a long association with John Ford—I think she did nine films for him, more than anyone but John Wayne. They were great friends and there was a standing invitation for us to go to his house in Bel Air on Sundays, that's when all his godchildren would visit him. We were there one Sunday around the time he was thinking about doing *Donovan's Reef* and he got the idea that I could play the part of Luki. The only catch was that I was this blonde, blue-eyed half-British American child and in the movie I had to be half-Hawaiian. They did some hair and makeup tests where they dyed my hair jet-black, darkened my skin and kind of slanted my eyes. Apparently my godfather thought I looked fine and I got the part. All my makeup was done by Bud Westmore, part of the Westmore family—there were about ten of them and they were the most famous makeup people of that era, from the '30s until the '60s. I was about seven years old and of course at that age you're very tied to your parents, especially your mother. As I was getting ready to film *Donovan's Reef*, my mother got a part in *What Ever Happened to Baby Jane*? [1962], which meant that she couldn't go to Hawaii with me. So my two older brothers, who were all of 12 and 13, came along as my guardians and my godfather threw them in as extras and gave them little bit parts in the movie. We were three boys on our own in Hawaii ... living large! It was a great adventure.

How did John Ford treat you on the set? Was he patient?

It's funny, on every movie John Ford would choose an actor or actress to be his whipping boy, and it didn't matter who they were. I mean, he'd pick on John Wayne or James Stewart or Henry Fonda, and there I was

It's just not cricket. Lee Montague and Dudley Sutton try to settle the score in Disney's *The London Connection* (1979).

on *Donovan's Reef* and he was wonderful to me, just as lovely as can be! I have a scene in the film where I'm meant to jump in a Jeep with the legendary Cesar Romero and a lovely actress, who I had a huge crush on, named Elizabeth Allen. In the scene leading up to that, Elizabeth Allen and Cesar Romero have a lot of dialogue and I'm eating a papaya. Well, it was quite warm and the papaya was a little overripe and I started to feel queasy, I didn't feel well at all. We got to the next scene, I'm sitting between the two of them, and right in the middle of the scene I suddenly had to throw up. I'm looking at Elizabeth Allen and I'm looking at Cesar Romero and I really don't want to throw up on Elizabeth Allen so I quickly turned and threw up all over Cesar Romero. Of course my godfather cuts and is absolutely in hysterics, Cesar Romero is humiliated and probably not very happy with me, but John Ford just thought it was the funniest thing in the world. This was like one o'clock in the afternoon but he wrapped for the rest of the day and told everyone to go home.

They took me to the hospital, he came to visit me and he couldn't have been kinder.

Did you maintain a relationship with Ford over the years?

Absolutely, all the way until his death. I'd go visit him every odd Sunday and was as close to him as any of his godchildren were. He was a lovely guy. As you know, I was a child actor and then completely left the business—I didn't want to do it any more, I wanted to be a normal kid. When I was a child actor my name was Timothy Stafford and at the age of eighteen I changed it, for many reasons, to Jeffrey Byron. Then about a year after that, I decided that I wanted to be an actor again and by happenstance I met the director Peter Bogdanovich, who was very hot at the time. Peter Bogdanovich idolized John Ford and when he became rich and famous he bought a beautiful house directly across the street from him in Bel Air. I met him at John Ford's house and afterwards I wrote him a letter, completely sincere, saying that I thought he was a wonderful director, and that he was bringing back a certain kind of a style in movies that hadn't been seen in many, many years. Lo and behold I get a note back from him saying he's about to cast a movie called *Nickelodeon* [1976] and he'd like me to be in it. Originally it was a very small part but Peter kept giving me more and more to do and although I was only contracted for one week I was on the film for something like seven. What was great about *Nickelodeon* was that we were shooting on a soundstage directly across from where John Wayne was filming his last movie *The Shootist* [1976]. He had cancer at that time, like the character he was playing, so it was a very poignant movie. I went to visit him on the set and he was in his dressing room, playing chess with his stand-in. I introduced myself, told him that I was Anna Lee's son and that I played Luki in *Donovan's Reef*. He gave me a gregarious hug and couldn't have been sweeter. I spent about a half an hour with him and it was great to be able to do that.

You grew up on movie sets. Any come to mind that readers of my book might like to hear about?

I went on the set when my mother did a film with James Coburn called *In Like Flint* [1967]. I was a big fan of his, he was such a man's man, and I got to walk around his red Ferrari which was very fun!

How did your approach to acting change as you moved from being a child to an adult?

As a child it's all instinct and frankly it's mostly about direction: The director acts out what he wants you to do and you mimic him. As you become an adult actor, it's more about the craft, I did theater and was in a class on and off for twenty years. I worked with some really great teachers and honed my craft so that when I showed up on set I had a pretty strong sense of what I was supposed to do. You still take direction but you're certainly not taking line readings like you would as a child.

Did your mother ever give you any acting advice?

My mother was very conscious of being in the moment, trying to get in touch with the reality of what's going on in the moment. I'd suggest that being real, being authentic, is something that every actor should strive for.

Did the fact that you grew up in the film industry make you less intimidated by the apparatus of filmmaking and by auditions and so on?

I never looked at it as easy or a walk in the park. In my twenties the big thing for a young actor was to get a television series, every pilot season they'd literally see thousands of actors, and then it would be down to six, then four and then finally two and I was often in that mix. You'd go to the network and walk into a room and you'd see twenty executives staring back at you. It was very nerve-wracking and very difficult to read a part and be in the moment when you're dealing with executives who, frankly, know little or nothing about acting and are just looking for a quality or a look or something.

Is there any way the audition process could be improved to make it less nerve-wracking for actors?

The process is always better if the director's in the room. They usually aren't, but if they *are* it gives the actor a sense of security because the director is there to help, the director is there to make you better. The casting director has one person coming in after another and they have to keep track of everything. Often, through no fault of their own, they're more like a policeman, whereas a director can take a little bit of time to nurture an actor and make them feel relaxed. The other side of it is that the actor has to walk into that room thinking that everybody in it is their friend; that will take a lot of the pressure off. It may not be true, but you have to convince yourself that it is. You don't want to think of them as your enemy because at the end of the day you're offering them a service. If they pick you, it'll mean you've just made their life easier because they don't want to sit in that room for weeks or months trying to figure out who they're going to cast.

You acted in an episode of McMillan and Wife *[1971–77] that was directed by Jackie Cooper. Did you compare notes about your respective careers as child actors?*
  Not really. I worked with Jackie a few times, he liked me and kept bringing me in for things. But those kinds of shoots are so quick, you do an entire episode in like six days, so when a director, especially an episodic television director, is on the set, his whole mind is consumed with getting the next shot, the next shot, the next shot.

Does that speed of production affect your performance?
  You're there to do a job and you have to be able to do it under any circumstances. You have to adapt to what you're doing whether it's a play or a one-hour television show or a movie. Six days is a walk in the park compared to what I did a few years later when I was a contract player on a soap opera. We'd do an entire episode in one day, thirty pages of dialogue in one day. Now that is daunting, that is tough! I remember going in for my first day and I was just a wreck, I called my agent in a panic at lunchtime and I was like "Get me out of here! I can't do this." But he calmed me down and the good news is I learned how to do it and within a week it had become second nature to me. You realize how powerful your brain is when you test it.

Charles Band also grew up in the movie business. Did you have a good rapport with him?
  I had a great rapport with him, he's a real character, a real … I don't know if the word *scalawag* is right but he was a very smart guy. He would literally go to the Cannes Film Festival and sell a movie that hadn't been made. He'd spend $5,000 on a really cool-looking movie poster, come up with a great logline, get all these pre-sales and make the movie with the money! *Metalstorm: The Destruction of Jared-Syn* was basically a 3D rip off of *Mad Max*. It was, again, a very physical part and I had a great

time making it. By sheer luck Universal was coming out with *Jaws 3-D* [1983] at the same time, it had cost them, I don't know, $25 million, which was the equivalent of 100 million today. It was released on 2,000 screens, and back then 3D films had to be shown on special screens. And it was done in two days, I mean, it was a total bomb. Universal was desperate to fill those screens and here's Charlie Band with this silly little film that I doubt even cost him a million dollars to make. Universal bought it for three million, released it on 1500 screens, which was unheard of for that kind of film, and it did really well. I mean, when I say it did really well, it probably made 15 or 20 million dollars but for a film like that…

Tony Russel
Actor

One of the best things about Italian genre movies of the 1960s is their international casts: In one fell swoop you get your favorite western/spy/sword-and-sandal/horror stars from Italy, Germany, Yugoslavia, Britain, France and anywhere else that cameras were rolling. As likely as not the lead will be an American: Ladies and gentlemen, Tony Russel.

Early in his career he appeared in a bunch of classic American crime and western television series like *The Lone Wolf* (1953), *Highway Patrol* (1955–58), *Broken Arrow* (1956–57) and *Peter Gunn* (1958–61), and in the superb John Sturges western feature *Last Train from Gun Hill* (1959).

He made his name as a leading man in writer-director Burt Topper's *War Is Hell* (1963) an independently produced Korean War movie that caused some controversy in the States but was much lauded in Europe. This led to Russel's relocation to Rome where he worked on every kind of action film going: from director Antonio Margheriti's sword-and-sandal epic *The Invincible Seven* (1963) to Alberto Leonardi's Bond "riproduzione" *Target Goldseven* (1966).

He turned down the lead in Sergio Leone's A *Fistful of Dollars* (1964) but earned his spaghetti western spurs by dubbing Franco Nero's voice for the English-language version of Sergio Corbucci's *Django* (1966). Returning to America, he guested on numerous action series such as *High Chaparral* (1967–71), *Death Valley Days* (1952–75), *Vega$* (1978–81) and *CHiPs* (1977–83), and reteamed with Burt Topper on several features including *The Hard Ride* (1971) and *Soul Hustler* (1973).

You're in the great John Sturges western Last Train from Gun Hill.
I played a very small part, I was a bartender, if I remember. I was kinda flattered because I was working, but it was only for three or four days, I was just getting started. I got it through a friend of mine, Earl

Holliman, who was a very well-known actor. I was at the Pasadena Playhouse with him, we were students at the drama school in California and then he got rolling pretty well. He had a close friend called Paul Nathan who was the associate producer to Hal Wallis. They were looking for someone to play this part, and he recommended me to the associate producer who recommended me to Hal Wallis. Then Hal Wallis took me in and introduced me to the director and that was it. I didn't have that much to do, I was just standing behind the bar over there.

War Is Hell was your first lead.
And that was through a kind of coincidence also. I'd joined the Screen Actors Guild in 1952 not long after I graduated from drama school. I did a picture called *Hiawatha* [1952] with Vince Edwards—remember Vince Edwards? He had that medical series *Ben Casey* [1961–66]. He was Mr. America, big muscleman, he was lifting weights up there on location. I was there for two weeks just playing an Indian. That's how I got my SAG card and that's how I met Burt Topper, who was also playing an Indian. Then in '59 or '60 I ran into him in a studio and he said, "Hey, Tony, I'm gonna do a picture called *War Is Hell*," although at that time it was gonna be called *War Hero*. We talked for a while and he just gave me the part and I subsequently did two or three other films for him. Sometimes it's who you know, not what you know.

He's a very interesting guy—an actor, writer, producer. What was his background?
He was with American International for many years as a cutter and an editor and a line producer for Arkoff and Nicholson, very successful. Then he went off on his own and did a couple of independent pictures and this was one of them. We shot it in two weeks in black and white.

It had a bit of a bumpy ride, didn't it?
Well, because of its content. It was about a Korean War platoon and it was almost … not anti–American, but it painted a picture of the American soldier as being a little weird. I played a psycho sergeant who, although the war was over, for want of recognition, goes around killing some of those North Koreans. At that time, films had to have the stamp of the government to be released, so nothing too vulgar or subversive got out, and they weren't going to release *War Is Hell*. But it got released

in France and Italy and all the European countries, got great reviews, and won an award out of competition at the Cannes festival.

And then they added the Audie Murphy prologue to get an American release.

Exactly, about a year later Audie Murphy did the prologue and said, "This is the story of one platoon, one man" and so on, and that's how it got released. That's the picture that launched me in Europe because the Italian producers and directors had seen the film. It was a small film but it had some good things in it.

Burt Topper's reputation was quite high in Europe. Was he ever tempted to follow you over?

In fact he did, he met with Carlo Ponti, the producer who married Sophia Loren. I met him while he was there, we had dinner together. But Burt Topper, he was so independent that he never relegated any authority to anybody else. That's why he was a producer-director-writer—he did everything, he moved the cables around! He'd hire a technician or a cameraman and he was always on his back, he wanted to do the whole thing. Actually he was a good producer, he wasn't a bad director, but he was a good producer, and he was a great editor more than anything else.

Was he the most independent-minded director you worked with?

Probably, because I worked with him for three years kind of co-producing things, but we never got anything done because every time somebody came up with an idea or had a story, he didn't like it, he wanted to write his story and I'd say, "Hey, Burt, you can't do it all." He was his own worst enemy as far as doing that, but he was really talented. He knew how to put a project together, economically too, that was his biggest asset. Then I think his father passed away and left him a lot of money, houses and apartments in Hollywood, so he kinda drifted away from the business completely. We became pretty close friends because, hell, we met in 1952, so it's been over fifty years since I've known him.

How would you compare the moviemaking process and what the directors wanted from actors in the U.S. and Italy?

I guess it depends on the budget of the pictures. When I went there, the budgets of the pictures I did were very small. Even though I was the star of the picture, I was the third nationality. If it was a Spanish-Italian co-production they were allowed one foreigner and I was usually the foreigner, the American star. I starred in about twelve pictures, and to be honest and objective they were all pretty lousy pictures. Lousy in the sense that they were always in a hurry to make them and I had the misfortune of being able to speak Italian fluently and was knowledgeable enough to be able to hear them talking about, "Uh, how much film have we got left in the can? Hurry up finish the shot." I mean, I became so budget-conscious that I was always in a hurry and good in one take, though it wasn't difficult to do it in one take because after every picture they go into the soundstage and dub everything. In America we're disciplined, we show up on set with our lines memorized. In Italy when they'd forget their lines they'd just go into "Uno, duo, tre, quatro," they'd just go into numbers, in the same mood, the same tone. There was one Italian actor who dubbed me into Italian all the time, he dubbed me in *War Is Hell* and from then on he was my Italian voice—great voice, great guy. In fact, I liked myself better in Italian than in English, that's probably why I was so successful in Italy!

Is it true that you turned down the lead in A Fistful of Dollars?

My agent was Fausto Ferzetti, Gabrielle Ferzetti's brother. One day he called me and said, "There's a director here, his name is Sergio Leone. He's seen some of your action pictures and he'd like to meet you." So I went to my agent's office and I met him and he said, "I'm going to do a western" which made me smile, because Italians doing westerns was kinda funny at that time. So he gave me a script and he gave my agent a script and about two hours later my agent called me and said, "Did you read the script, Tony? Isn't it the worst piece of shit you've ever read in your life? There's nothing there," and I agreed, it was terrible. Actors look for the meat of the character. I couldn't read between the lines, the blood, the music, all that, I couldn't see that, that's in the director's head, not mine. They weren't offering much money and I had another offer at the same time to go to Egypt to do a picture called *Secret of the Sphinx* [1964] with Maria Perschy, who was a big star in Germany. So we called and said I wasn't gonna do it. Before I left for Egypt I met Clint Eastwood on the Via Veneto, he'd taken the part and was going to Almeria, Spain. We shot our pictures in five weeks at the most and when we got back

Double O Sette. Tony Russel and Erika Blanc in *Tecnica Di Una Spia* **(1966), released in the U.S. as** *Target Goldseven.*

we got together and Clint said, "Oh, Tony, what a piece of crap I made, 120 degrees in the shade, no money," and he moaned and groaned. And when it got released, it was standing room only for six months in the largest theater in Rome!

Duccio Tessari, the director of Secret of the Sphinx, *was very talented.*

That's right. I had never seen Sergio Leone's film but I'd seen Duccio Tessari's, I can't remember what it was but it was a well-done picture. So when I had a chance to work with him, I jumped at it. They were giving me a lot more money, it was a better director as far as I was concerned, it was a James Bond–type thing, kind of comedic in a way, and I hadn't done one of those. And the idea of going to Egypt, the Nile, the Aswan Dam, Luxor and Alexandria fascinated me.

Were there Egyptian crew and actors involved?

Yeah, they picked up quite a few Egyptian actors that could speak English, haltingly but well enough so that when they were dubbed they could synchronize it. When I was doing my first film in Italy, *The Legend of Fra Diavalo* [1962], we had Mario Adorf speaking English, Yugoslavians speaking in Yugoslavian, Italians speaking Italian, a few Spanish actors there…

What's your opinion of post-syncing?

I never liked it. It was in my contract that I would speak English and I would get to dub myself. So if you watch any of my movies, you see that most of the time I am in absolute sync but the rest of the actors are out of sync because they're speaking Spanish or Italian or German or Egyptian or whatever it is. Post-syncing is really a chore. I directed several of those dubbing things and wrote some of the scripts, you spend eight hours in a little room at a Moviola trying to fit the words in and it's tough, really tough. I think when they dubbed *Fistful of Dollars* they dubbed it in New York and they had a lot of talent to choose from, but when you dubbed a picture in Rome there was a lot of English and Americans there, but they weren't all good actors, so you were limited. The only good thing about it was if a plane went over or there was a big noise, they just kept rolling.

There were a lot of American actors in Rome in this period.

Oh, yeah, there was Gordon Scott, he played Tarzan in a couple of pictures and he did some movies there. Steve Reeves made enough money to buy a ranch in Montana or something when he came back to the States. I used to hang around with him, he was Mr. Universe and he was so musclebound they had to help him on and off a horse sometimes.

He needed a musclebound horse!

That's right! *Hercules Unchained* [1960] started the whole thing. That's when I went to Italy: They were doing the Maciste films and I did a couple of those. Gordon Scott and Steve Reeves, they were names, really well paid, they did *Romulus and Remus* [1961] and we, the English Language Dubbing Association, dubbed it because neither of them had a very good acting voice. A lot of actors had a couple of lines here, a couple of lines there, but they made their living dubbing. There were three separate English dubbing organizations when I got there, all competing for the same work, so when I became president of the English Language Dubbing Association I got the other two to work with us under one banner. One time I came back from location in Spain and they were dubbing a picture for a producer who hadn't paid for the previous picture we'd dubbed for him. They were so starved for a couple of lira that they'd do anything. I told them not to dub for him until he paid for the last picture, and then he's gotta give us 50 percent up front. It was funny because when I was growing up, my dad used to talk about the war between the Turks and the Italians, and how the Turks would sneak in and sneak out, how their tents would be there one day and gone the next. As president my name was Tony Russo, and some of the producers didn't know that Tony Russo was also Tony Russel the actor. I was gonna sign for two pictures with the producer who owed us money but that didn't happen because when I stopped the dubbing and sequestered the soundtrack, we had a meeting, and when he saw that Tony Russo was Tony Russel he turned to his associate and said, "We have been invaded by the Turks!"

Did any of the dubbers go on to on-camera work?
Yeah, there was a guy called Frank Wolff.

He was a great actor.
Absolutely, he was a great dear friend of mine. He used to come over to my apartment and he'd play the guitar and sing songs, he was really talented. He turned down the heavy in *Fistful of Dollars*. He did some quality pictures, he worked with some good directors; I worked with decent directors but he was working with heavyweights because he was that good an actor. He was married to a wonderful Irish girl called Maureen, but they divorced and she went back to Ireland, and then he married another woman who became his manager and they had problems. He was emotionally disturbed, he had a drinking problem, his personal life fell apart and he killed himself. It was sad, really sad. Even though he was so talented, he had such lack of self-worth.

Tell us about directors Antonio Margheriti and Alberto Martini.
They were mechanics in a sense, they'd get the picture out. They were former editors and cutters and they knew exactly how to save money, and it was all about saving money. For instance, I did two science fiction pictures with Margheriti in five weeks. One of them was *Wild Wild Planet* (1965) with Liza Gastone, a very attractive, wonderful lady, and

Massimo Cerrato, who was Anna Magnani's lover. Imagine, five weeks to shoot two films! Fortunately I only lived about half a mile away from the studio so I said to them, "You call me when you're ready for me and I'll be there in five minutes," because I hated to sit around all day while they were working on the set. When they called me they'd tell me which picture we were shooting because they were both the same, with the same outfits and everything else.

Which studio was this?

De Paolis, the second biggest studio in Rome; the biggest was Cinecittà, I didn't do much work there although my son worked there on *Cleopatra* [1963]. Somebody knew that my son had done some work in the States and recommended him—they needed a little nine-year-old Caesarone, Cleopatra and Caesar's son. So he read for [director Joseph L.] Mankiewicz, who asked him what he'd done and he said, "If you go to the Archimedi Theatre you'll see me in *Tammy Tell Me True* [1961]," which was a movie he'd done with Sandra Dee. Well, they called and said, "We'd like to use your son," and I said, "What are you paying?" and they offered some ridiculous amount, and I said, "No, you're way off base, he doesn't work for that kind of money." See, I could do that for my son, I couldn't do that for myself, I'd say, "I'll take it! I'll take it! I need the money!" My son didn't need money. My son was crying because he wanted to work with Liz Taylor, Richard Burton, Rex Harrison and all those big people, and I'm going to ruin it. So they call back and made a few more offers and I said, "Okay, but I don't want taxes, that's net!" and every week we'd walk into this room full of lire to get paid, and he was on it for 14 weeks! I think he only worked for five days! I think everybody retired on that movie. The English actors who came over there were skiing in the Alps, Hume Cronyn was there for a year. It must've been nice to come home with that cushion, to be able to turn down roles you didn't want—I was always in desperate straits. "I'll take it! I'll take it!"

Peter DeAnda
Actor

Peter DeAnda is a playwright and theater actor of great repute. He's also done a lot of impressive work in movies and television and a good bit of it is in the action bracket.

He starred in the private eye pilot *Cutter* (1973), written by action television high-achiever Dean Hargrove, and appeared in episodes of the TV cop shows *Dan August* (1970–71), *Cannon* (1971–76) and *Police Woman* (1974–78).

He had a lead role in *Come Back, Charleston Blue* (1972), the big screen version of *The Heat's On* by Chester Himes, one of a series of crime novels about Harlem police detectives Coffin Ed Johnson and Gravedigger Jones, played to perfection in both *Come Back, Charleston Blue* and the earlier *Cotton Comes to Harlem* (1970) by Raymond St. Jacques and Godfrey Cambridge.

He also joined George C. Scott, Stacy Keach and a dream cast of supporting players, including Rosalind Cash, Ed Lauter, Roger E. Mosley and Clifton James, in director Richard Fleischer's *The New Centurions* (1972), an adaptation of ex-cop Joseph Wambaugh's bestselling novel about the pressures and absurdities of big city police work.

You worked with the great director Richard Fleischer on The New Centurions.

Richard Fleischer was having a lot of troubles with George C. Scott and I think he just wanted to get the hell out of there. The deal George made was that he'd do *The New Centurions* if the studio would fund a project of his called *Rage* [1972], but the part in *The New Centurions* was very small and George demanded that they make it bigger, which meant that all the other parts went to littlesville.

They were re-writing while you were shooting?

Yeah, they shot your scenes but when the film came out they weren't

Marlene Warfield and Peter DeAnda in the Universal Television detective pilot *Cutter* (1973).

in it because George's part had gotten bigger and they didn't have the room. I knew George from New York, every actor in that movie was from New York, Stacy Keach and everybody else, which pissed off the actors from L.A. who thought, "What the hell makes New York actors better than us?" George was a good guy. Some people thought he was a bastard but I understood him. His fight was with the powers that be, not us, but we suffered when he demanded what he wanted. I didn't care because that was a time when, even though my career was just beginning, I was starring in a lot of stuff. I'd done a soap opera called *One Life to Live* [1968–2013] and I was real big on that, but I hated doing it and left after about a year and a half.

Why did you hate it?

Because it was unreal and they played games, paying me very little for doing the same thing that whites were doing, but that's how it was at that time because the breakthrough for blacks had just happened. I was one of the first to forge ahead, along with Lou Gossett and Clarence Williams. Bill Cosby had come along shortly before, but when I did *Cutter* I was the only stand-alone black male star, without co-stars, in television.

How did you get the lead in Cutter?

I was on location in L.A., shooting *The New Centurions*, and I got a call to show up at Universal, at eleven o'clock at night, to read for it. I was about the hundredth and the last person to read for the part.

Who else was up for it?

Everyone who was about my age. I was thirty-two at the time, so everybody who was in their mid-twenties to mid-thirties, which would be everybody.

Can you remember anything about the shoot?

It went thirteen days in Chicago. To get permission to shoot there, the producers had to send a dummy script. Chicago had a reputation for guns and shooting and wanted to get away from it. Not that there was a lot of guns in *Cutter*, but my character does wear a strap holster in one scene and a guy comes at me with a gun in another—a Chicago actor who was drunk as a skunk so the scene took all day to shoot. I finished shooting the film and flew back to New York but I hadn't signed a contract. Peter Falk was getting $900,000 a season, Rock Hudson was getting $750,000 a season, Dennis Weaver was getting $500,000 a season, and what they offered me was $40,000 a season, and if I took it they'd basically own me. Anything they weren't paying me would have been going into their pockets as profit, and would have gone to paying the others. Not only would I have been getting far less than the white guys, I would have been paying part of their salaries as well. So I just said no and opted out and that's why *Cutter* didn't go any further than the pilot. I took out a couple of pictures in *Variety* and let everyone know I was available and not beholden to anyone. It caused me a few problems but I didn't care. I'm an activist—politically, socially and morally. They just didn't know me. Universal said I wouldn't work for them again, that I wouldn't work at all, but I was hot as a firecracker at the time and went right into *Come Back, Charleston Blue*, and no more than a couple of years later Universal cast me in another pilot. That's the old story of "I'll never hire you again … unless I need you."

What can you tell us about Come Back, Charleston Blue?

That was a silly shoot. It was a gangster comedy and there was a scene where white guys put on blackface and pretend to be black. The Black Muslims saw that and chased the company out of Harlem. It was no big thing to me, they were just mouthing off, rightly so, but no big thing. But the producers had to move the production down to the lower part of Manhattan and put up Harlem street signs. Godfrey Cambridge and Raymond St. Jacques were not the best actors. Godfrey was a comic, really, he'd act to make some money but that was about it. He used to eat seven steaks at one meal so no wonder he died of a heart attack at such a young age. Bontche Schweig, the writer, quit because they weren't doing things right—he didn't mean it to be so much of a comedy. So the producer, Samuel Goldwyn Jr., hired his wife to take over and she wasn't much of a writer, it was just a moneymaker for her. Things like that would happen a lot back in the day.

You appeared in a bunch of classic action shows. Can you remember anything about Dan August?

It was good working with Burt Reynolds, he was all right. I remember I had to throw him through a fence that was scored to break, but it didn't crack too easily and he got all cut up. Burt Reynolds liked to do all his own stunts. Fuck that! I did a scene where I almost got killed, for real. We were in an airplane and Burt Reynolds and Norman Fell were chasing us in a car. The guy flying the plane struggled to bring the thing to a halt and almost slammed into the embankment, with a full tank of gas. He was the instructor at the airfield and they hired him instead of bringing someone along because they wanted to save money. That's television.

What about Cannon *with William Conrad?*

That was a three-parter. I was playing a pimp. Conrad was kinda gruff but actors never did upset me, no one does. I take no guff from anyone.

And Police Woman?

I was an Eldridge Cleaver type. They had me in handcuffs and a rabid follower of mine was trying to break me free, so there was a lot of shooting, shooting up the motel. Angie Dickinson came up to me and asked me what I thought of the script and I said, "It's a script." She fired up, her eyes were burning, but I don't talk to people when I'm deep into my acting shit. It was a good piece, it was a wonderful piece, but I didn't look at it that way until after we'd shot it. I don't read scripts like that, I don't talk about it, I just let everything flow and I meld with the character, the ins and outs of what he's about.

Can you explain what you mean by "let everything flow."

I bury myself so deeply in a part that it just flows by itself. I'm totally immersed in the part and therefore it comes out naturally. I don't run lines with other actors, I don't do anything more than study the part myself and say things over and over again until I know it's going to come out right. I'm sort of a natural actor.

How would you compare acting for the stage with acting for television and film?

They're very different. With stage acting you're actually delivering ideas. Acting for the screen is good but it's not the same thing, it can't be the same thing. You're on stage for two and a half hours; with film you're shooting for ten weeks or more and it's a matter of cuts, you're just shooting bits and pieces. It's very tiring because it's very boring. Acting in movies is not an ongoing interest for me, it doesn't push anything in me that makes me think, "I gotta do film." If they ask and the script is tolerable, I'll do it, but I'm not searching.

Is it difficult to shape a performance that's edited together from lots of different takes?

No, I was more a one-shot genius. I did it all in one take, literally. Other actors say, "I need to do it again because I'm not feeling too good with that" but my mind works differently to that. I always felt good with what I did, I knew it would project when it was shown.

Could film and television directors learn anything from stage directors?

Not really because what they do is so different. They have to work very fast and take care of a lot of people. Television is just television, they're just trying to keep you in your seats so you'll buy the products they're selling. The actors have gotten better than they used to be but the projects are just as silly, and there's a lasting racism there. Look at the Emmys, it's practically all white. The Golden Globes, the Oscars and the Tonys are the same—a man could go snow-blind watching those things. That has to be addressed, it has to be rectified, and I wish people would bring it up instead of thanking God and all that stuff.

You studied at the Paul Mann Actors Workshop in New York.
After I got out of the service I lived with my family in Pittsburgh. There was a big recession at the time, there were no jobs to be had there, and I was spending a lot of time drinking. My mother knew I wanted to act and write and gave me twenty bucks to get out of there. I was on the bus to New York the next day. I worked for a duplication machine company for about a year, selling products and fixing machines, but I never sold anything. I'm claustrophobic and hated going up to the offices in the elevators. I used the time to do scenes with my classmates in the park instead. My boss called me in to fire me and I told him not to worry, I'd just been cast in *The Blacks*, which was the biggest hit in New York at the time. He was wonderful about it and just said, "Get your ass outta her and do it!" I took the place of Raymond St. Jacques, who left to do *Rawhide* (1959–66), and wound up playing six of the male parts over the course of two and a half years. I'd do another show and then come back. By that time I was married with two kids and it kept us going, kept us alive. I worked constantly for about seventeen or eighteen years, did about seventy-five plays in New York and received some of the best reviews ever. I started acting in 1963 but I was just getting the big push around 1968 when I wrote my play *Ladies in Waiting*. Then I had a writing career that was huge so I spent more time with that.

Have you written any screenplays?
I was hired to convert Marvin Gaye's "What's Going On" into a film. Stevie Wonder was behind that, I made tapes of myself doing all the characters and sent them off to him but it never went any further than that. The other guy that was involved in it was the guy who ran the dance show, Don Cornelius; he was the guy who first brought it to me. I knew him from *Cutter*, he had a bit part in that 'cause he was from Chicago—that's where his television show was done. I had another screenplay optioned, a western set during the Civil War, called *Bugler and the Rifleman*. We were gonna shoot it in Israel but it's a big piece, an epic piece, and it would have cost a lot of money. It fell by the wayside, but that's okay. I'm old now, 75, which is cool, and I have no hurts.

Linda Marlowe
Actor

Foxy ladies kicking ass were a staple of 1970s action movies, particularly in the low-budget sphere. America offered up the likes of Anne Randall in *Stacey* (1973), Connie Stevens in *Scorchy* (76) and Pam Grier in her AIP star vehicles. The best known British examples of the sub-genre are *The Big Zapper* (1973) and its sequel *Zapper's Blade of Vengeance* (1974), both starring Linda Marlowe. We're talking 1970s movies here so Emma Peel and Modesty Blaise don't count.

The man behind these movies was Lindsay Shonteff. An independent filmmaker of admirable tenacity, he specialized in bootleg Bond movies with leading men like Nicky Henson and Gareth Hunt, who biffed and quipped as expertly as the real thing. Marlowe didn't let the side down either. In Finland they called her "Lady Bond," in Hong Kong "Dirty Harriet."

Her pre–Zapper action credits include appearances on *The Saint* (1962–69), *The Informer* (1966–67), *Callan* (1967–72) and the Ted Willis-devised, 007-inspired period adventure series *Virgin of the Secret Service* (1968), and in numerous movies such as *Impact* (1963) for prolific B-movie producers Butchers, *The Man Outside* (1967) a British spy movie starring Van Heflin, the Stanley Baker-produced *Robbery* (1967), and Shonteff's *Night After Night After Night* (1969).

When did you leave Australia?

When I was ten. My parents were English, my dad was an actor and he decided that he wanted to come back to London so we all travelled on a boat and from then I never left London.

Did you have any friends in London's ex-pat Australian acting community?

Only Peter Finch. My father and he acted together all the time in Australia and they were very good friends. The Oliviers discovered Peter

Finch and brought him to England, and not long after that we left Australia. When we arrived in England, Peter Finch and his wife found us a flat near them, and we resumed our friendship.

Did you study acting?

I wanted to be a dancer first, I wanted to be a ballerina so I went to ballet schools, but then I wasn't going to be good enough to be a ballerina so I decided I would be an actress and I went to the Central School of Speech and Drama, one of the top drama schools in London. Then I went into rep, I even did weekly rep, which is a great training ground. If you go into a company for six months and you do lots of different parts, it's a wonderful way of learning your craft. Unfortunately people can't do that any more and they sit around waiting to be on television and some of them never really learn to be actors properly.

Did your parents help you pursue an acting career?

Yes. They weren't over the moon to begin with, they would have liked me to further my education and maybe do something else because they knew what a tough profession it was, but they didn't stop me and they let me go to drama school when I said I definitely wasn't going to do any further education and was going to be an actress, come what may. My mother's still alive, she's ninety-five. My father died twenty years ago, sadly. A lot of my success has come since he died, with the Royal Shakespeare Company, working at the Old Vic with exciting directors, and I wish he'd lived to see that. I think he would've been very proud that I was able to continue because his life wasn't as easy, he found it difficult to make money when we came to England. He worked as an actor for quite a long time, then got a restaurant, did other things. But I wish he was around because I feel I have had a successful career.

What can you tell us about the movie The World Ten Times Over *[1963]?*

That was one of the earlier ones. There was another one called *That Kind of Girl* [1963] and also I had a tiny part in *Becket* [1964] with Peter O'Toole and Richard Burton. They were all about the same time, literally in my first years out of drama school. On *The World Ten Times Over* I remember not liking the director very much, he was a bit of a bully, Wolf somebody or other.

Wolf Rilla.

I wasn't mad keen on him, he was a very unpleasant man. He put me down, he made me feel stupid, it wasn't a very happy experience. It was nice working with Sylvia Sims and June Ritchie. I've met Sylvia Sims in later life, we met up through her daughter who was a friend of mine, we worked together and then I met Sylvia again, probably about 18 years ago. I did a lot of that kind of film in the early sixties, genre films that were what they call B-movies.

Like Impact *and* Spaceflight IC1 *[1965].*

I enjoyed doing those. *Spaceflight IC1* was fun, I did it in one of the studios, I think it was Elstree, and I think I died in it!

You moved into bigger films with The Americanization of Emily *[1964] and* The Man Outside.

The Man Outside was with Van Heflin. He was a big film star, I certainly remember that! Van Heflin seemed very nice, he was very nice to me, very amiable, not difficult. I mean, I didn't get to know him, but…

He wasn't mean like Wolf Rilla.

Oh God no, he was lovely. No, I haven't thought of anyone who was mean apart from Wolf Rilla, so he obviously was really mean! I had a tiny, tiny part in *The Americanization of Emily*, I played one of the army girls.

How would you compare working on them to working on a B-movie?

Well, obviously they had a lot more time and a lot more money. I did a film called *Tam-Lin* [1971] with Ava Gardner and I was on it for eight weeks. I didn't have a big part in that but I was filming it for eight weeks. I got to know her because she was always asking us all out for dinner, she didn't like being on her own. Roddy McDowall was the director and he was lovely, I loved working with him, he was a sweetheart and a wonderful actor as well.

Do you think directors who have been actors approach their work differently?

I think so. In the theater too. They understand actors and they know how to get the best out of an actor, because they've learned from their own experiences.

How do you get the best out of an actor?
Well, you've got to be able to put yourself in their shoes, not make them feel foolish, give them an atmosphere where they feel they can dare to do things and it won't be wrong, that anything you try is right, because whatever you try is leading towards finding what's right in the end. There are a lot of directors who don't do that, they just criticize or they say, "No, you can't do that." You should be able to try everything and find what the best way is and I think that actors understand that.

What are your memories of Robbery?
I only did that for fun. My first husband Bill Marlowe, who's now dead, played one of the gang, and because I was married to him they asked me if I wanted to play his girlfriend. The sad thing about *Robbery* is that Stanley Baker really wanted to promote young actors and signed Bill up to his company, but then the British film industry virtually collapsed. Suddenly there was no money, and Stanley could no longer keep people under contract. It was an exciting time and then it all went bad and it took a very long time for the British film industry to recover and I'm not sure it ever did.

A lot of people remember you from The Big Zapper.
I did all my own stunts so that was fun. There was nothing like special effects in those days so if you had to look like you were flying, you had to jump on a trampoline, the higher you jumped the more they could make it look like you were flying through the air. Things like that, the physical stuff, I really enjoyed. I'm a physical actor, I'm a physical theater performer as well, I'm even a trapeze artist so I've always liked to do physically daring things.

The Big Zapper *must have been successful to warrant making the sequel,* Zapper's Blade of Vengeance.
Not in this country, in the Far East apparently, but they weren't very good films. Funnily enough the BFI is bringing them out on DVD, they seem to be very interested in all of these films that I did back then. *That Kind of Girl* is coming out on DVD as well. I keep saying, "But they're awful!" and they say, "No, they're not awful, they're very interesting films of the time and *That Kind of Girl* is actually quite a good film."

Lindsay Shonteff was a rarity at the time, a commercial independent.

Well, absolutely, and he managed to make films and put the money back in to make another film, so he was actually operating on his own and I admired him for that. I did three films for him, actually, I did the two *Zapper* films and I did another one as well, *Night After Night After Night*. I met up with him again after a long time and he was very sad because his wife had died and he adored her. He was a lovely man, I enjoyed working with him. He didn't make very good films, but I admired his enthusiasm and his desire to keep churning these films out.

Linda Marlowe bops a baddie in director Lindsay Shonteff's *The Big Zapper* (1973).

What about Alan Lake, your co-star in Zapper's Blade of Vengeance?

Alan Lake was lovely. I mean, he drank a lot and he lived hard and fast but he was a real sweetheart. He was married to Diana Dors and when I met her, at a party or something, she said to me, "Linda Marlowe, you're the sexiest woman in this room." I thought that was quite good coming from Diana Dors!

You've worked a lot with Steven Berkoff.

I met Steven Berkoff in the early seventies and that was a big change, my career went off in a different direction. I was his leading lady for some years, throughout the 1970s and '80s. I sort of killed my commercial work; I still managed to do television in between, some big series, but I did an awful lot more theater. Working with Steven in the theater became much more interesting for me than if I'd stayed doing more conventional work. He was the first person in England to bring physical theater to England, because of his work with Jacques Le Coq and his own imaginative style. He wrote a play for us to do together called *Decadence*, which was a huge success.

Would you say that both Steven Berkoff and Lindsay Shonteff were mavericks?

Absolutely, very much so. Very different and in a completely different way, but very, very maverick people, which is what attracted me to them, actually. Steven's work in the theater was always praised by the critics because it was so wonderful, but both of them were outsiders, they were never really part of the establishment. People always viewed them as a bit odd, they really had to fight for what they did.

Stanley Baker was similarly independent-minded.

He was, he was another maverick character. He got his film company together, employed young actors, put people under contract and tried to set up something like the American studio system. He was very ahead of his time.

Your career has been equally adventurous. You've had a go at everything.

Absolutely, I was always a bit of a maverick as well, I always wanted to do something different. For three years in the seventies I left acting and started a female rock group with two other girls, called the Sadista Sisters. We released an album and toured around everywhere and were quite successful. Then maybe ten years ago I decided to concentrate on doing solo shows. I'm getting pretty old and I thought maybe work was going to dry up, and in fact Steven said, "Why don't you do a solo show? take the power into your own hands." I did and it was so successful that I've now got six shows and my own company, and they take me all over the world. I'm off to Zimbabwe next week and I was in Georgia last week. I'm always busy because I created work for myself. I never stop working which is a pretty good thing in your late sixties, to be never stopping.

Peter Mark Richman
Actor

If you've watched any action television series from the period this book covers, chances are you'll know Peter Mark Richman's face; he appeared in more of them than anybody I could nominate, playing "smooth and steely" villains and hard-ass authority figures on well-remembered shows like *Combat!* (1962–67), *The F.B.I.* (1965–74) and *It Takes a Thief* (1968–70), and ripe-for-excavation shows like *T.H.E. Cat* (1966–67), *Search* (1972–73) and *The Silent Force* (1970–71).

He worked in live television in the 1950s, made movies with lofty names like William Wyler, Gary Cooper and Sophia Loren, and starred as Nick Cain in the gangster series *Cain's Hundred* (1961–62). The fact that Robert Altman, Irvin Kershner, Tom Gries, Sydney Pollack and Buzz Kulik directed episodes of the latter should tip you that it was kinda good.

Trying his hand at the super-spy bit, he headlined *Agent for H.A.R.M.* (1966), directed with typical visual flair by Gerd Oswald.

He was also one of the stars of *Longstreet* (1971–72), a series about a blind detective created by writer-producer Stirling Siliphant and featuring Bruce Lee in a recurring role.

Anybody who's watched any 1960s or 1970s television knows your face. You were always going up against Efrem Zimbalist on The F.B.I.!

I was a resident bad guy on *The F.B.I.*, I was nine or ten different bad guys throughout the years. That was one of my favorite shows and Quinn Martin was one of my favorite people. He was a terrific producer, a wonderful writer, and a very nice man, you could talk to him. He had a whole coterie of actors that he hired again and again and I was one of them.

Was it ever emotionally draining going to work and mustering all that villainous intensity?

Not really. I could turn it on and off. I had a poor childhood and a lot of stress growing up!

You worked with Robert Wagner several times, on It Takes a Thief *and* Switch *[1975–78].*

He was a good friend and a hell of a funny guy. He was also great to work with because he had good habits professionally. A lot of television stars forget what they're there for, they become imbued with the celebrity stuff. I remember doing *Gunsmoke* [1955–75] and being told that Jim Arness wasn't going to do off-camera lines for my close-ups, I'd be doing them with an assistant. I said, "The fuck I am! I'm going back to my dressing room and if Jim doesn't show up I'm not doing the show." Well, that got their attention! Not that Jim Arness wasn't a good fella, but sometimes assistant directors try and make points for themselves by not troubling the star with off-camera stuff.

You worked with Bruce Lee on the series Longstreet.

He was a nice kid but he was like a taut wire, very tense, like he was going to explode at any moment. We did a scene where he tried to show James Franciscus' character how to do kung fu and I say, "Stop all that crap" and try to give him a boxing lesson. We then had a little fight, which he won of course!

The first series you starred in was Cain's Hundred.

I was a New York actor doing live television, *Philco Television Playhouse* [1948–55], *Studio One* [1948–58], *Playhouse* 90 [1956–61] and shows like that. I was going out to California to shoot a lot of stuff, guest starring on television shows, but I didn't move out there until *Cain's Hundred* presented itself, because that was the first time I was offered a long-term contract. I played Nick Cain, a lawyer who represented mob figures but wanted to quit. They tried to bump him off and accidentally killed his fiancée so he started a campaign to get revenge, to indict and prosecute the top hundred gangsters, one by one. It was a very good series, before its time, but I only shot 30, 31 episodes. NBC was concerned about the level of violence on their shows and they cancelled *Cain's Hundred*.

Some talented directors worked on Cain's Hundred, *people like Irvin Kershner.*

Nowhere to run. Peter Mark Richman and guest star Barbara Eden sell the MGM series *Cain's Hundred* (1961–62) (courtesy Peter Mark Richman).

Irv Kershner was a very, very fine director, innovative and courageous. He took chances getting the shot, not always in favor of the actors. It was kind of a dangerous situation because he went to the edge. He did the pilot, that's when I first met him, and we became very close through the years.

Masters of the Shoot-'Em-Up

Working in television in the 1950s must have been very exciting.

The late '50s was innovative. Today the network executives have too much power, the wives of network executives have too much power, and all the shows are the same. The '50s was fresh and exciting, it was the beginning of television drama and comedy and it was a cauldron of very talented directors and actors, New York actors, building careers.

Directors like John Frankenheimer.

He was a terrific director. He hired me to do *Clash by Night*, the Clifford Odets play, for *Playhouse 90*. I came out to Hollywood to do it but when I went to the first reading they started cutting down my part, so I went back to the hotel, called my agent and told him to get me out of there. John Frankenheimer apologized and promised he'd bring me back in a couple of weeks to do another show. He offered me a part as a gunslinger in a show with Sterling Hayden called "The Last Man." My wife was seven months pregnant at the time and I told them that I didn't think I should leave her. They asked if she could act and I said, "Yes, she's a very good actress," and they gave her the part of Sterling Hayden's pregnant wife!

Television production was very fast in those days. Did speed have its advantages? Or did you prefer the slower pace of working on features?

It has its advantages and disadvantages, but I'm adaptable and sometimes there's too much time on a feature. When I did *Friendly Persuasion*, my first film, the contract was for nine weeks and I stayed for four and a half months. A lot of the time I was just sitting around.

It's pretty good to start your film career in a William Wyler film starring Gary Cooper.

I loved Gary Cooper. He took us to dinner at Romanoff's during the shoot and was terrific guy. He was very learned and well-read, the opposite of what you might think [because of his] "Yup, ma'am" image. Wyler saw a piece of film that I did, a *Philco Television Playhouse* called "The Bold and the Brave," his assistant showed him the kinescope, and Wyler said, "He's a good actor, but can he be a nice guy?" I was somewhere in Massachusetts at the time, staying in a cabin in the woods, touring in *The Rainmaker* with Eva Marie Saint. She knocked on my door and said, "You better call your agent because they want you in New York today,

Wyler wants to meet you." So I got a plane and it blew a tire on takeoff and I almost got killed, but I got to New York and had a very good meeting with Wyler at the St. Regis Hotel. He said, "Don't take anything until you hear from me" and a week later I got the part.

Dark Intruder [1965] sounds interesting.

It was a hell of a film. Harvey Hart, the director, was a Canadian, I met him when he hired me for a television show that was like a Canadian *Playhouse 90*. It was a terrific piece of work, I was very pleased with my part, and we really struck a relationship that was pure gold. I owned the rights to the Philip Roth book *Letting Go* and we formed a production company to make a movie of it. Harvey Hart broke down the book and I wrote a screenplay and we almost got it done.

You also worked very closely with director Ted Post.

I loved him, he was a dear man and there's nobody who accomplished more than he did in film and television. He directed me in *The Twilight Zone* [1959–65], *Combat!* and several other things. We became very good friends and much later I hired him to direct a piece I wrote called *4 Faces* [1999]. It was a play first, a one-man show where I played four different people. I was invited by Arthur Penn to perform it at the Actors Studio and did twenty-one performances. Then a very wealthy friend of mine, John Crean, may he rest in peace, put up the money to make a film. It's never been released commercially, I don't know why, maybe because it has no sex and violence in it! But I won an award for it and it played many film festivals.

Tell me about your involvement with the Actors Studio.

I got into it in 1954 after appearing in a production called *End as a Man*. It was a smash hit that ran for about six months and there were a lot of wonderful actors in it, people like Anthony Franciosa, who held my hat and said, "Yes sir!" I studied privately with Lee Strasberg and he was the guiding force behind the Actors Studio. Lee was a great teacher and solidified my approach to acting. He focused on an actor's individuality and gave them the confidence to use all the powers and abilities they had. Actors all have a method, many teachers contribute to that, and the longer you work, the more confident you get in your approach. But Lee Strasberg was a great influence on me.

Barbara Bouchet aims to please, while Peter Mark Richman gets to grips with Alizia Gur. An Italian "fotobusta" for Universal's *Agent for H.A.R.M.* (1966).

How do you go about creating a character?

I read the script many times, concentrating on the dialogue. I don't memorize it by rote, and I don't lock in how I'm going to say the lines too soon, but I try and become so familiar with it that it's not an appendage, it's the character speaking. Then, depending on whether it's a character role or a straight leading man, I might use a dialect or a walk or some other idiosyncrasy. Most people, if you watch them, have idiosyncratic characteristics that you can adapt for your part and I enjoy doing that.

Can you remember anything about making Agent for H.A.R.M.*?*

I was on a motorcycle a lot! Gerd Oswald was a good director, but the film was not very good. It was done as a pilot for me, and the next thing I know it was released theatrically. It made a lot of money for Universal because it was made relatively inexpensively. Alizia Gur was one of the femme fatales in it—she was Miss Israel, a beautiful girl. My wife and I are still good friends with her and she still looks terrific.

What are your memories of working with Sophia Loren on The Black Orchid *[1959]?*

She was unbelievable. I was standing on a set at Paramount, the steps of an apartment building, when I first saw her. She walked past in jeans and a tight sweater and she was the most beautiful, sexy broad that I have ever seen. We sat around a table and read the script for a week, and she'd look at me and bat her eyes and I'd just fall apart. My wife was pregnant at the time and I'd come home and tell her all about Sophia Loren, which probably wasn't a very nice thing to do to your pregnant wife!

How'd you get the part?

I already knew the director, Marty Ritt, from the Actors Studio. I was shooting a *Playhouse 90* with John Frankenheimer, we were doing a dress rehearsal and I got an urgent phone call from Marty. He said he had a part for me, but he wanted me to come in and meet the producers, Carlo Ponti and Marcello Girosi, first. I said, "Well, Marty, do you have a part for me or does it depend on the producers?" and he said, "Schmuck! You got the part!"

Bibliography

Brooks, Tim, and Earle Marsh. *The Complete Directory to Prime Time Network TV Shows, 1946–Present*. New York: Ballantine, 1985.
Gifford, Denis. *The British Film Catalogue, 1895–1970*. London: David and Charles, 1973.
Halliwell, Leslie. *Halliwell's Film Guide*. London: HarperCollins, 1996.
_____, with Philip Purser. *Halliwell's Television Companion*. London: Paladin, 1982.
Maltin, Leonard. *Leonard Maltin's Movie Guide*. New York: Plume, 2007.
Vahimagi, Tise, and the British Film Institute. *British Television: An Illustrated Guide*. New York: Oxford University Press, 1996.

Index

Numbers in ***bold italics*** indicate pages with photographs.

The A-Team 129, 143, 151–152, 157–158
ABC (U.K.) 6
ABC (U.S.) 154, 179
Academy Awards 154, 199–200
Accidental Family 101
The Actors Studio 211, 213
Adam at 6 A.M. 146–147
Adam-12 129, 133
Adams, Peter 80
Adams, Tom 118, 123
Adorf, Mario 192
The Adventures of the Wilderness Family 37
The African Queen 11
The Age of Consent 34
Agee, James 11
Agent for H.A.R.M. 207, ***212***
Albert, Eddie ***166***
Ali, Muhammad 114
Alias Smith and Jones 155
Allen, Dede 131
Allen, Elizabeth 182
Allen, Woody 4
Allied Artists 99
Almeria 190
The Alpha Caper 98, 102–104, ***103***
Altman, Robert 207
Alzado, Lyle 67
Amarcord 60
The Ambushers 161–***163***
American Film Institute 62, 63
American International Pictures 20, 129, 188, 201
The Americanization of Emily 203
Amicus 127
Anderson, Gerry 178
The Andy Griffith Show 101
Angels from Hell 129
Anhalt, Edward 147
Annakin, Ken 32, 35
Annett, Paul 118–128, ***127***
Annis, Francesca 122
Antonio, Lou 76

The Apartment 129, 162
The Arena 59, 61
Arkoff, Samuel Z. 188
Armitage, George 59
Armstrong, R.G. 59, 66
Arness, James 208
Arnold, Alan 81
Ashby, Hal 100
Associated London Scripts 26, 33
ATV 5, 119, 120
Avco Embassy 63
The Avengers 3, 6, 168, 176
Averback, Hy 15

Bacall, Lauren 20, 21
Bad Day at Black Rock 147
Badlands 68
Baer, Max 108
Bagge, Brian 124
Baker, Robert S. 91, 95
Baker, Stanley 168, 173–***174***, 201, 204, 206
Band, Albert 178
Band, Charles 178, 185–186
The Bank Job 44
Bardot, Brigitte 119
Baretta 129
Barker, Lex 29
Barker, Ronnie 45
Barnaby Jones 79
Barrett, Ray 31, 34
Barrett, Tony 101
Bartel, Paul 59, 62
Basinger, Kim 76
The Battle for The Battle of Britain 118–120, 122–123
The Battle of Britain 119–120, 122–123
Battles 151, 160
Battlestar Galactica 155
BBC 27, 86, 95
The Beast Must Die 118, 121, 126–128
The Beatles 170
Beatty, Warren 131

Index

Becket 202
Bellamy 80
Bellamy, Earl 73
Ben Casey 188
Bening, Annette 145
Bennett, Harve 101–102
Bennett, Joe 133
Bergen, Candice 13
Berger, Senta **30**
Berkoff, Steven 205–206
BFI 204
Big Bad Mama 10, 13, 59–62
The Big Valley 11
The Big Zapper 201, 204–***205***
Billy Jack 63
Billy Jack Goes to Washington 63
Birney, David 98
Blackbelt Jones 178
Blackfather 22
The Black Orchid 213
Black Rodeo 108, 114
The Blacks 200
Blake, Katharine 34
Blanc, Erica ***191***
Blier, Bernard 48
Bloody Mama 61
Bloom, Claire 95
Bluey 80, 89
Boardwalk 23
Bochco, Steven 102
Bogart, Humphrey 21, 172
Bogdanovich, Peter 178, 183
The Bold and the Brave 210
Bond, James1, 2, 26, 31, 36, 70, 98, 106, 118–119, 123, 135, 161, 163–164, 168, 175–176, 179, 180, 187, 191, 201
Bonnie and Clyde 10, 129, 131
Booth, James 168
Border Cop 51
The Borderers 121
Borgnine, Ernest 36, 38
Bouchet, Barbara ***212***
Box, Sydney 31–32
Boxcar Bertha 65
Boyle, Peter 110
Brackett, Leigh 16, 21–22
Bradford, Richard 3
Brando, Marlon 70, 72, 168
Brannigan 10, 15
Breakheart Pass 70, 73, 74
Bregman, Martin 107, 110, 113
Brennan, Walter 101
The Bridge on the River Kwai 45
Briggs, Johnny 170–173

Bringing Up Baby 21
Broccoli, Albert "Cubby" 36, 119, 164, 168
Broken Arrow 187
Brolin, James 36, ***39***, 43
Bronson, Charles 44, 74, 78, 161, 164–165
Browne, Howard 67
Bryce, John 6
Buchan, John 1
Buckstone County Prison 108
Bugler and the Rifleman 200
Bujold, Genevieve 14
Bullet Proof 59, 67
Bullitt 1, 143, 147
Bullshot 44, 47
Burke's Law 16, 18
Burton, Richard 87, 119, 194, 202
Busey, Gary 67
Butch Cassidy and the Sundance Kid 155
Butchers 201
Byron, Jeffrey 178–186, ***180***

Caan, James 145
Caesar, Adolph 51, 53–57
Caine, Michael 93, 120, 170
Cain's Hundred 207–***209***
The California Quarterly 11
Callan 121, 201
Callas, Charlie 161
Calvert, Phyllis 121
Cambridge, Godfrey 195, 198
Cameron, John 178
Camfield, Douglas 177
Cannell, Stephen J. 2, 70, 78–79, 132, 143–144, 151, 155–158
Cannes Film Festival 185, 189
Cannon 151, 160, 195, 198
Capone 59, 61, 65, 67–68
Capra, Frank, Jr. 63
Capucine 40
Carlisle, John 118, 123
Caron, Leslie 71
Carradine, David 65, 68, 104
Carson, Johnny 77
Carver, Steve 16, 22, 23, 59–69
Cash, Rosalind 195
Castellari, Enzo G. 1
Catch Me a Spy 44, 47–50, ***49***
"Caution, Lemmy" 91–92
CBS 24, 144, 147
The Central School of Speech and Drama 202
Cerrato, Massimo 194

Index

Champion 111
Chapman, Leigh 16–25, *17*
Charade 48–49
Charley Varrick 151–152
Charlie's Angels 151
Charro! 143, 145–146
The Chase (novel) 21
Chase, David 132
Chase, James Hadley 91, 94
Chicago Film Festival 57
The Children's Hour 163
Childs, Ted 6
CHiPs 187
Christie, Agatha 29
Cimarron 70
Cinecittà 60, 194
Clambake 15
Clark, Dick 131
Clark, Petula 119
Clarke, Cecil 5
Clash by Night 210
Cleary, John 32
Cleaver, Eldridge 198
Clemens, Brian 6
Clement, Dick 44–50
Cleopatra 194
Clouse, Robert 1, 178–***180***
Coburn, James 36, 38–***39***, 135, 166, 183
Code Seven, Victim Five 26
Codename: Jaguar 135
Cohen, Larry 98
Cohn Curtis, Bruce 45
Cole, Muriel 169, 171, 177
Colicos, John 68
Colla, Richard 102
Collins, Joan 122
Columbia 34, 45, 163
Combat! 16, 18, 207, 211
Come Back, Charleston Blue 195, 197–198
The Comedy Man 32, 97
Condorman 178
Connery, Sean 93, 163–164, 175–176
Connors, Chuck 99
Conrad, Robert 19, 70, 77, 143
Conrad, William 151, 160, 198
Constantine, Eddie 91–95
Convoy 10
Conway, Gary 80–90
Coogan's Bluff 155
Cooper, Gary 14, 100, 207, 210
Cooper, Freddie 50
Cooper, Jackie 185
Cop Shop 80

Corbett, Glenn 166, 178
Corbucci, Sergio 187
Cord, Alex 63
Corman, Roger 10, 13, 14–59, 60–62, 65, 67, 106, 108
Cornelius, Don 200
Cosby, Bill 73, 76, 197
Cotton Comes to Harlem 195
Courtenay, Tom 44, 46, 170
Craig, Bill 8
Crawford, Dorothy 80, 84, 88
Crawford, Hector 80–83, 88, 89
Crawford, Ian 81
Crawford Productions 80–90
Crean, John 211
Crenna, Richard 101
Crime Sheet 168
Cronin, Paul 83
Cronyn, Hume 194
Crossplot 91, 95
The Cruel Sport 130
Culp, Robert 73, 76, 77
Curtis, Tony 168, 174–175
Curtiz, Michael 145
Cushing, Peter 123
Cutter 195–197, ***196***, 200

Daley, Robert 130
Damon, Mark 59–60
Damon, Stuart 91
Dan August 161, 164, 195, 198
Daneman, Paul 123
Danton, Ray 135, 137
Dark Intruder 211
Darker Than Amber 178
Davenport, Nigel 178–179
David Cassidy—Man Undercover 24
Davis, Sammy, Jr. 119
Davison, Bruce 78
Davy Crockett and the River Pirates 70
The Day of the Cobra 1
Dead Center 59
Dead Reckoning 105–106
Dean, James 104
DeAnda, Peter 195–200, ***196***
Death Valley Days 187
Decadence 206
Dee, Sandra 194
Deeley, Michael 173
De Masi, Francesco 60
Demme, Jonathan 59
De Paolis Studios 194
The Desert Rats 87
Desilu 71

Index

Devane, William 137
Dial 999 26–28, 91
Diamonds Are Forever 161, 163
The Diary of Anne Frank 100
Dickinson, Angie 62, 198–199
Dierdrich, John 90
Dillon, Carmen 47, 50
Directors Guild 145, 153–154
Dirty Harry 152
Dirty Mary Crazy Larry 16, 20–22
Disney, Walt 181
Division 4 80, 82, 84–86
Dixon of Dock Green 6
Django 187
Dobson, Tamara 155
Doctor Who 33
Doel, Frances 14
Dog and Cat 70, 76
Dog Day Afternoon 107
Doleman, Guy 31
The Don Is Dead 70
Donner, Richard 2, 133, 145
Donovan, Terence 80, 85–86, 89
Donovan's Reef 178, 181–183
Don't Sleep Alone 106
Dors, Diana 93, 205
Douglas, Gordon 76
Douglas, Josephine 119
Douglas, Kirk 44, 48, *49*, 108, 110–113, *112*, 115–117, *116*
Douglas, Michael 74–*75*, 146
Douglass, Charley 101
Dreyfuss, Richard 12
Drum 59, 61, 68
Drummond, Bulldog 44, 47
Dryer, Fred 78
The Dukes of Hazzard 108, 110, 151
Durning, Charles 117

Eastenders 5, 118, 121, 126
Eastwood, Clint 24, 78, 190–191
Echo Four-Two 26
Eddie Macon's Run 108, 110–115, *112*
Eden, Barbara *209*
Edwards, Glyn 168
Edwards, Vince 188
Eischied 24
Ekberg, Anita *106*–107
El Cid 71
Elios Studios 60
Elphick, Michael 177
Elstree Studios 203
Embassy Pictures 109
Emergency-Ward Ten 123

The Emmy Awards 199, 200
End as a Man 211
The Enforcer 178
English Language Dubbing Association 192
Enter the Dragon 1, 178–179
Eon Productions 118–119
The Equalizer 178
Espionage 26
Euston Films 80
The Expendables 117
An Eye for an Eye 59, 63–*64*

Falk, Peter 197
The Fall Guy 129, 151
Fassbinder, Rainer Werner 92
Fast Charlie, the Moonbeam Rider 59, 65, 68
The F.B.I. 207
Feldon, Barbara *103*
Fell, Norman 198
Fellini 60
Ferzetti, Fausto 190
Ferzetti, Gabrielle 190
Fever Grass 29
Fields, Sid 22
Finch, Peter 201–202
Finch, Scot 126
Fine, Mort 80
Fink, Rita 16
Finlay, Frank 168
Finney, Albert 92, 170
A Fistful of Dollars 187, 190–193
Flatt and Scruggs 131
Fleischer, Richard 70, 195
Florance, Sheila 89
Fonda, Henry 98, 102–104, *103*, 181
Forbes, Bryan 178
Ford, John 178, 181–183
Foreman, Carl 45
Foster, Barry 168, 173
Foster, Meg *75*
4 Faces 211
The Four Preps 155
Franciosa, Anthony 135, 159, 211
Francis, Raymond 168, 172
Franciscus, James 208
Frank, Harriet 16
Frankenheimer, John 129–130, 133, 210, 213
Franklin, Richard 80
Fraud Squad 3, 118, 120–121, 126
Frazer, Shiela 52–53
Freebie and the Bean (series) 70, 129

220

Index

Freedman, Jerrold 12
The French Connection 1, 114
Friendly Persuasion 99, 100, 210–211
Frost, David 29

Galton, Ray 26
Gambon, Michael 121
Gantman, Joe 105
Gardner, Arthur 10–11, 13–14
Gardner, Ava 203
Gardner, John 26
Garfield, John 149
Garner, James 132
Gastone, Liza 193
Gator 10, *13*
Gavin, John 36
Gaye, Marvin 200
Gazzara, Ben 67–69
Geeson, Judy 124
George, Christopher 166
George, Roger 68
Gerber, David 24
Get Christie Love 151, 154–*155*
The Getaway 70, 73, 76
Ghost Squad 26
Girosi, Marcello 213
Godard, Jean-Luc 92
The Godfather 21
Golan, Menahem 59
The Golden Globes 199–200
Goldwyn, Samuel 119
Goldwyn, Samuel, Jr. 198
Gomer Pyle, U.S.M.C. 101
'good ol' boy' movies 1, 10, 13, 108
Goodbye, Mr. Chips 119
Gordon, Larry 76, 131
Gores, Joe 2
Gossett, Lou 197
Grade, Lew 3
The Graduate 109
Granada Television 27
Grand Prix 130
Grant, Cary 48–49, 100
Grass 118, 124
Graves, Teresa 154–*155*
The Great Escape 147
The Great Locomotive Chase 70–71
Green, Les 104
The Green Berets 20
Greene, Lorne 98, *103*
Greenhill, Georgie 90
Greif, Leslie 24
Greyn, Clinton 168
Grier, Pam 61, 155, 201

Gries, Tom 70, 73–74, 207
Griff 98, 102–*103*
Grills, Lucky 80, 89–90
Grosvenor, Dennis 80
The Grundy Organisation 80
Guardino, Harry 68, *155*
Guest, Val 168
Gunfight at the O.K. Corral 108
Guns in the Heather 178
Gunsmoke 76, 208
Gur, Alizia *212*

Hackman, Gene 13, 110
Hagman, Larry 98, *103*
Hale, William 74
Hamilton, Guy 118, 120, 123, 164
Hamilton, Ted 89
Hammond, P.J. 8
Handmade Films 47
Hannibal Brooks 44
The Hard Ride 187
Hard Times 51
Hardcastle and McCormick 143–144, 151
Hargrove, Dean 2, 70, 195
Harris, Ben 51
Harris, Richard (actor) 72
Harris, Richard (writer) 3–9
Harrison, Doane 129, 163
Harrison, Rex 194
Harry-O 98
Hart, Harvey 211
Hawaii Five-O 151, 159
Hawks, Howard 16, 20–22, 129–130, 133, 143, 145
Hayden, Sterling 210
Hayes, Isaac *20*
Hazell 3, 6, 7
HBO 1
Heart of Darkness 14
The Heat's On 195
Heflin, Van 201, 203
Hempel, Anoushka 26
Hendry, Ian 6
Henry V 47
Henson, Nicky 201
Hepburn, Audrey 49
Hepburn, Katharine 18, 21
Herbert, Percy 178
Herbie Goes to Monte Carlo 179
Hercules Unchained 192
Herman, Gary 53
Herman, Norman 21
Heston, Charlton 63, 166
Hiawatha 188

Index

Hickey & Boggs 76
Hickman, Gail Morgan 178
Hickox, Douglas 10, 15
High Chaparral 187
High Noon 45
High Risk 36–42, **39**, **41**
Highway Patrol 187
Hildyard, Jack **127**–128
Hill, Phil 130
Hill, Walter 76
Himes, Chester 195
Hitchcock, Alfred 62
The Hitter 51–58
H.M. Tennant 5
Hoffman, Dustin 104
Holden, William 40, 171–172
Holliman, Earl 187–188
Homicide 80–85, 87–88
Hopkins, Anthony 179
Hough, John 16
How the West Was Won 71
Howard, Trevor 34, 40
HUAC 11
Hudson, Rock 104, 197
Huggins, Roy 2, 155
Hunt, Gareth 201
Hunter (Australian series) 85
Hunter (U.S. series) 1, 70, 78–79, 143, 151
Hunter's Walk 3
The Hunting Party 10, 13
Hyde-White, Wilfrid 29

I Spy 73–74, 76, 78, 101
The Ice Pirates 36, 42
Impact 201, 203
Impulse 24
In Like Flint 135, 183
The Informer 201
Innes, George 176
International Detective 26
International Velvet 179
The Invincible Seven 187
Irma La Douce 162
The Iron Horse 16
It Takes a Thief 16, 129, 207–208
ITC 3, 91

Jackson, Glenda 122
Jacobi, Derek 169
Jaffe, Sam 63
Jake and the Fatman 70, 151, 160
James, Clifton 151, 195
James, Donald 168
Jarrott, Charles 122

Jason King 168, 176
Jaws 3-D 186
The Jericho Mile 179
Jessica 33
Jigsaw 168
Jobert, Marléne 44, 48–**49**
Johnson, Don 133
The Jokers 44
Jones, Freddie 45
Jones, Ian 81, 85
Jones, L.Q. 59, 66
Jones, Tom 119
Jordan, Patrick 168, **174**
The Judas Goat (novel) 135

Kanew, Jeff 108–17, **116**
Kansas City Bomber 12
Kaplan, Jonathan 59
Karloff, Boris 29
Karlson, Phil 108, 162
Kate 121
Katzin, Lee 101, 148
Keach, Stacy 195–196
Keith, Brian 14, 144
Kelly, Daniel Hugh 144
Kennedy, Gerard 80, 85
Kershner, Irvin 207–209
Kessler, Bruce 129–134
Kid Galahad 165
Kidder, Margot 179
Killers Three 129, 131
King Creole 145
Kinnear, Roy 178–179
Kirgo, George 105
Kirkpatrick, Maggie 80
Knots Landing 137
Kojak 2
Kolchak: The Night Stalker 132
Koslo, Paul 151
Kramer, Stanley 99–100
Kramer, Stepfanie 78
Kruse, John 95
Kulick, Buzz 207
Kung Fu 98, 104
Kwouk, Burt 178

Labro, Philippe 1
Lacey, Ronald 47
Ladies in Waiting 200
Lady Frankenstein 59
LaFont, Bernadette 48
La Frenais, Ian 44–46
Lake, Alan 205
Lakin, Rita 102, 105, 107

Index

Lamb, Irene 45
Lancaster, Burt 11, 108, 115, 117
Lange, Claudie 91
Larson, Glen A. 2, 151, 154–156, 161
The Last Bride of Salem 105
The Last Man 210
Last Train from Gun Hill 187–188
Laughlin, Tom 63
Lauter, Ed 195
Laven, Arnold 10–11, 13–14
The Law of the Lawless 16
Lawrence, Quentin 122–123
Lazenby, George 119
Le Coq, Jacques 206
Lee, Anna 181, 183–184
Lee, Bruce 179, 207–208
Lee, Christopher 93
Lee, David 81, 82
The Legend of Fra Diavalo 192
The Legend of Nigger Charley 114
Lehman, Val 80
Leigh, Vivien 201
Leitch, Chris 51–58
Le Mans 143, 147–148
Le Mesurier, John 29
Lemmon, Jack 163
Leonard, Sheldon 78, 101
Leonardi, Alberto 187
Leone, Sergio 64–65, 187, 190–191
Lethal Weapon 133
Letting Go 211
Levin, Henry 162
Levy, Jules 10–11, 13–14
Lewis, Jerry 145
Lewis, Robert M. 98–107, ***106***
Liberace 119
Licensed to Kill 118
The Lion 40
The Liquidator 26, 31
The Little Hut 169
Lloyd, Euan 126, 168
Logan, Robert 77
Lom, Herbert 29, 93
London, Jack 11
The London Connection 1, 178–182, ***180***
London Weekend Television 123–124
The Lone Wolf 187
Lone Wolf McQuade 59–60, 63–64
The Long Duel 32
Longstreet 207–208
Lord, Jack 159
Loren, Sophia 100, 189, 207, 213
Louis, Joe 99
Lucky the Inscrutable 135

Lye, Reg 31
Lyon, Francis D. 70

MacDonald, John D. 178
Maciste 192
MacLaine, Shirley 163
Macon County Line 108
Mad Max 178, 185
Magnani, Anna 194
The Magnificent Seven 22, 147, 161–162, 165, 167
Magnum PI 151
Maibaum, Richard 98, 106–107
"Make It Australian" campaign 89
Malden, Karl 72, 74–75
Mallick, Terrence 109
A Man Called Sloane 70, 77, 79
The Man from U.N.C.L.E. 16–***17***, 135
Man in a Suitcase 3
The Man Outside 201, 203
The Man Who Loved Cat Dancing 14, 143, 149
The Man Who Would Be King 93
Mancini, Ray "Boom Boom" 67
Mankiewicz, Joseph L. 194
Mann, Anthony 70, 71
Mannix 1
Man's Favorite Sport? 130
Margheriti, Antonio 187, 193
Marlowe, Linda 201–206, ***205***
Marlowe, William 168, ***174***, 204
Marshall, Roger 7, 8
Martin, Dean 76, 161–***163***
Martin, Quinn 2, 70, 74, 77–79, 161, 164, 207
Martini, Alberto 193
Marvin, Lee 62, 178
Mary Queen of Scots 122
Mason, James 34, 87
Massacesi, Aristide 60
Matlock Police 80, 83–85
Matt Helm 135
Maxwell, Marilyn 111
McClain's Law 129
McCloud 132, 151, 154–156
McDowell, Roddy 203
McEachin, James 98, ***103***
The McKenzie Break 10
McLaglen, Andrew V. 70
McMillan and Wife 98, 102, 165, 185
McQueen, Steve 19, 65, 73–74, 78, 143, 146–148
McStay, Mike 168–177, ***169***, ***174***
Mean Streets 151–152

223

Index

The Mechanic 161, 164
Medford, Don 13, 148
Melinda 151
Mellion, John 31
Men in War 70-71
Metalstorm: The Destruction of Jared-Syn 178, 185-186
MGM 31, 42, 71, 209
Miami Vice 133
Midway 161, 166-167
Miles, Sarah
Milestone, Lewis 72
Milius, John 14
Miller, Mark *103*
Miller, Ron 181
Milligan, Spike 26-27
Mirisch, Walter 65, 148
The Mirisch Company 129, 148
Mission: Impossible 16, 149
Mr. T *157*
Mitchell 70
Mitchum, Robert 13, 166
The Mod Squad 98, 101-102
Modesty Blaise 201
Montague, Lee 178, *182*
Moore, Roger 91, 95, 168, 170, 174-176
More, Kenneth 32, 97
Morituri 72
Morricone, Ennio 60
Mosley, Roger E. 195
Moving Violation 10, 14
Mozambique 26
Mulinar, Rod 88
Murder Bag 168
Murder in Texas 74
Murphy, Audie 189
Murray, Billy 118, 124
Mutiny on the Bounty 70, 72

Nathan, Paul 188
Nation, Terry 33
Natural Enemies 109-110, 114-115
NBC 179, 208
Neighbours 89
Nelson, B.J. 63
Nero, Franco 187
Nero Wolfe 151, 160
Never Say Never Again 44
The New Centurions 195-197
New Scotland Yard 6, 118, 123-124, 126
New Wave 92
Nicholson, Gerda 89
Nicholson, James H. 188
Nickelodeon 183

Night After Night After Night 201, 205
Night Crawler 20
Night of the Juggler 10
The Night They Took Miss Beautiful 98-99
Nimoy, Leonard 98, *103*
Nitro 12
No Hiding Place 3, 26, 168-177, *169*
No Room to Run 98, 105
Norris, Chuck 16, 23-24, 59, 63, *64*, 68, 70, 79
North, Sheree 98, 148
North by Northwest 91
Norton, Bill 10-15, 62
Norton, B.L. 10
Norton, Ken 67-68, 151, *157*
Nyby, Christian 73

Oates, Simon 176
Oceans of Fire 59, 66-67
O'Connell, Patrick 118, 121
The Octagon 16, 23
Octopussy 36
Odets, Clifford 210
O.K. Yevtushenko 118
Olivier, Laurence 47, 120, 201
O'Mara, Kate 177
On Friday at Eleven 91, *94*-95, 97
On Her Majesty's Secret Service 118-119
Once Upon a Time in the West 65
One-Eyed Jacks 72
One Life to Live 196
O'Neal, Ron 51-57
O'Neal, Tatum 179
O'Neill, Eugene 11
Ordinary People 113
The Organization 143-148
Orion 64
Oswald, Gerd 207, 212
Otley (book) 45
Otley (movie) 44-47, 50
O'Toole, Peter 119, 202
Our Man Flint 135
Our Man Flint: Dead on Target 135, 137, 141-142
Our Man in Marrakesh 26, 29-*30*
Outlaw Blues 10
Owensby, Earl 108

Pacino, Al 98, 104, 107
Palmer, Nicholas 121
Palmer, Tom 77
Panavison 147
Paramount 15, 129, 213

224

Index

Parker, Fess 71
Parker, Robert B. 135, 139-*140*
Parker, Colonel Tom 165
Parks, Gordon 53
Passport to Shame 91-93
Pate, Michael 80
Paul Mann Actors Workshop 200
Paul Temple 168
Peck, Gregory 63
Peckinpah, Sam 10, 59, 62, 70, 73-74
Peel, Emma 201
Penn, Arthur 129, 131, 211
Pennington, Jon 31
Peppard, George 71-72, 104, *157*
Perschy, Maria 190
The Persuaders! 26, 33, 91, 168, 174-175
Peter Gunn 187
Peyton Place 102
Philco Television Playhouse 208, 210
Phillips, Sian 173
Pinewood 180
Play for Today 123
Playhouse 90 208, 210-211, 213
Plummer, Christopher 179
Poe, Edgar Allan 63
Poitier, Sidney 52, 143, 148
Poldark 125
Police Story 24
Police Surgeon 6
Police Woman 195, 198-199
Pollack, Sydney 11, 12, 207
Ponti, Carlo 189, 213
Porridge 44
Post, Ted 211
Potter, Peter 5
Powell, Michael 34-35
Powell, Robert 176
Pray for the Wildcats 98
The Predator 1
Preece, Michael 70-79, *75*
Prentiss, Paula 105
Presley, Elvis 15, 143, 145-146, 149, 165
Preston, Mike 80
Previn, Andre 175
Previn, Steve 175-176
The Pride and the Passion 99
Prisoner 80, 88, 89
Probation Officer 27
Producers Guild 153
The Professionals (movie) 16
The Professionals (series) 1
The Protectors 178
Public Eye 3, 5
Pull the Other One 177

The Pulse of Danger 31

Quilter, Victoria 80
Quinn, Anthony 36, 38-39

Radio Times 5
Raffill, Stewart 36-43
Rage 195
Raiders of the Lost Ark 36
The Rainmaker 210
Rakoff, Alvin 32, 91-97
Randall, Anne 201
Rank, Arthur 32
Rawhide 200
Ready, Steady, Go! 170
The Real McCoys 101
Rebel Without a Cause 104
Red Balloon 130
Red Dawn 14
Red Line 7000 20, 130, 143, 145
Red River 21
Redcap 3
Redgrave, Vanessa 122
Redifussion 169
Reed, Carol 72
Reed, Oliver 13, 51
Reeve, Christopher 180
Reeves, Steve 192
The Reivers 147
Relyea, Robert 146, 167
Remy, Bob 63
Rennie, Michael 26
Requiem for a Heavyweight 93
Reunion Day 34
Revenge of the Nerds 109, 115
Revolver 1
Reynolds, Burt 10, 12-14, *13*, 36, 76, 143, 149, 161, 164, 198
Reynolds, Debbie 71
Richman, Peter Mark 207-213, *209*, *212*
Ride the High Country 116
Rilla, Wolf 202, 203
Ring of Passion 99
Rio Lobo 21
Ripcord 16
Ritchie, June 203
Ritt, Martin 213
River of Death 59
Robards, Jason 73
Robbery 168, 173-*174*, 201, 204
Roberts, Marguerite 16
Robertson, Cliff 106
Robinson, Hugh A. 151
The Rockford Files 129, 132, 143-144

Index

Rodgers, Anton 26
The Rolling Stones 170
Roman Holiday 99
Romanoff's 210
Romero, Cesar 182
Romulus and Remus 192
Rossiter, Leonard 45
Roth, Bobby 57
Roth, Philip 211
Route 66 74
Rowan & Martin's Laugh-In 154
The Royal Shakespeare Company 202
The Royal Theatrical Fund 172
Ruddy, Al 24
Ruff, Garfield 51
Russel, Tony 187–194, ***191***
Ryan 80, 88

Sacristan, Gregorio 60
The Sadista Sisters 206
The Saint 3, 91, 95, 170, 201
Saint, Eva Marie 210
St. Jacques, Raymond 195, 198, 200
The St. Valentine's Day Massacre 61
Saltzman, Harry 118–120, 168
Sam Whiskey 10, 12
Santean, Antonio 22
Sapper 44
Sara 75
Sarafian, Deren 149
Sarafian, Richard C. 14, 73, 149
Sargent, Joseph 13
Satlof, Ron 151–160
Savalas, Telly 2, 51
The Scalphunters 10–12
Scanlan, Joseph 135–142
Schmeling, Max 99
Schmidt, Tommy 146
Schneider, John 108, 110, 113
Schneider, Romy 45
Schulz, Dwight 157
Schulz, Ted 70
Schweig, Bontche 198
Scorchy 201
Scorsese, Martin 65, 151–152
Scott, George C. 195–196
Scott, Gordon 192
Scott, Peter Graham 118
Screen Actors Guild 188
Screen Gems 18
Script Clerks Guild 70–71
Search 207
Seaton, George 63
Secret Agent Super Dragon 135

Secret of the Sphinx 190–191
Segal, George 48
Selleck, Tom 166
Sellers, Peter 119
Serling, Rod 93, 95
Serpico (movie) 107
Serpico (series) 98
Sewell, George 168, ***174***
Shadow Squad 26–27
Shaft 51
Sharif, Omar 107
Sharkey, Ray 145
Sharp, Don 29–30
Sharp, Henry 19
Sharpe, Cornelia 98, 107
Shatner, William 62, 78
Shaw, George Bernard 11
S+H+E: Security Hazards Expert 98, ***106***–107
Shear, Barry 167
Sheldon, Les 143–150
Shepperton Studios 127
The Sheriff of Cochise 71
Shonteff, Lindsay 201, 205–206
The Shootist 183
Siegel, Don 151–152
Siegel, Jerome M. 161–167
The Silent Force 207
Siliphant, Stirling 207
Simpson, Alan 26
Sims, Sylvia 203
Sinatra, Frank 100
The Six Million Dollar Man 165
Skullduggery 76
A Small Town in Texas 10
Smith, William 151
Smokey and the Bandit 108
Solar Productions 143, 146–147
Sollima, Sergio 1
Solomon, Joe 129
Sometimes a Great Notion 102
The Sopranos 132
Soul, David 168
Soul Hustler 187
The Sound of Speed 129–130
Spaceflight IC1 203
Spacey, Kevin 145
Speight, Johnny 26–27
Spelling, Aaron 78, 98, 101–102
Spenser: A Savage Place 135, 139, 141
Spenser: For Hire ***140***
Spenser: The Judas Goat 135, 139, 141
Spielberg, Steven 36, 104
Spooner, Dennis 3

Index

A Spy at Evening 168
Spy Trap 118, 123, 125–126
Spyder's Web 3
Stacey 201
Stander, Lionel 177
Stapleton, Terry 80
Star Wars 155
Starsky and Hutch 168
Statham, Jason 44
Steel 16, 22–23, 59
Steiger, Rod 91, **94**–**95**
Stella 34
Stephenson, Pamela 80
Stevens, Connie 201
Stevens, George, Sr. 63, 100
Stevens, Stella 98
Stewart, James 181
The Stick Up 168
The Sting 155, 161
Stoll, John 127
Stoner, Lynda 80
Strasberg, Lee 147, 211
The Streets of San Francisco 70, 74–**75**
Strode, Woody 108
Strouse, Charles 131
Studio One 208
Sturges, John 143, 145, 147–148, 161–162, 164, 187–188
Subterfuge 118
The Subterraneans 71
Superfly 51–53
Superman 180
Suppose They Gave a War and Nobody Came 14
Sutton, Dudley 178, **182**
The Sweeney 3, 5–6, 168, 176–177
Swink, Robert 99–100
Switch 129, 155, 161, 165–**166**, 208
Sykes, Eric 26–27

Tam-Lin 203
Tammy Tell Me True 194
Tanaka, Prof. Toru **64**
Tarantino, Quentin 61
Target 3, 6
Target Goldseven 187, **191**
Tarzan 40, 192
Taylor, Elizabeth 119, 194
Taylor, Rod 31
The Tell-Tale Heart 63
Ten Little Indians 29
Tenafly 98
Terry-Thomas **30**
Tessari, Duccio 191

That Girl 101
That Kind of Girl 202, 204
Thaw, John 6, 177
T.H.E. Cat 207
Thick as Thieves 44
The Third Man (series) 26
Thomas, Danny 101
Thorson, Linda 6
Thunder and Lightning 108
Thunder Road 13
Tingwell, Bud 31, 87
T.J. Hooker 70, 78
The Todd Killings 167
The Tony Awards 199–200
Top Secret 26–27
Topper, Burt 187–189
A Touch of Frost 4
Touchstone 16
Tough Guys 108, 115–117, **116**
Towers, Harry Alan 26, 28–31, 91
A Town Has Turned to Dust 95
Trader Horn 10
Treasure of San Teresa 91–93, 96
The Treasure of the Sierra Madre 147
Trenchcoat 178
Truck Turner 16, 19–21, **20**
Trumbo, Dalton 11
TV Guide 145
20th Century Fox 105, 156
24 Hours to Kill 26, 28
The Twilight Zone 211
The Two-Five 133
Two for the Seesaw 166

UCLA film school 99
Uhnak, Dorothy 151
United Artists 13, 14, 108, 119–120, 164
Universal 63, 65, 74–75, 102–103, 112, 141, 143–144, 156–157, 159, 165–166, 186, 196–198, 212
Urich, Robert 36, 43, 135, 139–**140**

Vaccaro, Brenda 75
Vance, Leigh 95
Van Cleef, Lee 16
Van Der Valk 26
Van Gyseghem, Joanna 118, 121
Van Peebles, Melvin 53
Variety 197
Varsi, Diane 131
Vega$ 187
Venables, Terry 3
Vennera, Chick **41**
Vertue, Beryl 26–27, 33

Index

Villain 44
Virgin of the Secret Service 201
Vogel, Virgil 77

Wagner, Lindsay 36, *41*
Wagner, Robert 36, 161, 165–*166*, 208
Walker, Texas Ranger 1, 24, 70, 79
Walking Tall 108
Wallis, Hal 188
Walt Disney Productions 1, 39–40, 70–71, 108, 117, 141, 178–182
Wambaugh, Joseph 195
War Is Hell 187–189
Warbeck, David 118
Ward, Tony 85
Warden, Jack 149
Warfield, Marlene *196*
Warner, Jack 119
Warner Brothers 140
Warren, Charles Marquis 145
Waterman, Dennis 6, 123
Wayne, John 10, 15, 20–21, 63–64, 178, 181, 183
Weaver, Dennis 132, 155, 197
Webb, Jack 2, 133
Weintraub, Fred 19
Welch, Raquel 12–13
Wendkos, Paul 73
West, Adam 36
West, Red 151
West Side Story 167
Westmore, Bud 181
Weston, Jack *13*
What Ever Happened to Baby Jane? 181
Whatever Happened to the Likely Lads 44
What's Going On 200
Where the Bullets Fly 118
The Whirlybirds 71
White Lightning 10, 13, 108
The Wild Geese 126
Wild Wild Planet 193–194
The Wild Wild West 16, 19, 143

Wilder, Billy 129–130, 133, 162–163
Wilder, John 74
Willes, Peter 173
William Morris Agency 17–18, 110
Williams, Clarence, III 197
Williams, Gordon 3
Willis, Ted 3, 6, 27, 201
Wilson, Richard 76
Wilson, Sheree 79
Wincer, Simon 80, 88
Winner, Michael 164–165
Wise, Herbert 27
Wise, Mike 12
Wiseguy 143–144
Wolff, Frank 193
Wonder, Stevie 200
The Wonderful World of Disney 179
Woods, James 75
Woodvine, John 118, 123
Woodward, Edward 121
Wopat, Tom 108
The World of Suzie Wong 171–172
The World Ten Times Over 202–203
The Wrecking Crew 161–162
Writers Guild 12, 35
Wyler, William 99–100, 163, 207, 210–211
Wynn, Keenan 137–138

Yates, Peter 168, 173
Yeldham, Peter 26–35
Yorkshire television 121
Young, Freddie 120
Yucatan 147
Yuill, P.B. 3

Z-Cars 168
Zapper's Blade of Vengeance 201, 204–205
Zieff, Howard 145
Zimbalist, Efrem 207
Zodiac 26

www.ingramcontent.com/pod-product-compliance
Ingram Content Group UK Ltd.
Pitfield, Milton Keynes, MK11 3LW, UK
UKHW041945140426
5217IPUK00014B/664